Memoirs of a Physicist in the Atomic Age

Memoirs of a Physicist in the Atomic Age

WALTER M. ELSASSER

Science History Publications
New York   1978

Adam Hilger Limited
Bristol   1978

First published in the United States by
Science History Publications
a division of
Neale Watson Academic Publications, Inc.
156 Fifth Avenue
New York, N.Y. 10010

Published in the United Kingdom by
Adam Hilger Limited
a company owned by
The Institute of Physics
Techno House
Redcliffe Way
Bristol B81 6NX

Library of Congress Cataloging in Publication Data

Elsasser, Walter M   1904–
   Memoirs of a physicist.

   Bibliography: p.
   Includes index.
   1. Elsasser, Walter M   1904–
2. Physicists—United States—Biography. I. Title.
QC16.E58A35   530'.092'4 [B]   77-16583
ISBN 0-88202-178-8 (Science History)

ISBN 0-85274-400-5 (Adam Hilger)

Printed in U.S.A.

*Even if I could be Shakespeare,
I think I should still choose to
be Faraday.*

—Aldous Huxley (1925)

Contents

List of Illustrations

Preface

I had the good luck to live through a period which to future generations will no doubt appear as the Golden Age of Science, or at least of
Atomic Science. Since I became acquainted with an unusual number of
the great and famous among my colleagues, I have often been asked to
put my recollections on paper. In these pages are accounts of my
meetings with Heisenberg, Schrödinger, and Pauli, with the Curies
and Joliot, with Millikan and Oppenheimer, and with others who had
a role in developing atomic physics.

I have tried to steer a middle course between an anecdotal account
and a more technical exposition, neither of which seemed satisfactory
by itself. The result is essentially a subjective autobiography telling
particularly about my own gradual growth in scientific understanding.
I thus hope to have provided some insight into how a scientist thinks.
And, by minimizing technical details, I expect that my story can be read
by those who have little or no background in physics.

In accordance with the autobiographical emphasis, I have made
every effort to record just what I succeeded in recalling and not to yield
to a desire for elaboration or embellishment. Also, I did not prepare
myself by reading about the history of science, other people's biogra-
phies, etc. Such few books of a biographical character as I have drawn
upon are listed in the notes. To make sure of dates in a few cases where
I was in doubt, I have consulted a suitable reference work.[1]

The reader might be surprised by my frequent preoccupation with
"natural philosophy." This is an old English term for physics; it
perfectly expresses the prevailing spirit of that earlier European society
in which I grew up. This distinct philosophical attitude was replaced
during my own lifetime by an almost purely pragmatic one; the earlier
age ended abruptly in the smoke of Hiroshima. I believe that by now
such pragmatism has overshot its mark, that science is meant to be far
more than a tool for the improvement of material conditions. Such
ideas are touched upon at several places in the later parts of this story.

My hearty thanks are due to the publisher, Mr. Neale Watson, and
his accomplished staff, especially Mrs. Anne Pietropinto who saw the
work through press with unfailing courtesy and Mr. Gerald Lombardi
who carefully read through the entire manuscript for style and im-

proved it in many particulars. Almost all of the photographs are taken from the collection of the American Institute of Physics and are reproduced with their permission. I wish to thank Dr. S. Weart, Director of the Center for History of Physics, for his kind assistance in this. In addition, I am indebted to Mr. Wolfgang Pfaundler, of Innsbruck, for permission to reproduce the photograph of Erwin Schrödinger, and to Mr. Alan Richards, of Princeton, for allowing me to use the photograph of von Neumann and Oppenheimer.

Walter M. Elsasser

October, 1977
Department of Earth and Planetary Sciences
The Johns Hopkins University

1

Background and Youth

At the time I was born my family had been living for some generations in the southwestern part of Germany called Baden, in which I spent the first nineteen years of my life. This region extends on the east side of the river Rhine from the Swiss border in the South, through the Black Forest, to a stretch of fertile hills, at the end of which lies the town of Heidelberg.

My ancestors, so far as I know about them, belonged to the middle class, mostly engaged in commercial pursuits. About one of them, my paternal great-grandfather, I happen to have detailed information: When I was in my late teens I developed a certain interest in family history, and to find out more I visited a distant relative who lived in the city of Karlsruhe. He was a childless, elderly widower, living in uneventful retirement, who was only too happy to be visited by a young relation. He promised me a unique experience: a visit to the grave of my great-grandfather who was also his own forebear. This man had been buried in an ancient forest-cemetery, a burial place for Jews of previous generations but now disused. Early next morning we took off by taxi and after travelling for an hour arrived at a group of graves in a clearing of a large forest. The cemetery, although no longer used, was well tended. The tall crowns of the surrounding trees rustled in the wind, and there was an atmosphere of great, unearthly peace. I found it hard to concentrate, even to watch my relative's efforts at deciphering the Hebrew letters on the simple grave-stone.

I learned that cemeteries such as this had been widespread in olden times among Jews who lived in the country. They were placed at the largest possible distance from all Christian habitations, in conformance with ancient non-Jewish superstititions. I also learned that my great-grandfather had been a peddler who travelled up and down the highways and byways of southwestern Germany. As peddlers go, he was not too badly off since he owned his horse and wagon. From all I had seen I concluded that my ancestor must have followed the age-old traditions of Jewish religious life.

This man's son, my paternal grandfather, was caught in the great wave of economic prosperity that swept Germany, as it did the rest of Western Europe, in the nineteenth century. In his youth he migrated from his native hamlet to a small town on the road to Heidelberg farther north. That country is ideally suited for fruit trees, and my grandfather founded and operated a distillery for the making of liquors from fruit. He accumulated a fair amount of wealth in this way; he must also have acquired some social status, as he was a City Councillor during most of his later life. But it seems quite clear that along with this growth of wealth and status, he rather thoroughly abandoned the traditional Jewish ways, although he retained a formal association with the Jewish community. There were then many signs of the breakup of the ancient faith. My own parents became Protestants when I was still very young; of my father's two younger sisters, one eventually joined a group similar to the Ethical Culture Society of the United States, while the other married a non-Jew and moved away. My grandfather must have died before I was old enough to remember him, but I have seen his grave in the City cemetery. It was a fairly large and clumsy pile of stone decorated in the Victorian manner.

My father, Moritz Elsasser, was a different personality altogether. He was rather easygoing, always willing to live and let live. He grew up in a small town and after graduating from high school proceeded to study law in Heidelberg. He ended up by acquiring a doctor-of-law degree. This was not, however, designed to tax his intellectual capacities, as he later told me more than once. He first became what was known as a notary, a full-time government employee, whose function is to advise and assist members of the public in preparing legal documents for specified fees. In this function my father spent some years living in a small town in the Black Forest. There, he befriended an ex-army officer of the minor nobility who had followed the family tradition by joining the army early in life. But since he cordially hated all things military, he retired with the rank of captain; he and his wife then bought the "Big House" of the town and settled down to be country gentlefolk. Later on, these good people became my and my sister's god-parents in the Protestant faith. Since, however, their preoccupations with things religious were minimal, this did not amount to much. I remember more than one summer vacation when I was still a little boy, spent pleasantly in their large house and idyllic garden with the fir-covered hills of the Black Forest looking down on us and a babbling creek carrying its water toward the Rhine.

Soon after 1900, my father was transferred to Mannheim, then a thriving and large commercial town, twenty kilometers to the northwest of Heidelberg. Here he met my mother, Johanna Masius; they fell in love and married. About a year later, in 1904, I was born, and three years later my only sibling, my sister, Maria. My maternal grandfather as a young man had come from the region of Mecklenburg on the Baltic coast; he had founded and developed a mill for the weaving of burlap and the making of burlap bags. He had married into an old, local family. His business prospered, so that he could raise his five children very comfortably; my mother, for example, was sent at sixteen to a French-speaking boarding school in Lausanne in Switzerland, to acquire social polish. While I know little about this school, my impression is that it catered to the daughters of the upper bourgeoisie, Swiss, French, and German, mostly with a Christian background, and it must have given my mother some impression of gentility that she could not have gained otherwise. Later, when my parents married, grandfather Masius gave them a large dowry.

My mother was a very determined woman, with strong convictions which she carried through. She was a rather quiet, restrained person of few words; one could call her puritanical. She was not interested in politics, unlike my father, a lifelong student of public affairs and history. The marriage was long and harmonious, and I do not remember any serious quarrel between my parents. While my father intensely disliked open arguments, my mother in turn kept her feelings under close control. Thus, family life proceeded on an even keel.

I had a nursemaid, excellently chosen and later transferred to my sister: Louise was an unmarried young woman who stayed with us for about six years until we left Mannheim; she was adored by all and was treated as a fullfledged member of the family. My mother, being rather well-off before the First World War, had two maidservants (not including Louise). This number was later reduced to one.

We lived, as I said, in Mannheim which is a remarkable architectural curiosity. Some 200 years earlier, about 1690, the region called the Palatinate, consisting of much of the upper Rhine valley and the flat country to the west, had been systematically devastated by the French in one of Louis XIV's wars. Not only were all the cities destroyed, but every village and every single house was put to the torch or levelled. This extended even to Heidelberg, farther west. The avowed intention

was to create a glacis that would allow future French generals to
control any military access to the French heartland from the east. In the
early eighteenth century, Mannheim was rebuilt using a plan of
unified city architecture. The streets cross each other at right angles as
in a chessboard; the city is surrounded by a broad, circular boulevard
except where there rose the vast baroque castle, a colossal, half-mile-
long, three-story building with over a thousand rooms. Old guide-
books described it as the world's largest single building. Even to a
youngster like myself, it stood as a silent witness to the formidable
power that an absolute monarch of the eighteenth century could exert
over his subjects. In my youth the castle was still in an excellent state of
repair and in use. I once penetrated into the interior because a distant
relative of ours who was a judge in the Superior Court had living
quarters there. The rooms were huge and well cared for, and I saw a
large hall that had been decorated in a sumptuous rococo manner by
Italian painters and artisans. One could well see in the mind's eye a
company of elegantly garbed ladies and gentlemen of an eighteenth-
century court listening to a concert, but one could not quite fit this
period-piece into the modern world.

Some years later my father was made a judge in the Court at
Mannheim. In Germany, judgeships are appointive, not elective. He
did not, however, much enjoy exercising the functions of a judge, then
or later, since being a very peaceable man he found it disagreeable to
preside over people quarrelling or arguing, even in the highly stylized
manner of a court of law. In the fall of 1910, my father was transferred
to be judge in the town of Pforzheim, a town about thirty kilometers
east of Karlsruhe. There, for the first two or three years, we lived in a
suburban house with a charming garden, but before the outbreak of the
war we had moved into a large, new, rented apartment in the center of
town. Such frequent moving no doubt helped to give my later life a
certain nomadic character: I have, as an adult, never held a position or
residence for more than seven years, and mostly for not longer than
five.

I remember my grammar school rather clearly. This was a public
school, private schools being almost unknown. Pforzheim was a
factory town, and most of its 70,000 inhabitants were first or second
generation factory workers. The social level of my school was therefore
quite new to me: There was at least one boy in every class, often more
than one, who had not been properly toilet-trained, and who, by the
end of an hour, had a puddle of urine under his seat. How the poor,

harassed teacher, invariably a male, could force any knowledge into these heads has always mystified me; but it seems he did for many children succeeded in mastering the three R's. Compulsory public education extended to the age of fourteen; those who wanted to go to high school were first placed at age nine in a separate class of the elementary school for a few months.

At about that age, I began to develop a passion for modelmaking. Plastics were not yet used, so the models were made from heavy white paper on which were printed the contours of the object such as a battleship or an airplane; these were cut out and the models glued together. I eventually acquired great proficiency in this activity. A little later, I became enthusiastic about "tin" soldiers which were in fact cast from lead rather than tin. The technique was extremely simple, requiring a gas burner, a small ladle to melt the lead, and the forms, of which a vast variety could be bought.

Needless to say, my preoccupation with soldiering was, psychologically speaking, purely romantic; as a matter of personal experience soldiering and war did not exist for me. I had the same romantic relationship to Westerns and other adventure stories which I began to read avidly at about that time. I was introduced to this kind of literature by a school friend whose father, a wealthy manufacturer, had accumulated a vast collection of such books. I borrowed these in the evening but had to return them next morning so that they could be slipped into their place again. My parents knew nothing of this and would have considered it low-brow literature. So I developed in this period into a stealthy, rapid reader and would go through a volume of an adventure story in one night in the privacy of my bedroom. This is the first occasion I remember when I did an extensive amount of reading. As I grew older, I became a voracious reader and spent a large part of my life poring over books. Since I read comparatively few novels, mostly heavier literature, I never tried to become a rapid reader but forced myself to read slowly.

I was ten years old at the outbreak of the First World War. One had been prepared by the newspapers, but the actual rush of events was rapid, starting with the declaration of war by Austria on Serbia, in midsummer of 1914. Immediately thereafter, the German government decided on mobilization. Overnight, posters appeared at all public places with "Mobilization" printed in huge block letters on top of lengthy instructions for those about to be called into service. My own parents were relatively composed, but the atmosphere among the milling crowds in the streets was far from quiet. There was a general air of intense expectancy. The words "ein frisch-fröhlicher Krieg" (a fresh-and-jolly war) were repeated endlessly in the newspapers and by the public speakers who sprouted everywhere like daffodils in spring. In the first two days of mobilization, the populace in the streets seemed a little stunned, which is understandable since Pforzheim was a factory town and most people's feelings were probably akin to the socialist party that had little sympathy with Imperial dreams of glory. But these feelings turned increasingly into enthusiasm as the streets began to fill with uniformed soldiers. Soon, the anticipation of a fresh-and-jolly war to be followed by a quick-and-easy victory became dominant.

The schools had closed for vacations a few weeks earlier. But word was spread that every able-bodied boy would be enrolled by the Red Cross if he reported to the railroad station. Since the station was within easy walking distance from our apartment, I did this at once and spent most of the ensuing days there. A major railroad line passes east-westerly through the town; it now deployed German troops toward the West. Some hours after mobilization was proclaimed, trains started rolling westward and within a day or two such traffic was incessant: A train filled with troops passed about every half hour for all of the day and most of the night. We boys were assigned to distribute lemonade to the soldiers during the few minutes each train stopped in the station. We did this until we had to stop from exhaustion. For me this was simple, since when I became too tired, I could always reach my home rapidly and rest there. Others who lived farther away were not so lucky. The one recollection that stands out from that period is the incessant and interminable singing. I presume such has always been the habit of soldiers going to battle.

But I was not in the least prepared for the reversal that began about a week after the start of this traffic. Suddenly there appeared hospital trains moving in the opposite direction. They were marked with red crosses, an occasional uniformed nurse was in evidence; but most of the curtains were tightly drawn and one could see little of what went on inside except when a curtain was left half open and one glimpsed bandaged, grim-looking soldiers. All this was made even more emphatic by a heavy pall of silence. Some of the wounded would leave the train at our station, to be transferred in local vehicles to improvised hospitals. Clearly, youngsters were not welcome in this part of the war effort; when I moved too close to a hospital train, I was harshly shooed away. In the second week of August, the number of hospital trains increased markedly, and the number of troop trains moving westward dwindled; so I soon felt that small boys were not longer required or were downright undesirable at the railroad station. Nobody had time to keep track of them; by the third week in August my participation in the German war effort ended. A short time later school started again.

The family lived in Pforzheim for another two years, but nothing was quite the same. Wounded and crippled soldiers became an everyday sight. Gradually, supplies began to run short; rationing, first of foodstuffs, then of clothing, was introduced. A period of history had come to an end. I should here mention one effect of the war upon my family about which I heard only years later: My maternal grandfather was a firm believer in the grandeur and reliability of the Bank of England. He was a wealthy man and his entire fortune was invested there, including my mother's dowry. Early in August, 1914, when England declared war on Germany, all property of German citizens in England was confiscated. We never saw any of it again.

At that time I was old enough to read newspapers and official publications. It was, indeed, hard to escape the din of the German propaganda machine which specialized in showing the technical superiority of the German Reich over its enemies. It was very unsubtle propaganda, since few people at any level of education will accept mere technical wealth and proficiency as a token of preeminence.

During the six years we lived in Pforzheim my parents had succeeded in developing a congenial social circle composed mainly of young lawyers and their wives, many of them with small children. They came mostly from good, settled, Protestant families of the area. My parents kept in touch with some members of this group for many years after they had left Pforzheim. I mention this because although the matter of the family's Jewish origin could not be avoided only a few years later, unless I am completely mistaken, the question just did not exist before the shattering events of World War I. My parents considered themselves then fully assimilated to German ways of life. But this did not last.

In the winter of 1915–1916, my father was called into the army. He had been in the reserve, and his group was among the oldest to be called up during that war; they were men in their early forties. His unit was sent to the Swiss border. Fairly soon, he found himself at a desk at the headquarters of the military border guard, the army having discovered that he was a lawyer. But he had troubles with his health:

Years earlier he had developed a large stomach ulcer, for which there was then no remedy. Having now to eat barracks food, in place of my mother's diet, he had incessant pains. Since apparently he did a useful job, he obtained permission to have his wife join him. In the fall of 1916, my mother took her two children, packed some furniture, and moved with us to the seat of the headquarters of the border guard. This was a rather smallish town situated in a charming southern valley of the Black Forest and almost within walking distance of the ancient Swiss City of Basel. Because of the war, one could not cross the border without a special permit. But by 1916 the food shortage in Germany had become severe, and the Swiss had then allowed the Germans that lived close to the border to come over at regular intervals; not only could one take back certain amounts of staples, but when children were allowed to come along, they could eat their fill on the spot of chocolates and pastries, then unknown inside Germany.

The military detachment that guarded the Swiss border consisted of several battalions. These were under the orders of an elderly general who had been brought out of retirement. The general, being too old to be very active, had two adjutants who did the work. The first was a colonel in charge of the troops and of military affairs; the second was in charge of administration, including the relationships with the civilian public. This second person was my father, Sergeant Elsasser, who was never promoted to officer's rank.

It was, of course, very exciting for a boy of eleven when my father told me that he was familiar with every trail crossing the border on which smugglers as well as spies could move in or out of the country. It was less edifying when he told me about the inconveniences that resulted from his being only a non-commissioned officer. Not infrequently, some higher officer would appear at my father's desk with a request for a visa, usually a man about to be moved to the front, who wanted a few days' vacation in Switzerland before he went off. My father would have to go through a routine of refusing the man's request, and then would have to remain standing at attention until the officer walked away, usually furious and showing it.

My father's counterpart on the other side of the Swiss border was another lawyer, by the name of Kaufmann. He had been a native of Baden, had studied law in Heidelberg, and had then settled in Basel, where he had opened a banking business that became quite successful. He was about my father's age, and the two men at once took to each other and became lifelong friends. From that time on, Mr. Kaufmann took care of whatever financial transactions or investments my father wanted to undertake.

I found myself transferred to a new high school. This was a simple matter since schools in this part of Germany were thoroughly standardized. But there was in this small community a neighborly spirit. The other boys at school accepted me as one of their gang without a preliminary fight; after some weeks I began to feel at home and to relax. This was the only residence in all my youth where I had a strong feeling of this kind. Unfortunately, it was not to last. In the spring of 1917, after the family had been there for only some six months, headquarters were shifted to the city of Konstanz, eighty kilometers farther east. So we packed again and moved there.

The change I experienced was radical. There was a high school that I could enter without difficulty—but the atmosphere seemed to be full of suspicion and hostility. I do not remember having found any friends at all in the year we lived in this town. My father's activities were transferred intact. Food shortage was severe by then; to counteract this, the family collected and dried mushrooms that grew in great abundance in the woods.

At first sight Konstanz strikes one as a clean but rather sleepy provincial town. But although it was once much more, there are no spectacular ruins to testify to it. But on my walk to school, I passed a rather large rectangular edifice, the so-called Council building. It is one of the few buildings in central Europe that is still in its original state, having escaped destruction by fire or war. On entering it one finds oneself at once in a very large hall about three ordinary stories high, whose ceiling is supported by a series of horizontal oaken beams so large that there would be no oak trees in Europe at present to cut them from. The impression, to me at least, was totally medieval, and more than once I felt that a company of knights in heavy armor must be clanking not far away. In that building the Council of Constance was held for four years (1414–1418) when Konstanz was one of the most important bishop's seats north of the Alps and also a major commercial center with trade all over Europe. So it was only fitting that there should be an Ecumenical Council in this town. It became, in fact, one of the largest ever held. In these days the fate of the Church was as much the concern of laymen as of priests. The throng that assembled and stayed for four years was tremendous. Thousands of priests and monks from all over Europe and numberless dukes and counts with thousands of knights in their retinue gathered there. The good burghers of Konstanz kept records of the food and lodging they dispensed to that scintillating crowd; even the number of whores, which they estimated at 7,000, has come down to us.

In its prime function, the stabilization of the Church, this Council was a failure. But it happened to do away with John Hus, the Czech reformer. He was the first of those remarkable men who created Protestantism; he was over a hundred years earlier than Luther and Calvin. John Hus came to Konstanz as a result of two independent guarantees of safe conduct, one by the Pope, another by the German Emperor, both of whom jointly presided over the sessions of the Council. Barely arrived in Konstanz he was arrested and thrown into a grisly dungeon attached to a large monastery. He was accused of heresy and after a short trial was found guilty and promptly burned at the stake in the middle of town. A hundred years later the glory of Konstanz was at an end. Trade moved to other towns better located geographically, church administration was hampered by wars with the Protestants, the population dwindled, and Konstanz turned into a small provincial town.

Toward the end of the year 1917 my father's illness had become so bad that the army decided to muster him out. Some time after his return to civilian life he had a surgical operation, then rather a novelty, which cured this illness permanently. Shortly thereafter, he was promoted to a judgeship at the Superior Court in the city of Heidelberg where we moved at about Christmas of 1917. First, we lived in a rented house south of town in a suburban village; about two years later we moved into a comfortable apartment house in town where the family lived for the rest of their stay in Heidelberg.

In 1918 food shortages were severe. My father, who had spent most of his younger life in this region (his hometown was not too far from Heidelberg) and who knew the ways of the local populace to perfection, managed by various deals, this side of the legally permissible, to provide potatoes, vegetables, and meat, so that the family was almost always well fed during these hard times.

The city of Heidelberg was a thriving center of some 70,000 people. It had long been the mecca of many British tourists (this was before the era of the American tourist), and when they disappeared at war's outbreak, the elegant hotels kept on operating with a clientele closer to home. Then, there was the old and famous university. Like all German universities it tended to induce a certain social stratification, but it was not severe. I knew a few of the professors' children, but my snobbery was not so developed that I desired to "crash" their social circle; I just met some of them occasionally. On the whole, I found Heidelberg not inhospitable. My parents managed to build up a modest social life, although it never returned to what it had been before the war.

Some time after we had settled in Heidelberg, I witnessed a spectacular historical event: the collapse and retreat of the German army in November, 1918, and the accompanying revolution that deposed the Kaiser and the smaller princes and started the Weimar Republic. When the retreat began in earnest, we schoolboys (I was then fourteen) were alerted to serve as guides for the troops from the time they entered the town at its western end until they left it on the highway beyond that ran eastward. We were also instructed to do our best to persuade the soldiers to deliver their weapons to a central depot in the railroad station. I can still recall the mountainous piles of rifles interspersed with occasional machine guns and other weapons. In the few days it had taken the troops in their vehicles (by then the army was fairly well motorized) to traverse some two hundred kilometers from the front to Heidelberg, political control had passed into the hands of the "revolutionary councils of workers and soldiers." Our scout-troop of guides almost automatically came under their authority, and I became acquainted with some not very impressive representatives of the new order.

The mood of the returning soldiers was remarkably uniform. They were not a "bedraggled lot" as one might imagine. They had been rather well fed, and many had fairly clean and well-kept uniforms, but one could sense that they were finished with war: no more killing, no more watching one's cronies die, no more 24-hour vigilance. All they wanted was a normal, quiet, regular life. They couldn't have cared less about who had won what and who had lost what. It was in this ambiance of total psychic exhaustion that the Weimar Republic was born.

The period of retreat and revolution did not last long. After a couple of weeks, it became quiet again, no longer did military vehicles pass through town. Life returned to its usual routines, including school. The later parts of the war had left traces that were visible everywhere; I remember in particular two of our teachers who had been at the front and had returned home before the war was over.

One was a man in his mid-thirties who had been badly wounded. Both legs and one arm had been shot up, but the surgeons had succeeded in piecing him together, so that he could hobble around on two crutches. Although it was clear that everything was done with pain and effort, his teaching remained spirited. He was a constant reminder to us boys of what war was really like. After a couple of years, he disappeared, and I do not know what became of him.

The other teacher had also come back from the trenches before the war ended, but he was a psychological not a physical casualty. It had made him into a total cynic. He taught history, and I remember how he described the decline of the Roman empire and the spread of Christianity, claiming that there was a bitter struggle for supremacy between it and Mithraism. In that area, diggings had long since unearthed innumerable relics of Mithraism, the chief cult of Roman legionnaires. But the teacher treated the subject with complete cynicism as if it were a story about a woman having to choose between two hats. He made it perfectly clear that he thought of Christianity as just a human foible, a crutch for the weaklings. This kind of mentality was then rapidly spreading in Germany, and I saw many examples of it later on. The seedbed of Hitler's domination was in this cynicism.

In the spring of 1919, I was confirmed in the Evangelical Church. (This name had been given to the official unification of Lutherans and Calvinists. Underneath this the two historical denominations continued, at least at that time. My church was Calvinist; later, I could find no distinction between it and the Presbyterians in the United States.) The minister was a very fine man, sensitive and intelligent, who gave me some personal attention, which I shared with another boy, who was the son of a professor at the university.

I had become well acquainted with this particular boy and found him sympathetic and interesting. His family came from northern Germany, and his father specialized in oriental languages, all of which gave the boy an air of mild but rather attractive remoteness from the local children. But then, one day this boy asked me, for no perceptible reason, whether I did not have any Jewish ancestors. I told him that I just didn't know and never had thought about it. I then forgot about the matter, but a few weeks later he suddenly asked me the same question again, without in any way leading up to it. This time I asked my father, only to receive an evasive and altogether unsatisfactory answer: Nobody could be sure of his ancestry. (One hears the student of the Code Napoleon, still a highly significant document when my father had studied law: "The inquiry into paternity is prohibited.") Moreover, he said, who could know what sinister things might have happened during the Thirty Years' War (a monumental event in German history but then 300 years in the past). There was evidently nothing to be learned from him; how can a fifteen-year-old adolescent argue with an experienced lawyer? I then set out to make discreet inquiries of my own and through some favorable incidents arrived at clearcut results within about a year: My four grandparents had been Jewish, and since there had been no utterly violent civic or military events for at least a century, it was safe to assume that all my ancestors had been Jewish.

This was to be higly important to me in that age of rising anti-Semitism. Before this I had had no notion whatsoever of Jews as a separate group, either as a religion or as a nationality. The Jews in Germany were a small minority, about one percent of the population, and not overly conspicuous, despite their contributions to economic and cultural life. It was quite easy for a boy to grow up without ever having heard of Jews as a distinguishable element. But looking back, I can clearly see that my parents must have enjoined their relatives, all Jewish, with whom they were, on the whole, on quite good terms, not to mention Jewish matters to me or my sister, and it is also clear that these relatives complied. Neither of my parents were formally religious; I saw them in church only two or three times on ceremonial occasions. For me the Jews were simply the people of the Bible, and that was, after all, very ancient history. My parents always had some Jewish friends, but I became aware of their Jewishness only much later in life; earlier, they were only individuals or family friends. Judaism, or any religion for that matter, was just not discussed in my home.

It seems clear that my parents had achieved a successful social adaptation, but only at the expense of a major split: As individuals they were on a very high level, endowed with principles and integrity, with much decency and goodness. I am not just indulging in retrospective fancy; I am trying to condense what I heard as a boy and young man from people whose judgment I trusted. But there was another side to them: They were children of the nineteenth century, an age that had not precisely invented Reason, but had put her on the market place, within popular reach. This goddess had told them that Progress inevitably would soon do away with such ancient minorities as the Jews, and they believed it uncritically and unreservedly.

At this same period, my father's patriotism had some unpleasant consequences. He had invested everything he owned in German war bonds. With the lost war and the ensuing extravagant inflation, all this was lost; after the war, the family had to live on the salary of a judge, which was, of course, quite adequate but by no means overly generous.

In the spring of 1921, in my last year of high school, my father approached me one day with a suggestion: When he was a student he had been a member of a fraternity. He felt that I was too much of a lone wolf, that I needed some "social polish." He believed that there was an excellent opportunity to acquire it by my joining his former fraternity with which he was still connected as a member of their alumni association. The fraternity had not had duels in his time and had only taken up duelling later, but it was still not compulsory, and there would be no unpleasant consequences if I declared that I was not interested in it. Evidently, my father's emotions were heavily engaged; he must have thought of this as a last chance to turn his son from an oddball into something closer to an ordinary, good German citizen. On my part, I felt that one can always readily dissolve a purely social association; so after a series of further mild proddings from my father, I agreed that he could contact the fraternity and ask them to put my name on their roster for the coming year. After some time a reply came back: To the deep consternation of my father it was flatly negative. The outcome of a meeting with the heads of the fraternity made things clear: They held no grudge against people of Jewish extraction; in fact, the preceding fall they had accepted a couple of students of the Jewish faith. They had, however, thereby violated the so-called Nürnberg articles adopted in 1919 by a national organization of fraternities, one of which specified that persons of Jewish descent were inadmissible as members. In my case that could simply not be handled by ignoring the person's religion or "race." There lived in Heidelberg a medical practitioner, Dr. Elsasser, well known to every child in town as a Jewish doctor. This man was a rather distant relative of ours, but it still was difficult to deny our "race." My father was crestfallen.

When my graduation from high school approached, I had made up my mind to study physics. Given the economically bad times, I was to begin by living at home and studying at the University of Heidelberg. The professor of physics there was a celebrity, Philipp Lenard. Years earlier, after he had received the Nobel prize, the university had offered him a chair and had built him a magnificent institute on the slope of a hill; it was the most conspicuous landmark in Heidelberg apart from the castle. It was also within easy walking distance from both my home and my high school, so for some time I had now and then missed an hour of school to sit attentively in the back of the physics lecture hall watching Lenard's admirable performance of demonstration experiments.

Lenard had by then a well-established reputation as a crank and also as an active collaborator in right-wing political movements. However, the day was still ten years in the future when Lenard was to retire from his professorship to devote himself entirely to the Nazi Party. Hitler duly rewarded him by making him President of the Nazi Academy of Sciences.

But in the fall of 1922, politics was far from my mind when I sat in the large lecture room waiting for my first regular class in physics to begin. Every seat in the hall was taken. In walked Professor Lenard wearing an impeccably tailored suit; to his left breast there was fastened a silver swastica of gigantic proportions, perhaps ten centimeters square. This was most unusual, if one remembers that in spite of war and revolution, Germany had then still remained a place of law and order. A distinguished senior professor was most certainly not expected to brandish symbols of political extremism in class. But the students thought otherwise. They applauded intensely. They clapped, and then they shouted; they kept on clapping and shouting, on and on and on. How long this continued, I cannot say precisely, but it was certainly the most dedicated and loudest ovation I ever witnessed in my life, before or after.

So here it was: The German academic youth had voted. They had voted clearly for the swastika. Perhaps this was a staged performance; one would not put it beyond the Nazis even at that early moment. But then, the hall remained filled at later lectures, so most of them must have been registered students.

It was only a few minutes from the physics lecture hall to my parents' apartment. I found them both at home ready to sit down for the midday dinner, which is the main German meal. At that moment I lost my composure. I started screaming, tears rolled down my cheeks: "I will not go to that lecture again. I will not. . . ." It took my father several days to quiet me down while he explained to me that I was only damaging myself, nobody else. He added that if I wanted to get out of Germany, the time was after I had gotten a university degree, not now. So, finally I relented.

During the year a number of people approached me, often unexpectedly, and told me that I must absolutely leave Heidelberg after the first year. The reason was clear and simple: After the one-year course in basic physics I would have to enter the laboratory, and Lenard was frequently seen in the laboratory. He was completely unpredictable, and he was very likely to attack me physically, take me by the scruff of my neck, and throw me out of the laboratory bodily. He was known to have done similar things before. It was clear that these good people, many barely knowing me, did not try to frighten me but were really concerned.

So in the fall of the year 1923 I moved to the University of Munich where I stayed for three semesters. At that time I wanted to become an experimental physicist; it was only about three years later that I switched to theoretical physics. By the third semester I was doing fairly advanced experiments. The professor of experimental physics was Wilhelm Wien, also a Nobel prize winner. He had built up a laboratory that was fairly large for those days, with some five junior faculty members around him. Early in my third semester in Munich, in 1924, one of the assistant professors approached me somewhat officiously and told me this: It was apparent that I was thinking of getting a Ph.D. at the institute. He wanted to point out certain things that were not clear on the surface—every single member of the faculty with the exception of the director and himself was a cardcarrying member of the Nazi party. So he, without having any personal interest in the matter, wanted to advise me that it might be decidedly better if I studied at another university. For instance, Göttingen was not only very good, it was "full of Jews."

At that time everybody knew about the Nazis. They had made their entrance into the larger world with the abortive "beer-hall putsch" that was engineered jointly by Hitler and Ludendorff, the former Chief of Staff of the Germany army during World War I. It took place in Munich in November 1923, shortly after I had arrived there. It seemed that an extended sojourn in an institute almost exclusively staffed by Nazis was going to be difficult, indeed. An inquiry with the director only made it perfectly clear that he would go to any length to avoid a scandal. Early in 1925, with the beginning of the spring semester, I moved to Göttingen.

Shortly after I had left Heidelberg, my parents had also left. My father had become involved with a then novel undertaking; it was what one would call a credit-union for government employees. He eventually resigned his judgeship and ended up as the chief legal adviser to their office in Berlin. The organization was popular and growing rapidly. My parents moved to Berlin around 1924. The corporation, being technically a private undertaking, gave him a considerable sum as severance pay in return for his giving up his tenured judgeship. He turned most of the money over to his friend Kaufmann in Basel who invested it outside of Germany. It suffered considerably during the Depression, but enough remained to help me after 1930.

Around 1934 father retired and my parents went to live in the Black Forest, but a few years later they had to leave Germany. After a year in a camp for refugees in England, they came to the United States where they first lived in Michigan, then in Chicago, where they both later died and are buried.

In my last years in Southern Germany, toward the end of high school and at the beginning of my university career, I became very fond of travelling and hiking. Much of this could be done not too far from home. I developed a practical system in which I combined travel on local trains with hikes, and since I soon learned the art of living on little during these trips, they were not expensive. There was no chance for a person of my background and upbringing to make money, however little, by working. Fortunately, my parents were generous in this respect. I saw a good deal of southern and central Germany and, after moving to Munich, began to wander often in the northern fore-Alps.

2
The Road to Science

A youngster growing up today can hardly believe that fifty years ago, and especially in Europe, the scientist was far less highly regarded than he is now. Not that science was looked down upon—it was just something that nobody in his good senses would choose as a profession. The old, traditional style of high-school education was based upon the classics; the type of school that had gradually developed for this study was called the "Gymnasium." (The term has no connotation whatever, in German, of physical exercise, as it has in English.) As a result of the rapid growth of the middle class in the nineteenth century, another type of curriculum had then appeared, based on science, mathematics, and modern languages, which was called the "Real-schule" and in my time was an alternative to the Gymnasium in many towns.

The Gymnasium had a nine-year curriculum (corresponding roughly to the fourth to twelfth grades in America, though more advanced at the end). In the first three years, one had nine hours a week of Latin. In the third year French and history were added, in the fourth year Greek and mathematics. Then the number of hours of Latin was slightly reduced, but otherwise these five subjects continued undiminished until graduation. There were some minor subjects such as natural science which began with natural history and eventually included a smattering of physics and chemistry. There was some physical education and some singing, from which I was soon excluded as totally unmusical. There was also, from beginning to end, a subject called "religion," taught for two hours a week. In the later years of school in particular, these classes were taught by young clergymen, in my case, by Protestant ministers. This instruction was compulsory unless the parents were officially registered as "without religion." But in nine years of high school, I never heard a minister talk even for an hour on a subject germane to the Christian religion; the talk was for weeks or months on end about marginal subjects that one may call "cultural history"—Byzantine art and the political development of Islam, for example. There was no required instruction in English; but during the last three or four years before graduation, a class in English was offered. My English, therefore, was abominable until I learned the language after immigrating to the United States and marrying a native American.

The men who taught the chief "cultural" subjects, Latin, Greek, history, while quite competent on the whole, were rarely inspired. That is to say, they transmitted very little to us of the spirit and greatness of classical antiquity, although they were convinced to a man of this greatness. The instruction in the early years consisted largely in the rote-learning of Latin and Greek grammar, declension, and conjugation. Eventually, of course, one read some of the classical writers, and then the quality of the teachers who supervised this activity improved. Even apart from this, however, it is impossible to hide the poetic grandeur of Homer in Greek or of Horace in Latin if a student is confronted with the text day after day. Nevertheless, the instruction was sufficiently inadequate to prevent me from learning to read Latin with fluency. But I did manage Greek, whose grammatical construction is simpler. I remember that I could read Homer without much difficulty, and I also remember that in my university years I could read stretches of the gospels in their original Greek.

As I now remember these years in the Gymnasium, I wonder just what this particular form of education did to a youngster like me. Such an educational scheme, no matter of what quality, is far from pragmatic. True enough, Homer praises the courage of his heroes, and Plato praises the philosophical depth of Socrates; but their circumstances are too far removed from modern life to be a useful example. This, however, I feel very strongly, is not the case for the personages depicted in the Bible, who are as close to us as if they lived today—but perhaps I am prejudiced. One thing is clear to me: This unpragmatic immersion into a past world must have tended to bring out in me the introverted features that I undoubtedly possessed long before.

I think that all this has a direct bearing upon the practice of science. Clearly, science has a pragmatic aspect; one usually thinks of engineering as "applied science." But science has also what I shall call, for lack of a better word, a philosophical aspect. Both aspects are necessary, complementing each other. To say, as some people do, that pragmatic science is good and that philosophical science is just an empty sport, is a sad misunderstanding. My own background and upbringing clearly directed me into the philosophical aspects of science, this being undoubtedly the main influence of my early German environment. Germans have predominantly thought of science as a philosophical enterprise. The English used the term "natural philosophy" from the days of Newton to well into the twentieth century; it seems to me excellently chosen.

Germans, however, have not forgotten the pragmatic side of science. To remind me of this in my youth, there was the vast complex of factories centered in the town of Ludwigshafen, across the Rhine river from Mannheim. This was the home of the famous German chemical trust, no doubt then and perhaps still today one of the largest industrial undertakings of the world. I was aware of its existence, of course, but toward the end of this period there arose a unique opportunity to see some of it at close quarters, in consequence of a tremendous explosion that occurred at Oppau, in 1921. Oppau is a village adjacent to Ludwigshafen on its north side which had long since been absorbed by the sprawling colossus of the chemical works. The explosion took place early in the morning. I was just beginning to get dressed. My windows were leaned-to. Suddenly there was a big, protracted boom as if from a distant explosion, and then my windows opened ever so slowly and steadily as if pushed by an invisible hand. There was a shattering of glass, then silence. I saw that a large shop window had been broken. Since there was nothing more, I went to school; everybody had heard the boom but nobody had been able to locate it. Radios then barely existed and there was no public broadcasting, so one had to wait until early next morning when the newspapers carried the definitive data: Within the area of the chemical trust, near the village of Oppau, a large store of ammonium nitrate had exploded all at once and caused great havoc. It turned out, in fact, somewhat later, to have been the biggest man-made explosion before the atomic bombs. It seems that the safety precautions had been adequate for many years without mishap; so, vast quantities of the material, tons and tons of it, had been stored in a large warehouse until that day in 1921 when the whole storehouse exploded.

My teacher of mathematics and science determined that his pupils should have a close-up view of an event which probably would not recur in their lifetime. He managed to organize an excursion, only two days after the explosion. Some buses took us to Oppau which is about twenty-five kilometers from Heidelberg as the crow flies. The buses deposited us there and left; we were supposed to find our own way home, by means of trolleys and commuter trains. When we arrived in Oppau we saw a sight that must be familiar to those who have been to Hiroshima or Nagasaki: where there had once been a huge steel construction of towering reaction chambers, all was now smashed to pieces; steel pipes, half a meter in diameter, were twisted into bizarre shapes as if they were so many delicate wires. If there were once wooden shacks such as are usually found on the grounds of factories, they had all disappeared, and the ground was bare except for some flattened rubble. But one comparatively new-looking three-story building of concrete seemed totally intact except for its many large windows. These were completely empty, not a scratch of glass or woodwork had remained, but the steel-concrete structure itself seemed quite unaffected. After we had seen these sights I left the group; I wanted before returning to see something of the living conditions of industrial workers. I saw them: Tract after tract of small houses intermingled occasionally with clearly older, more agricultural settlements. The expressionless, gray, and grim faces of the industrial workers were something I had rarely observed before. There were also those men about whom I had heard stories: Those who work at the dye vats and absorb the dye ineradicably in their skins. There were men with blue skins, with orange skins, with pink skins, quite a number of them. They walked with great dignity as if God had created them that way.

The man who had taken us to see Oppau was Karl Reinig, who first became my mathematics teacher around the eighth grade. Physics, however, did not appear in the curriculum until later. On closer acquaintance I found Reinig to be a self-made man. His father had been a miller in a small village of the fertile country southeast of Heidelberg, not too far from where my great-grandfather had lived. Reinig had strong political opinions, but he never spoke of them to me. I found out from others that he was a lifelong devoted socialist; presumably he didn't credit me with enough background and discrimination to understand the circumstances that make a man a socialist. Reinig must have been near fifty at that time; he was a bachelor who lived alone and was cared for by a housekeeper. Reinig was highly educated with a Ph.D. in mathematics. This was unusual; there was only one other Ph.D. among the teachers, a younger, slightly consumptive-looking man who had a passion for Sanskrit. But since the university paid him very little for whatever he did, he had to teach languages at our school to help feed a whole house full of children.

Reinig very soon discovered my interest in science and mathematics, so that our relations became more personal. He took me into his confidence, although he did not speak to me about his private life. He developed the habit of asking me to accompany him on long walks through the wooded hills that surround Heidelberg. We spoke about everything concerned with science and the nature of scientific inquiry, so far that is, as I was able to understand these things at my age. It was also clear that Reinig derived considerable satisfaction from these discussions. In the ninth grade the chief subject of mathematical instruction was solid geometry. Reinig turned to me one day and said: This is all rather primitive and boring stuff which you can learn in a fraction of the time that I am forced to devote to teaching it. Why don't you spend this time to learn calculus? If you get a book of calculus problems and do three of the problems for every class of mine, I will accept this as your mathematics homework and absolve you from solid geometry. So I procured a textbook of calculus and a fairly elaborate collection of calculus problems through which I worked one by one. Long before I graduated from the Gymnasium, I had an extensive working knowledge of calculus.

This was a challenge to me, the more valuable as there was a remarkable dearth of challenges in my young life. I ought to enlarge on this: My school was large, so for each year there were two parallel classes. Girls were admitted, but their number was usually very small, one or two per class. But in our year there happened to be nine girls, all in my class. These girls were more industrious than the boys, but since there were so many they could cling to each other; I saw comparatively little of them, except perhaps during the last year in school. That left about twenty boys in a class that can only be described as mediocre. In fact, my class had a reputation, remarked on by many teachers, Reinig included, for being the dullest crowd that had ever been seen in the school within human memory. I would not put it beyond some smart school administrator when the two classes were first formed (some years before I came to Heidelberg) to put all the talented boys into the parallel class to avoid competition between boys and girls. Hence at an age when young people do begin to ask questions about their world, nobody in my group asked any. There was also no latitude in one's scholastic program: Throughout high school the program was rigidly fixed, and no individual variations were permitted.

Combine this with the cynicism that pervaded much of the German middle class at that time, when all values were greeted with a sarcastic sneer. In the middle class of Central Europe, traditional values were, of course, based on Christianity. This was now constantly derided, but other values were not recognized. The socialists had shown their hand in the 1918 revolution, but had not gone very far; most of the middle class had only contempt for them. Other values, such as those of the Far East, which are so widely cherished in America, were simply unknown except to a few literati.

The more I saw of this cauldron of utter sarcasm, the more my interest in science deepened, if only as a psychological reaction. At that time my parents had ceased to take much interest in my scholastic program; they were satisfied if my grades did not fall below the standard "good," which I usually could achieve with very little effort. They had a struggle of their own to adjust to their new environment. After the 1918 revolution, my father had worked enthusiastically for the newly founded Democratic Party. This party was to the left of the National-Liberal party, the mainstay of the German middle class, and to the right of the socialists, the party of the working class. My father's main associate in this undertaking was a talented grammar-school teacher and his even more talented wife. This lady came from a very simple background and, without formal schooling which was unavailable to her, had by sheer determination acquired a remarkable erudition, including fluency in several languages (she read Greek philosophers in the original Greek). Since these people did not live too far from our own home, we became close friends. I well remember them as never too far from genteel poverty. Whatever the lady could gain on top of her husband's salary by tutoring and the like went to educate their two sons, first for their tuition in high school and later at the university.

Mostly, however, these people, Hofheinz was their name, were genuine idealists. Their idealism was of the practicing kind that had been preached by Greek philosophers: If you have recognized what is true and good, go out and do it; do not just talk about it. The Hofheinzes and Reinig were the only people I felt I could genuinely admire in the critical period from my fifteenth birthday, after I came to Heidelberg, to my twenty-first birthday, when I settled in Göttingen. Years after my own boyhood days in Heidelberg, when the Nazis came to power, Mr. Hofheinz was forced into a somewhat premature retirement. Both of them died a few years later of what in novels is called a broken heart. The Democratic Party had only a very mild success. While I was not a very passionate bystander, it seems to me that if any significant member of the bourgeoisie, such as a wealthy manufacturer or a well-known professor had joined the party actively, I could not have failed to hear about it.

But to return to science, at that age I began to look through the scientific "cabinet" of my school for instruments, but there were almost none. Most of the very meager instrumentarium consisted of demonstration equipment, which students were not permitted to touch. One day I found an old theodolite in excellent condition. A theodolite is a small telescope mounted on a tripod, with a device for measuring angles. This one must once have been an unusually expensive surveying instrument; God knows how it found its way into the Gymnasium. So I decided to take it into the field and carry out a triangulation of the city. Heidelberg is ideal for that since the city is surrounded by rather steep hills on which one can find many easily accessible lookout points. I succeeded in persuading a couple of my school fellows to join me in making lengthy numbers of measurements; the results were entered into a big, black notebook. At that point my friends deserted me, and I spent many weeks in smoothing data by means of statistical methods— which provided an excellent means of learning such methods.

Since the yield of the science "cabinet" in school was so meager, I became more anxious to build things myself. I used to ask my parents regularly to give me tools as presents for Christmas and birthdays. They were always very generous with presents, mostly books; among them, again, the German classics preponderated. After Goethe and Schiller, other poets and writers began to appear, and there seemed to be no end in sight, so that I was not successful in my request for tools. I am sure that neither my mother, having grown up in a city, nor my father, the lawyer son of a well-to-do businessman, had a very clear idea of how tools are used; but they were sure that tools were for manual activities which belonged to the "lower" classes. They had grown up in the rigidly stratified Wilhelmine society, and although this society had crumbled, its concepts survived. So on asking for tools, I invariably received toys, and I found in time that it was impossible to make the distinction between a tool and a toy clear to my parents.

I have always believed, for reasons whose psychological roots have remained obscure, that the use of tools is an indispensable step in human education. On my arrival in the United States in 1935–1939, it was with utter delight that I found an entire nation steeped in the usage of tools as a matter of course. Even the spoiled son of very wealthy parents seemed to find it natural to don overalls and to repair his automobile. But now, sad to say, this beautiful trait of American life has largely been lost through rapid urbanization.

At that time I had, besides Reinig, another guide toward my future activity in science: the books in my parents' library. There existed at that time in Germany a journal of popular science called *Kosmos* that was roughly on the level of our *Scientific American*. My father had the issues of this journal from about 1900 to the beginning of the First World War. Every year there had appeared some four or five small monographs about 100 pages long. These covered all branches of contemporary science, and their authors had been very carefully chosen: They not only knew their subjects thoroughly, but had a knack for popular presentation. I read most of the volumes; those dealing with physical science, atoms and crystals, light and X-rays, stars and galaxies I read twice, if not more often. With a little effort these books were quite understandable to an interested youngster, so that when I graduated from high school in 1922 I had a fairly good intuitive understanding of what the avant-garde of physical scientists of that time were thinking.

That, of course, did not settle my personal future. There was hardly any prospect that I could become full-time scientist, that is to say, a professor. Such positions were reserved for two kinds of people: prodigies—and I knew nothing that would qualify me as one—or those with connections to professorial society, which meant in practice marrying a professor's daughter. I could not think of the latter as a plausible career. In the preceding generation it had often sufficed to have had reasonably well-to-do parents, but with the lost war and the disappearance of all my parents' wealth, there was not enough money left to support me even for a few years. I began, therfore, to think of becoming an engineer, until in the last year of school Reinig changed my mind. He pointed out that there was a new profession, that of industrial physicist, comprising people who worked in the research laboratories then being developed by some of the larger industrial corporations. This would allow me to study at a university and to avoid much of the drudgery, such as learning engineering drawing, that was connected with a career at an engineering school. In Germany, the latter schools, while having the rank of universities, are physically separated from them; they are called "Technische Hochschulen" which I shall translate by the usual term, Polytechnic Schools. When I came to Munich, I registered simultaneously at the university and at the Polytechnic School which was about fifteen minutes' walk away; I took some of the engineering-drawing and other courses, but abandoned this after a few semesters. With the exception of that little sideline, my entire advanced education took place at universities; but at that time no fixed curriculum had as yet become consolidated for physicists. It existed for chemists who were already numerous at universities; this was carefully worked out, with a series of examinations along the way, and a diploma for those who didn't want to go on to the Ph.D. But there was nothing at all in physics; one was just a student and a free agent. I remember that in a few science classes one was given problems, and at the end of the semester one could get a certificate for having worked enough of them. As a result, I only had one examination in my career as a student, the Ph.D.; it was oral and lasted an afternoon.

In my father's library, I had also found a few books of a philosophical character. One of them has remained vividly in my memory: the zoologist Ernst Haeckel's *The Riddles of the Universe* (*Die Welträthsel*) subtitled, *Popular Studies in Monistic Philosophy.* It was the statement of a very coarse rationalism, one might call it straight materialism. This book had swept the German-speaking world. (I recently found a copy of the book in a local library. The preface is dated 1899, and that copy was the seventh edition, dated 1901, which seems to justify the term, "swept.") The coarseness of the work is very clearly expressed in the innumerable invectives against the Roman Pope as the representative of superstition on earth, which fill its later pages. There can be no doubt, however, that as a zoologist Haeckel was a savant of the first order, whose name ranks with the best in the history of biology. If, nevertheless, the official recognition of Haeckel was somewhat limited, it was clearly because the ruling group of the German Empire, still officially Christian, could not identify with a man who was so openly materialistic.

But the impact of Haeckel's philosophy upon the middle class was tremendous. When I first read it at age sixteen or seventeen, I was struck by the grandiose, monolithic simplicity of Haeckel's "world-view," although its very simplicity made me uncomfortable. My father made it very clear that he had no use for this or any other form of excessive rationalism; to prove this to himself and others he remained all his life a collector of stories about telepathy and other para-psychological phenomena, although he emphasized that it was too early to let these observations congeal into a scientific scheme.

Much as I disliked the crude philosophy of Haeckel, I can now see in retrospect that it was the shock I received from it that first opened my eyes to the genuine problems in the philosophy of science which occupied much of my thinking in later years. When I first read Haeckel I had no ideas about scientific research, let alone about the philosophy of science. Nor was I familiar with the famous aphorism of Mark Twain: "Isn't science wonderful? Such a towering edifice of speculation erected on such a slender base of fact." As I matured intellectually, I began increasingly to recognize the great and ever-present temptation of the scientist, namely, to lose sight of the empirical facts and to put method and simplicity first. In special fields of scientific research, one is usually close enough to the facts to keep this harmless; it is when the scientist begins to generalize and philosophize that he can most easily fool himself.

At that time of my life, under the pressure of anti-Semitism, I had begun to take my forebears seriously. To give these feelings a specific expression, I identified these forebears with the authors of the Bible. These men, clearly, were unanimous about one thing, whatever their other divergences: The understanding of nature, of man, or of God, was not a wholly intellectual matter. But it was altogether clear that in Haeckel's world there was nothing but Haeckel-like intellects trying to comprehend the world intellectually. He made it altogether clear that the authors of the Bible were just so many ignorant savages dwelling in superstition when the world had not yet been enlightened by modern science, by Lavoisier, Darwin, and, presumably, by Ernst Haeckel himself.

Stimulated by such quasi-philosophy I began to think about philosophy. I can best express myself here in terms of a word of the famous philosopher Hegel: He has said that if in some field quantitative differences become very pronounced they tend to turn into differences in quality. But as the great philosophers of science have made clear, the scientist in his methods has no place for qualities; qualities pertain to philosophy proper or, as it is usually expressed, to "metaphysics." Thus when the scientist encounters a quality, he will try to inquire into its quantitative, mathematical as well as logical, background. Let me give an example: The notion of heat appears to us first as a quality vouchsafed by our perceptions. But physicists have shown that for them heat is motion of the molecules, and that the properties of warm and cold bodies can in all detail and quantitatively be accounted for by such motion.

As the philosophers of science tell us over and over again, the purpose of the scientific method in its more philosophical versions is to order and to structure the multifarious data of experience. The most common superstition among scientists is that this structuring is "simple" or "obvious." Let me introduce an example: For thousands of years some of the cleverest and wisest men have studied the motion of the stars and developed mathematical descriptions, which had one thing in common: They were complicated. Around 300 B.C. the Greek astronomer Aristarchos proposed a scheme according to which the earth was a sphere rotating about itself and also moving in an orbit around the sun, as did the other planets. But the society of that time was not ready for this view. Aristarchos' scheme has only come down to us in the technical literature. Otherwise, for eighteen centuries, up to Copernicus, it was ignored or dismissed as idle speculation.

This demonstrates that two ingredients are essential in a major scientific development. One is pragmatism, a mastery of the technical aspects; the other, equally important, is harmony with the prevailing ideas of society. But society is controlled by unconscious tendencies, and there is no evidence that we can readily learn to control these tendencies, in turn, by rational volition. So, in order to find out what makes science tick, we might well have to mobilize sensitivities whose nature is not yet fully understood. The current unrelieved and brutal dominance of pragmatism in science, often clothed in terms such as political or other "relevance," is frightening. Since I have had a unique opportunity to see much of modern scientific development at first hand, I have had the urge to put these observations into a philosophical framework of my own making, of which more later.

To return to my story: For some time my mother's family had suggested that I join the commercial enterprise left by my grandfather. After his death the business had been carried on by my mother's brother and brother-in-law. It was quite prosperous, but it was felt that the enterprise needed some young blood, and I was my grandfather's only male descendant. There were also various sidelines of this particular commercial activity that an active young man could develop. Thus, after some prodding, I agreed to spend the summer of 1922 in Mannheim to try a commercial career. I was surprised by how much I liked this occupation. I presume that this was primarily because I was given a framework for my activities, definite working hours during which I was expected to produce at least some work, just enough to prevent the idle dreaming whereby one could fill the hours listening to a pedagogue hold forth about Greek literature. I was also paid a small salary every week and found having money in my pocket and the possibility of taking out a girl now and then, most gratifying. I found the complexity of commercial interrelationships surprisingly interesting, and also likely to keep me busy for a long time. Mostly, I liked the idea of becoming an adult member of society almost instantly instead of having to wait on the sidelines for many more years, as I would have to do, and actually did, to become a professional scientist. On the other hand, there were great losses on leaving the pursuit of science. I would have to abandon that deeply satisfying feeling of intellectual adventure that is the glory of any scientist with an inquisitive mind. I had already at that time become deeply committed to scientific activity, as I now discovered. What with other limitations, due partly to my innate disposition and partly to the hostility of the society into which I was plunged, preoccupation with science already had turned into one of my mainstays. So I returned from this commercial apprenticeship with a renewed determination to become a physicist.

I have already described my first class that fall with Philipp Lenard and how it turned into a political demonstration. This class continued throughout the year and was of a remarkably high caliber with respect to science and in the performance of numerous experiments. But Lenard's personality did not attract people of any note; therefore, I never had to go into the large physics building except for this one class. It was only in 1932, when Walther Bothe, the nuclear physicist, had become Lenard's successor that I got a close-up view of the laboratory. I was visiting Bothe in the late fall of that year, and he took me around the laboratory. The building dated from the early years of the century, and its inside architecture would have satisfied the dreams of an early movie director bent on showing the public what a scientific laboratory is like. The most outstanding features were the numerous and big electric meters placed everywhere as if part of the interior decoration. There must have been hundreds of them. As we walked along, now and then Bothe would whip out a pen knife and would begin to scratch the surface of one of these meters. Then he explained: It was one of Lenard's fixed ideas that the unit of electrical current was unjustly called the ampere. When the international conference was held, where the names of the electrical units had been fixed, the German delegation had appeared with the intention of calling this unit the weber, after a famous German physicist, but they had been outvoted. So Lenard had little labels printed with the word "weber," that were pasted on the face of each meter to cover up ampere. Bothe explained to me that he had already shown some dozen visitors around the laboratory since he had taken over but every time he discovered three or four meters that he had overlooked.

When I entered the university of Heidelberg I had decided to pass the examination which licensed me to teach science in high schools. The regulations for the State of Baden prescribed that a candidate had to take one course and one laboratory in each natural science. I therefore, took the main course and laboratory in botany at Heidelberg and was so successful that those who supervised the laboratory tried to talk me into making botany my chief subject. Later on, in Munich, I took a course called "historical geology," and still later, in Göttingen, I took a course and a laboratory in zoology that were very instructive. Ultimately, I passed the licensing examination two years after my Ph.D., but in Berlin, for the high schools of Prussia rather than of Baden, and with different requirements. I was examined in physics and mathematics—no other subjects were required—but there was a compulsory minor in philosophy. For some months previous to the examination I "crammed" philosophy but I failed to memorize sufficiently the terminology that the then leading professor of philosophy had established; so I failed in the examination. But my performance in physics and mathematics had been so outstanding that the examiners in philosophy were embarrassed; they merely told me emphatically that my grasp of modern philosophical terminology was inadequate and let me get by.

During the year in Heidelberg I became friends with a fellow student of physics. Siegfried Rösch was the child of a local family, who, being a few years older than I, had been drafted into the war and had lost one of his lungs in a gas attack. He had adjusted well, however, and managed to live a long and satisfactory life. He was well ahead in his studies, working under the professor of mineralogy on a thesis about crystal optics. Through Siegfried I became acquainted with the fascinating field of optics and with the devices employed there, as well as with some of the procedures used in physiological optics. This was valuable to me since my esthetic sense (not to say artistic interest), although well developed, was essentially visual, my sense for music being totally inadequate. But in everything visual, from optical experiments to painting and sculpture, I felt very much at home.

After his graduation Siegfried joined the Leitz Company, a well known manufacturer of microscopes and became one of their chief research scientists, working in the physics and physiology of colors. He was the best type of learned man, the German "Gelehrte," as sweeping and infectious in the enthusiasm for his field as he was industrious and self-critically fastidious in all the details of his work.

At the end of two semesters at Heidelberg, my father surprised me: He had by then begun to make a number of external contacts, which eventually, about a year later, would lead him to resign his judgeship and move to Berlin. Among them was a man, an industrialist or financier, who also owned a small machine shop in a southern suburb of Berlin. My father had evidently come to understand the benefits of manual training for a prospective physicist, and he agreed with the gentleman that I could serve as an apprentice for a couple of months in this machine shop, without pay on either side; my father would take care of my personal expenses in Berlin. Since I had never been away from home for any length of time, this sounded attractive enough. When a few weeks later I presented myself there, I found a conventional shop with a work force of half a dozen men, all rather distinctly proletarian in dress and demeanor. It was easy to see that they would not be interested in making the acquaintance or a young bourgeois. After I had located the foreman he remembered that the owner had given him vague instructions about me; they could hardly have been more than a request to keep the young man busy. I never laid eyes on the owner while I was there. The foreman told me that there was a time-honored beginning for the apprenticeship of a mechanic: to make a perfect cube with a file. He handed me the materials, a shapeless piece of soft steel about the size of a fist, and a big file with a wooden handle, led me to a workbench with a large vise, and told me to start work. Since I soon found that any communication with these men was hopeless, and since I was as much as ever financially dependent on my father, it was a choice between filing my cube and trying to see and enjoy as much as I could of Berlin, or else of returning home and admitting to what must have looked very much like defeat. I chose to remain. I continued filing every day; toward the end of my stay the piece of metal had been reduced to a cube-like small box the size of a hazelnut.

This year, 1923, was the peak of inflation for the German currency, when a loaf of bread cost 100,000 marks one day and a million marks several weeks later. In order to make me independent of this, my father had appealed to his friend, Kaufmann, the banker from Basel, who had established for me an account in American dollars at a large bank situated on the street *Unter den Linden*. Once a week I took half a day off to go downtown by subway and withdrew my allowance in marks; and it was more each time, of course. Returning to my rented room, I at once bought enough food staples to last the week, for within three days, all the prices would rise appreciably, by fifteen percent say, so that my allowance would have run short and would not have permitted such small pleasures as an excursion to Potsdam or to the lake country on Sundays. I had rented a garrett room, adjacent to a studio that belonged to a lady, who in her younger days had been an active artist. She was very motherly and helped me in my first attempts toward personal independence.

I was too young, much too callous, and too inexperienced to understand what this galloping inflation must have meant—actual starvation and misery—to people who had to live on pensions or other fixed incomes, or even to wage earners, especially those with children, whose pay lagged behind the rate of inflation. One heard occasional comments on the bad things the inflation did, but the main mood seemed to be fatalistic. The government was dominated by the Social-Democrats who had come to power in the 1918 revolution. Their voters, the laboring men were the people who suffered most from the inflation. Ultimately in the fall of 1923 the inflation was stopped and a new, stable currency introduced by government decree. This reorganization of public finances introduced much further suffering during the months of the adjustment period; the profiteers got richer, and the poor kept on starving. By the time the government brought itself to act against the inflation, it was psychologically already too late: The image of a do-nothing government of the left had settled firmly in the popular mind.   The savings of the little people had disappeared while the possessions of the landed proprietors and the industrialists had never been touched.

In the fall of 1923 I moved to Munich where I had no one who could advise me about the study of physics. But Munich was by far the largest and best university in southern Germany, and closer to Heidelberg than the larger universities in the north. I did not particularly enjoy living there, and I made no friends that lasted beyond my stay. I also developed no sympathy for the more or less ritual operation of beer-swilling carried on every fall in dimly lit halls, where the effect of central heating is supplemented by the animal heat of the assembled bodies.

From Munich it is only about sixty to eighty kilometers to the range of the fore-Alps that lie between the Bavarian plain and the Inn river in the Tyrol. Since these mountains are easily and cheaply reached by train, and contain numerous, inexpensive youth hostels. I spent many pleasant weekends there. Innumerable trails go to the top of mountains often two kilometers high which provide magnificent views. I never tired of them. About the middle of my three-semester stay in Munich, in the early summer of 1924, I made a trip to Italy staying in Rome for two weeks and then for some days in Florence.

My stay in Munich gave me the first insight into the structure of German universities: They are primarily feudal, an array of little kings, based on talent. I shall adopt consistently the English equivalents of the then current German terminology. A major professor in the natural sciences almost always heads an "institute." The academics who surround him are his "assistants"; in the American equivalent this includes everyone from an instructor to an associate professor. There was a powerful economic basis for the system: Tuition was paid for individual classes, and a large percentage of this money went to the teacher. This, of course, created an economic incentive for the professor to teach an attractive class, and also discouraged him from delegating teaching functions to others. It also forced the universities to be very circumspect in choosing major professors: They had to be talented enough to ensure that they would not simply become professional classroom teachers after their appointments. The reverse of this system was the "Privatdocent," a position that entitled its holder to teach classes, but not to receive a salary. This "privilege" was acquired through an elaborate ritual during which one had to submit significant research papers. Obviously, a Privatdocent was very limited in what he could teach since he had to have the permission of his professor, who could be counted upon not to let the young man teach subjects that would reduce attendance at his own classes.

The life of a student who did not follow one of the well-trodden careers such as medicine, law or, lately, chemistry was utterly free. There was neither the personal supervision nor the counselling that prevails in universities within the Anglo-Saxon tradition. The English system does not exist on the Continent. But while in France, as I found out later, there is an annual overall examination sufficiently stiff to force the student to work hard all year in order to remain competitive, there was no such thing in Germany; neither were there exams connected with individual classes nor overall examinations of any kind. I cannot speak of other and older forms of academic study; so far as I remember there were examinations for medics as well as for engineers.

In physics there were two kingdoms at the university of Munich. There was first the Physics Institute directed by Wilhelm Wien, a famous experimentalist. There I did considerable experimental work which I enjoyed very much; in fact, I did everything I could lay my hands on. During my third semester, I worked assiduously on such complicated matters as the Millikan oildrop experiment and the electrostatic quadrant electrometer. These terms might not be too meaningful today, but they were household words for physicists in my youth. This association terminated by my going to Göttingen, under conditions that I have described toward the end of the first chapter.

The other institute was that of Arnold Sommerfeld, professor of theoretical physics. Sommerfeld was as brilliant a teacher as he had been during all of his younger years as a research man. He taught a cycle of theoretical physics courses lasting six semesters; when I arrived he was at the last semester, which I just couldn't follow. The next semester the cycle began again, and I took its first two semesters, the best university classes I ever attended. Sommerfeld lectured without a textbook or without typed notes given to the students; he wisely only brought out his series of books, which are essentially the text of this cycle of classes, when he was about eighty years old. This technique, I think, has considerable pedagogical advantages because it forces the student to learn from handwritten notes, which involves his nervous apparatus and memory much more intimately than if he used a printed text. This was not unusual at the time; I do not remember any teacher from my student years who used a printed or typewritten text. Sommerfeld never used an eraser in his classes. He would stand in front of a very large fourfold blackboard that covered one wall of the classroom; two of these boards could be rolled up to expose two others behind. In a meticulous hand he would write formulas as he developed them; sections were separated from each other and some formulas emphasized by boxing them in with straight lines. At the end of the hour, the boards were almost filled with formulas, and no matter how difficult the mathematical process, it had seemed a major esthetic experience.

The mainstay of Sommerfeld's academic activity was his weekly seminar on contemporary atomic physics in which his assistants and a small number of students participated. Small as this group was, it was extremely lively. Sommerfeld had written a semi-popular book entitled

Atombau und Spektrallinien (*Atomic Structure and Spectral Lines*) which was immensely popular both among neighboring scientists such as chemists, engineers, biologists, and also among physicists themselves. It had been revised in a number of editions to keep it abreast of modern developments which in the 1920's were coming very fast. In fact, every year several papers would appear in the scientific literature that opened quite unexpected vistas on the nature of material bodies, from atoms to molecules to crystals to stars. Each week one of the seminar's older participants, often Sommerfeld himself, would give a carefully prepared lecture about one such recent scientific event; Sommerfeld's quick mind would seize on the significant and novel points and a lively discussion would almost always ensue. In that period it was still possible for a physicist to think of himself as the intellectual guardian for an understanding of all the phenomena of inanimate nature. In his book Sommerfeld showed incomparably how one came from this broad sweep to the study of the atom as the central phenomenon. Of course, that age has passed and cannot be revived. With the successes of applied science during the Second World War, scientific pursuits became fashionable, and the very nature of scientific research as a social enterprise changed radically as tens of thousands began to study science. This led to tremendous specialization and often to a shallow philosophical attitude—pure pragmatism.

Although my knowledge of Arnold Sommerfeld's rise as a scientist is only second-hand, it is worth recounting since he was one of the first men who became a full-time, theoretical physicist when this specialty developed around the turn of the century. Up to that time, professional physicists had existed only within universities. To make a living outside of teaching, a man had to be practical enough to call himself an engineer. In order to teach a university physics course, one had to be able to manipulate apparatus; those who could not were considered mathematicians. With the growth of knowledge and the penetration of both physics and mathematics into engineering, this changed in the second half of the nineteenth century. A little later, by about the First World War, almost every university in Germany had a professorship of theoretical physics in addition to the older chair of general physics which was then often renamed experimental physics. Sommerfeld's career fell right into this transition period; in fact, he was one of its pioneers.

Sommerfeld, born in 1868, spent his student years and some years thereafter in Göttingen where he was influenced by a great master of mathematics, Felix Klein. His first major work, entitled *Theory of the Top (Gyroscope)* appeared under their joint authorship. It is a 1,000-page treatise that was published in four installments, from 1897 to 1910. But if one reads the sundry prefaces of these four volumes, one sees that Klein, while starting the whole enterprise by teaching a class on it, must have left most of the hard work of elaboration to Sommerfeld. The subject had long been recognized as one of the most difficult, perhaps the most difficult in traditional mathematical physics. Ever since Leonard Euler had, in the middle of the eighteenth century, formulated and then solved the equations of motion of a gyroscope, the subject had been favored among mathematicians. But Sommerfeld, disregarding much of the already mountainous literature, wrote a treatise of extraordinary simplicity in spite of some rather advanced mathematics. He carried the treatment from elementary models over higher mathematics to all kinds of engineering applications. It was one of the first books to demonstrate what is meant by theoretical physics or, as some call it, applied mathematics: a treatment that joins purely abstract, mathematical insights to pragmatic results. The book also, of course established Sommerfeld's position in the scientific world.

In 1900 he was made professor of mechanics at the Polytechnic School in the city of Aachen, near the Western border of Germany. While mechanics is an ancient engineering subject, Sommerfeld used his position in an original manner, which became almost legendary in later years. He asked his engineering colleagues to point out problems on which he could exercise his mathematical skill. From this there arose a novel branch of theoretical physics: the mathematical treatment of the propagation of electromagnetic fields and waves. Beginning with the propagation of an electric disturbance along a wire, he proceeded to such intricate problems as the propagation of a radio wave from an antenna over the earth. These and a host of similar ones yielded to mathematical analysis; this subject has long since become familiar to those electrical engineers who are involved with the art's more subtle theoretical aspects.

In 1906 Sommerfeld was appointed professor of theoretical physics at the University of Munich, staying there until his retirement in 1940. He now turned to atomic physics. In 1919 he published the large, semi-popular work already mentioned, which I studied in great detail as a student. It soon became my major source for the precise understanding of modern atomic physics. Years later, when quantum mechanics had been consolidated into a general mathematical scheme, Sommerfeld

Arnold Sommerfeld

wrote a supplementary volume, but by then he was beyond his prime, and it did not have the phenomenal success of the earlier book; it was also much more technical in style, so that it did not differ radically from the numerous other textbooks that became available after 1930.

Stimulated by Sommerfeld's seminar I began to read some scientific literature on my own. I particularly remember a paper by James Franck, then in Göttingen. Franck had observed higher spectral lines of a very rarefied luminous gas, lines that involved highly excited states of the atoms. This rarefied gas was embedded in a much denser but still dilute atmosphere of an inert, noble gas. One could easily calculate that the higher states of the luminous atoms corresponded to large orbits of their electrons, so large, in fact, that the electrons which produced the observed radiation would have to penetrate through several of the neighboring atoms of the inert gas. Nevertheless, the spectral lines corresponding to the excited states remained fully visible. But this was altogether incomprehensible from a simple mechanical viewpoint. If the electron was like a little billiard ball, it would be deflected on crossing another atom, and there would be no spectral line at all. Here was an unexpected glimpse into a different order of nature in the minute dimensions of the atoms. This would soon be expressed naturally in the mathematical language of quantum theory. In the summer of 1924, when it had been made clear to me that future experimental work in Wien's Institute would be unsalutary, I asked Sommerfeld to write a letter of introduction to James Franck on my behalf, a request to which he at once acceded. Thus, when I arrived in Göttingen early in 1925, Franck accepted me almost immediately as one of his Ph.D. candidates.

In Munich, I also attended classes in theoretical physics given by one of Sommerfeld's assistants, Karl F. Herzfeld, whom I was to meet again, many years later, in the United States. Herzfeld was a specialist in the kinetic theory of gases for which he was already distinguished when I knew him in Munich. Later, after some years at Johns Hopkins University, he joined the Catholic University of America in Washington where he became chairman of the physics department, then very small; over the years he built it up in a remarkable fashion. It was one of the few physics departments I have seen that after the war did not become unbalanced by an excess of nuclear and high-energy physics.

The suite of offices that made up Sommerfeld's Institute opened upon some central rooms that were comfortably furnished and served as commons room as well as library. Current scientific periodicals in several languages were spread around, and the bound volumes were shelved along the walls. One could sit there and read, and also meet others informally. A fellow student whom I remember was a man who would be hard to forget: Werner Heisenberg. Our studies overlapped for one semester, the fall semester of 1923, after which he obtained his Ph.D. and left for Göttingen. When a year later I also went there, Heisenberg was only one semester away from leaving for Copenhagen where he stayed with Niels Bohr until being appointed professor of theoretical physics at the University of Leipzig in 1927. He frequently visited Göttingen, so that, although I rarely got to see him, I heard now and then through third parties about his doings and his work. I did not talk to him again until nearly half a century later, at an official function in Washington, D.C., around 1972, where we exchanged a few pleasant words of mutual recognition. He died a few months before this book was written.

Very soon after I came to Munich, I heard the stories that circulated among the students of physics, about Heisenberg's beginnings. His father was a professor at the university and a specialist in Byzantine culture and history, a subject not generally required in any curriculum. When Werner was close to graduating from high school, his father one day came to see Sommerfeld and said: I have a very difficult problem on my hands—my son is a scientific prodigy. He then demonstrated that this was not just a conceit of either father or son. Don't worry, said Sommerfeld, when he comes to the university send him to me; I will take care of him. The story may well be apocryphal, but it shows what his schoolfellows thought before he had even finished his studies. When the time for Heisenberg's thesis came, Sommerfeld said: You will be busy with atomic physics for the rest of your life; so you might as well learn that there are other things in science. He gave him a subject in the theory of turbulence, a branch of fluid mechanics. Heisenberg turned out a not overly inspired, but altogether incisive, piece of work, which has since been quoted numberless times in the literature on the subject.

When I encountered Werner Heisenberg he was a young man of medium height, of solid if not sturdy build, with a smooth, freckled face under a bush of straight, brownish hair. His naturally pale skin was sunburnt from his very frequent weekend excursions into the Alps. I had the impression, from such stories as I heard, that Heisenberg's chief ambition was to become an accomplished climber of rocks and mountains. He was easy in manner, not at all stiff, but there was some backdrop of reserve which he never quite seemed to lose on the occasions when I saw him. I had several casual exchanges on physics with him at Sommerfeld's Institute. Once I wanted his opinion about some half-baked ideas of mine on a subject of spectroscopy. I had the impression that he had given thought to the subject himself, and he strongly advised me not to let the matter rest with general thoughts, but to carry out some intricate mathematical calculations. At that stage of my training, I found the problem rather forbidding, and before I could rally my efforts Heisenberg had left.

One thing has engraved itself into my memory: On several occasions I heard Heisenberg say that he liked to do physics because doing physics was "fun." This was a great revelation to me. Having grown up in the stolid environment of the German middle class, I could think of scientific research as a matter of duty, or of personal ambition, or just to make money; or perhaps, if one had a classical education, one could think of oneself as driven by the demon of which Socrates always talks in Plato's dialogues. But to think of doing science "for the fun of it" was a new insight into the joy of life that left me exhilarated and deeply impressed.

After Heisenberg had written the article that made him famous, he referred to it often as "The Great Saw." and when asked what this meant he said it was the tool to saw off the limb on which the old physical theory rests. This work started the entire mathematical development of quantum mechanic, and the development was extraordinarily rapid. Heisenberg's paper has properly been compared with Einstein's famous paper of 1905 which started the theory of relativity. Both of these articles aim specifically at revising physics from the viewpoint of a critical philosophy that would eliminate "metaphysical" constructs, as the founder of the philosophy of science, Ernst Mach, had put it in the 1880s. I do not know of any other papers in the realm of theoretical physics that would compare to these two in philosophical impact. But while Einstein's paper had been carefully worked out and polished, so that it is in definitive shape and can still be read to advantage, Heisenberg published the raw idea, as it were, which then was made into a comprehensive theory with the help of others, particularly Born and Jordan, Dirac, and Niels Bohr.

When Heisenberg settled in Leipzig, it must have been a surprising, perhaps traumatic, experience for him. Leipzig is a sprawling commercial and manufacturing town set in a somewhat uninspiring flat landscape, very far removed from the majestic Alps near Munich or from the placid charms of the Baltic at Copenhagen. But Leipzig is also an old city; it was traditionally the musical capital of Germany, the home of the Bach family; and its concerts were famous. Heisenberg had to give up mountain climbing and must have returned more emphatically to the first great love of his life, music, which he seems to have cultivated even before his passion for physical science developed. By then he had an income that freed him from economic problems, especially since he was young and unmarried. But I am still baffled by his later decision, when the Nazis came to power in 1933, to endure Hitler. Everyone else in Germany who had connections abroad knew by then that Hitler was as bad as Genghis Khan or Attila had been in their time. Heisenberg's decision was one of these processes that we cannot fathom and call irrational His assistant, Felix Bloch had to leave on "racial" grounds. Bloch was Swiss and had grown up in Zurich; he went to the United States and became professor at Stanford University where he remained for the rest of his life. Heisenberg had become very famous by then and he had received offers from many distinguished universities in Europe and America. Everyone knew that the Nobel prize was just around the corner; it arrived in the fall of 1933. Heisenberg had been travelling and lecturing in many countries, so that he was not a recluse, ignorant of the world. Whatever unexpected psychological complexities had been brought to the fore by his rapid rise, we do not know and are unlikely to find out.

Some years later Heisenberg made a radical change. He felt disinclined to continue theoretical physics during the war in the way he had before; but he did not retreat into a similarly abstract subject for which he would have been ideally qualified, keeping to it until Hitler had blown over. Instead, he wanted to be practical and ended up supervising the German program to build a nuclear reactor, as Fermi did in the United States (about whose work Heisenberg, apparently, knew nothing). His labors in this field are a matter of record. It was a most unlucky story: Each time he came close to the point where the reactor would have gone "critical," he was bombed out by Allied air attacks and had to start from the beginning elsewhere. After the war he was director of the Max-Planck Research Institute in Munich for many years. He collected many honors and into his last years actively followed the progress of nuclear and high-energy physics. But some of the luster had gone out of him.

3

The World of Göttingen

When I arrived in Göttingen there were three professors of physics there, an unusual number for that time. They were Robert Pohl, James Franck, and Max Born, the theoretician. Of these, Pohl was teaching the general course for beginners. Pohl was also very active in his line of research, which was the study of color centers in crystals, a subject that a quarter-century later began to assume technological importance when the processes that had been studied in Pohl's Institute were used to produce colors on the face of television tubes. When many years later, after the Second World War, I worked at the RCA Laboratories in Princeton, I found that among those dealing with television tubes, Pohl's name was widely known.

Physics had its own building at Göttingen, a large, fairly new, brick construction situated at the southern end of town, some ten minutes walk from the center where the main university buildings were. The tenants of this building were Pohl and Franck. Pohl, who ran the First Physical Institute, had a bevy of Ph.D. candidates working in the upper floors of the building; Franck, whose laboratory was called the Second Physical Institute, occupied the ground floor. It often seemed to me that without the quite extraordinary personality of James Franck there would probably have been a less peaceful atmosphere than actually prevailed within the confines of the physics building.

Franck himself did not lecture much. He usually gave some specialized class on atoms and molecules that was held in a small lecture room of some twenty-five to thirty seats, which precluded a large attendance. Franck was extremely restrained in any public activity; even in this small class, he rarely raised his voice beyond the ordinary conversational level, so that one had to listen carefully to follow him. Fairly soon after I arrived, Franck assigned me a research subject, and I found myself with a room of my own. But James Franck's office was usually open; it had in it a very old, very battered sofa on which I sat often enough. In fact, my own notion of a scientist's paradise is pretty clearly circumscribed by this battered sofa, with Franck sitting at one end of it, myself at the other, and a rather lively discussion between us. Franck's main interest was the study of atoms and molecules by the simplest possible means, of which there are two: electrons and light. Earlier, Franck had experimented with electrons passing through a highly rarefied gas; he had shown that the electrons transfer energy strictly in lumps or packages. For this achievement James Franck together with his younger collaborator, Gustav Hertz, received the Nobel prize for physics in 1925. This was less than a year after I had arrived in Göttingen. It was characteristic of Franck that there were minimal celebrations: Franck had no detectable personal vanity.

After this great discovery that had occurred before the war, Franck had been gradually studying atomic and molecular behavior by means of light. That is to say, he and his students investigated optical emission, absorption, and fluorescence. In fluorescence the elementary process is composite: One quantum of light is absorbed while another quantum of a slightly different energy is simultaneously emitted. I had received a subject for my thesis dealing with fluorescence. While I was trying to make all the required technical preparations, I would drop in, now and then, at Franck's office and question him about atomic physics. More often than not, this became a discussion, and I have long come to regard Franck as my main teacher of science.

Most days, in the morning, Franck would make the rounds of his laboratory accompanied by his assistants, of whom I remember four. The senior was Otto Oldenberg, a tall, dignified looking, and very quiet man. He was the son of a long-term professor at the university who was already famous for his translations of certain Sanscrit scriptures hitherto inaccessible to the West. Otto himself was a distinguished physicist who was offered a visiting professorship at Harvard around 1931. After this visiting year, Harvard gave him a permanent position, and he remained there for the rest of his life. There was also Miss Herta Sponer, smart and well organized; she kept Franck's laboratory running on an even keel and she did as well in this as in her science. In 1938 she became professor of physics at Duke University, where she remained. Later, after the death of Mrs. Franck she became Franck's second wife.

Franck was greatly interested in physical chemistry, especially in how molecules are built up from atoms with the electrons providing the glue, as it were, to hold the molecules together. Since there are so

James Franck with Herta Spóner, Otto Oldenberg in back

many types of molecules, there was material for analysis lasting for endless years. When Franck settled at the University of Chicago after having done a tour of duty at Los Alamos during the war, he concerned himself mainly with questions of basic chemistry.

All those I have met in my own life who had the opportunity of coming close to Franck, agree that he was one of the most remarkable individuals they ever met. If I were asked to specify the main feature of his personality, I would say that he showed a certain gentle humility that he never seemed to lose even under provocation. I never saw him overwrought and rarely angry even if there was ample reason for anger; he described the cause of his feeling in such dignified words as to make it appear rational rather than purely emotional. But if he felt that something exceeded the morally permissible, he could express himself in perfectly clear and precise terms. There was nothing provincial about Franck's universe; he came from a rather well-to-do Hamburg family which might have had a cosmopolitan outlook since the name "James" is English and does not exist in German (the nearest equivalent is the biblical "Jacob"). From all I heard, the personal relations between Max Born and James Franck were very close; it always astounded me how two such radically different personalities could live in proximity without friction. But that it could be done was, in my opinion, the chief foundation for Göttingen's position as the center of world physics during the 1920s.

I was able to make some friends among the students in Franck's Institute and among some of the neighboring groups. These people were youthful representatives of all the types found in the German middle class. If there was anything special, it was because physics was still a relatively new subject. There was also plenty of room in Göttingen for those who wanted more practical, industry-oriented work; in addition to Pohl's laboratory, there were a number of institutes of applied science, an activity in which Göttingen had been pioneering, prodded by the famous mathematician Felix Klein, to whom I shall revert later. The relations of Franck and Born and their people to this applied end of the spectrum were tenuous; I do not remember meeting more than a few representatives of the applied sciences, and these only very rarely.

Among those whom I befriended, there was one student of Franck's, a tall fellow with abundant red hair. He came from Westfalen and, after he had obtained his Ph.D., he joined a steel works near his home where I once visited him. He explained to me how he was developing

measurements of the temperature at which iron melts where previously
one was dependent on the word of an iron master. But the whole
rough-and-tumble of an iron foundry was to me so novel that it was as
if he had emigrated to a foreign country; I eventually lost touch with
this man.

I had a more enduring relationship with another friend, Fritz
Houtermans. He had come to Göttingen before me and was already a
Ph.D. candidate of Franck's. We became and for long remained
intimate, seeing each other at least once a day. His background was
rather different from mine: His father was the somewhat stodgy
director of the provincial branch office of a large bank. His mother was
a Viennese intellectual, with Fritz the only child. Predictably, the
marriage did not endure, and Fritz grew up in Vienna with his mother.
The mother, being partly Jewish, frequented a circle of "progressive"
intellectuals, mostly Jewish, that flourished in the earlier years of the
century. Fritz had been extensively exposed to this environment and
affected its mannerisms. He was, moreover, a very witty man, in fact,
the most witty man I had yet met. He also possessed an almost
inexhaustible store of Viennese Jewish stories and jokes. It was only
toward the end of my three years in Göttingen that I began to discern a
certain repetitive streak in these stories. But the trick that they imply,
the application of the accumulated wisdom of a group to novel
situations, is very useful. I was almost totally unacquainted with such
anecdotes and with the ideas coming from the rich Jewish tradition,
and Fritz used to tease me not infrequently for being the most extreme
case of a "goy" (non-Jew) he had by then encountered. Fritz has the
unquestionable merit of having introduced me to Viennese coffee-
house life. He discovered something that could substitute for the
Viennese original: At a walking distance of about five minutes from the
physics building there was a "Konditorei," a pastry shop that included
a tea room. The latter consisted of half a dozen marble-topped tables
where coffee and tea were served. Fritz, by virtue of his superior
experience, tried to lay down the law that the only nutrient worthy of a
true intellectual was strawberry shortcake with whipped cream. I could
never quite accept this, less because my taste was different, than because
my allowance was considerably less than his. My upbringing was also
considerably more "bourgeois." I did not know then that earlier, while
in Vienna, Fritz had long been very close to the extreme left; whether he
was actually a Communist party member or only a sympathizer is
uncertain, since he never mentioned this aspect of his life to anybody in

Göttingen. When Hitler came to power, he had to leave Germany at once, for, had he been arrested for political reasons thereafter, he would hardly have escaped alive.

Another close friend was Wolfgang Harries, who could not afford to indulge in bohemian habits, since his father had several sons to educate. Wolfgang lived in a furnished room, like all of us, but his was of puny dimensions; it had just one chair, since another would hardly have fitted in. When I visited him, one of us always had to sit on the bed. But his good humor and his exuberant health made him an excellent companion. He went into industry after his Ph.D. and for some years worked for the Schott Glass Company. During the war he did some indifferent research work for the German military; then about 1950 he suddenly appeared in the United States, having been brought over by the U.S. army in that mass transplanting of a great many, carefully selected scientists and other technical specialists. He managed to embark on a second, successful career, this time in the electronics industry. His five children who came with their parents are all well settled in this country.

Wolfgang taught me that a man could love his country without being a brutal nationalist. His father was an attorney in the town of Kiel, and there was no sympathy for Marxism or socialism in the family or in him. He seemed to attribute a certain tolerant breadth I found in him to his home town's proximity to the Danish border and the ocean. In fact, I often found that the patriotism of coastal people was much more broad, accepting, and tolerant than the narrow, dogmatic, and exclusive nationalism of the upper-middle class Germans farther south. Farther south, among the Swiss, one again finds a more tolerant political attitude.

Then there was Charlotte. As the only woman in our circle she was automatically in the center wherever she went, but she understood the art of keeping her femininity discreetly in the background whenever it would have been a disturbing ingredient. She came from a town in Westfalen, outside of the industrial region, where her father was a newspaper editor. She must have inherited this man's curiosity and intellectual skill, for she was always well informed about many things, some scientific but even more literary. Her scientific interests were certainly rather unusual for a woman in the society of that day. Mostly, she had an extraordinary capacity for friendship. She took her Ph.D. with a physical chemist, Tammann, where the thesis was somewhat more a routine than with Franck, but she spent most of her time among

the crowd in Franck's Institute. After her Ph.D. she went for a while to
the United States where she taught at Vassar College among other
places, but apparently without the success that came later; eventually,
she returned to Germany and married Fritz Houtermans.

Franck and Born had become known among English-speaking
physicists, and a few years after they had settled in Göttingen a
pilgrimage of young physicists from the West, from England and the
United States, began. The Rockefeller Foundation and similar organizations had instituted fellowships, and it was possible for an ambitious
and eager young man to secure the means for such a trip. Since I only
remember some of these men clearly, I shall describe only a few here.
The earliest American physicist whom I can recall was Robert Brode,
later to teach for many years at Berkeley. An excellent physicist, he was
also a very jovial man, the life of every party. I remember in particular
one story he told us: Americans when they came to Europe wanted to
visit many countries, but at that time, a few years after the First World
War, each required a separate visa. Brode soon tired of going around
Paris, from one consulate to another, while waiting endless hours for
the officials to prepare the visa, so he invented a short-cut. He had
visiting cards printed which said, under his name, "Member, International Adiabatic Commission."[1] Brode and his companions tried this
scheme on a number of consulates, invariably with success. They
would hand the visiting card and their passport to a clerk, requesting
that the card be transmitted to the consul. A few minutes later the
passport would reappear and no fee would be charged. If they had an
interview with the consul, as happened occasionally, it never went
beyond courtesies; so great was the respect paid to Americans at that
time that no one ever inquired as to the functions of that mysterious
commission.

Since he was somewhat older than I, I did not get to know H. P.
Robertson, the cosmologist, well although he spent a considerable
length of time in Göttingen. He introduced an American classic, the
song "Clementine." It was not long before every physicist in Göttingen
was singing, humming, or whistling, "O my Darling Clementine."
For a while it became almost an epidemic. This was the first piece of
genuine Americans I had ever encountered, and I think that my love
affair with America started with it.

Another man who appeared somewhat later was an Englishman,
Patrick Blackett. As opposed to the gay, extraverted Americans, he
seemed a somewhat glum introvert, but perhaps only by comparison.

He certainly seemed to use words sparingly, and my recollection of him does not include conversations of great length. Blackett was accompanied by his wife and a friend, Dymond, also a physicist. For nearly a year, one could see this trio at about any time of day in the streets of the town or on the roads and trails in the surrounding woods. The two gentlemen of equal height, with their lean and lanky figures clad in similar darkish suits, invariably flanking Mrs. Blackett in a symmetrical manner, were quite a sight in that small town. In all that time I never saw either of the two men alone except inside Franck's Institute. Patrick Blackett later became the mastermind, or one of the masterminds, behind British war research in World War II. I did not keep in touch with Blackett, but Houtermans and his wife did. Many years later at Mrs. Houterman's, I met the Blacketts once more, a few years before his death. He had still not become a conversationalist, but it was pleasant to watch an "elder statesman" visibly relaxed and enjoying himself.

Another frequent visitor to Göttingen for more or less extended stays was Paul Dirac. He was tall, gaunt, awkward, and extremely taciturn. He had succeeded in throwing everything he had into one dominant interest. He was a man, then, of towering magnitude in one field, but with little interest and competence left for other human activities. In conversation he was invariably polite, but it did not follow that he could comprehend his interlocutor. One was never sure that he would say something intelligible. In other words, he was the prototype of the superior mathematical mind; but while in others this had coexisted with a multitude of interests, in Dirac's case everything went into the performance of his great historical mission, the establishment of the new science, quantum mechanics, to which he probably contributed as much as any other man.

Dirac had been educated at Cambridge and stayed there until his retirement. He later married the sister of the theoretical physicist, Eugene Wigner. I remember many, many years later, visiting the Diracs in Princeton when he spent a year at the Institute for Advanced Study; I also met one of their daughters and was surprised how much her delicate features resembled those I had known in her father when he was much younger.

By the spring of 1926, rumors had reached Göttingen that we would soon meet an American scientific genius who was then in Cambridge, England. His name was Robert Oppenheimer. When he appeared, I found a man of medium height, of the same age as I, then 22, with something of the lean and delicate look that one associated with young poets. This was accompanied by impeccable manners. It was clear that he had enjoyed the best of everything and had also had the native capacity to benefit from it. His range of interests was tremendous, although at that time these interests were only literary and not at all political.

In the beginning of our acquaintance, he repeatedly told me about his interest in modern poetry and especially in T. S. Eliot. In 1926, I had never even heard Eliot's name and certainly had no knowledge whatsoever of the trends in modern English poetry. German poetry was dominated by R. M. Rilke, some of whose works I knew well enough. In my personal opinion, shared by many others, he was the greatest and most profound of all German poets, apart from the unique Goethe. But Rilke was from Prague, and there was the stirring of a Slavic "soul" to his poetry that gave it a certain breadth and depth absent from the classical tradition of German poetry. The latter was rooted essentially in an eighteenth-century society living in small towns. This was about all I then had become acquainted with, and since Robert's knowledge of German culture was limited, we soon had to abandon this subject of conversation.

As I became better acquainted with Robert, he mentioned on occasion what must have been a fairly recent fling considering that he was only twenty-two, namely his interest in Hindu literature and his having learned Sanscrit to read the basic Hindu scriptures in the original, chiefly the Bhagavad Gita and the Upanishads. The little I knew about those documents came from the works of the German philosopher Schopenhauer. But there had been only limited resonance to Hinduism on the European continent, at least up to that time. I remember the remarks that a French friend of mine made later when he spent some time in New York. One of the most outstanding peculiarities of the Americans, he said, was their extensive interest in the Orient. It seems to me that Europeans did not share this until after the Second World War. I do not know who or what induced Robert Oppenheimer to study Sanscrit, but I remember that two or three times in this period he quoted and then translated sonorous verses from the Sanscrit.

It would be hard, I believe, to overestimate the influence of this preoccupation with Hindu cosmology (or should one say, religion, mythology, philosophy) upon Robert Oppenheimer. He had steeped himself profoundly in the world of the ancient Hindus. From the beginning of our acquaintance, I felt as if he were an inhabitant of

Olympus who had strayed among humans and was doing his best to appear human. He must often have had similar feelings himself, which he carefully concealed, but which surfaced now and then. For instance, when I visited him on his ranch in New Mexico ten years later, he happened to have acquired a brand-new sports car of a fiery-red color. "This car has a name," he told me, and he pronounced it when we happened to be alone. All I remember is that it was lengthy and very sonorous. When I asked for an explanation, he said, "That is the name of Vishnu's vehicle." Since this was ten years after our conversations in Göttingen, where similar ideas appeared fleetingly now and then, and nineteen years before the explosion at Alamogordo when Robert felt impelled to quote the Bhagavad Gita, I am sure that his involvement with Hindu cosmology was deep and personal, very far from a literary flirtation. Robert had grown up without a religious affiliation. His parents had abandoned Judaism and had joined the Ethical Culture Society of New York which, in my personal view, is much less than a religion. Robert was merely ahead by some years of the many Americans who have turned to Oriental religions for the fulfillment of their spiritual needs. If was C. G. Jung who said, and said most emphatically that the religious urge is a primary urge of human beings, and, if I understand him correctly, not reducible to any other urge.

In everyday life Robert Oppenheimer was a chainsmoker. Combined with his extreme courtesy, this led to a scene familiar to all who knew him in his younger years: When anyone, especially an older person or a lady, pulled out a cigarette, before he or she could have time to find a match, he would stand there with his cigarette lighter at the ready. I have seen this scene many times, and for me it is much more symbolic than the famous hat. I also often observed his recurrent, heavy cough. It seemed not just a smoker's cough but to indicate weak lungs. I suspect that in other times and climes he might have developed into what is so picturesquely called a consumptive. As it was, from late 1927 on, Robert lived in the extremely healthy climate of California, and shortly thereafter he acquired his ranch in the mountains of New Mexico, an almost perfect climate for anyone with weak lungs. Not so many years later, antibiotics were discovered, but by that time, I think, Robert's health had become quite stable.

There were two features of Robert's character affecting social intercourse that could hardly be missed: his high degree of self-control and his extreme discretion. These were, of course, exactly the qualities that enabled him to play with such virtuosity his historical role at Los

Alamos: to be the director, administrator, and father figure for perhaps the largest assembly of scientific primadonnas ever gathered together in one place, and to produce results fast. His capacity for discretion was apparent at a young age. Although he was rather unwordly at that time, leading a troglodytic existence where he often retired to his lair, perhaps to write scientific papers or poetry, as he sometimes claimed, he also must have had social contacts of which he hardly ever breathed a word. As a well-to-do American, he lived differently from anyone I had known before. He would disappear for a few days and then remark that he had been visiting in Copenhagen, in Leiden, or in Paris, trips which I considered in my provincial mind as involving vast expense and formidable preparations.

This brings me to the subject of his generosity: At one time he told me that he was going to spend a week in Paris. From Göttingen, this required not much more than an overnight trip with the express train, and it is none too strenuous if one has a first-class sleeping car—but this, of course, was an American perspective, not that of the impoverished Europeans of the age. At that time I had become enamored of the classical writer Plutarch but could not find a good German translation. I asked Robert whether he could pick up an inexpensive French translation of Plutarch in the bookstalls along the famous banks of the Seine. This was quite casual, and I forgot all about the incident. Ten days later he handed me his purchase: a set of fifteen small volumes dated 1811 containing a translation by a famous classicist of the Age of Louis XIV. He most firmly refused to discuss any payment, and I had no choice but to accept it. This beautiful set is still in my library.

A similar incident was later told to me by Charlotte: One day in 1926 she joined a group of physicists going to a Physical Society meeting in Hamburg. Robert Oppenheimer was of this party. Charlotte casually remarked to Robert about the elegance of his suitcase. His immediate answer was, "Would you like to have it?" She, of course, said no. But a few days later he delivered the suitcase to her and refused to take it back, resisting all arguments. I do not think it occurred to him that such munificence might be embarrassing to the girl who received it, and even less that it could be misconstrued by people of a devious mind.

I mention these traits because they seem to be intimately connected with his later downfall. With his lack of understanding for the deviousness of common people, and with the idea in the back of his mind that he was a stray from the Hindu Pantheon, he found it naturally very difficult to maintain any specific untruth, except for the two or three cases where gross security officials maneuvered him into it, and where he wanted to save his cause, a friend, or himself.

It seems to me that he courted extreme danger when he suffered Lewis Strauss, a man of an evidently pedestrian mind, to be his superior in the two chief activities of his life: first as a member of the Board of Trustees of the Institute for Advanced Study, of which Oppenheimer was the director; secondly, as the Chairman of the Atomic Energy Commission for which Oppenheimer served as the chief consultant. This permitted Strauss to checkmate Robert while maintaining the self-image of a noble and generous citizen. While giving tacit approval to Oppenheimer's elimination from the national political scene, he, nonetheless, left untouched the latter's functions as an educator and thinker, namely as director of the Institute for Advanced Study in Princeton.

I saw Robert again, after 1927, and shall return to these occasions. As I was writing this, there flashed through my mind the last occasion when I met him. It was in 1967, when I was living in Princeton, teaching geophysics. After a telephone warning, Charlotte suddenly appeared—she must see Robert at once. She may have had a premonition, or else an explicit warning from one of his intimates. There were widespread rumors that Robert had cancer (eventually, this turned out to be cancer of the throat), but I had no access to more concrete information. Charlotte phoned him at once from my home, and he invited her for the same afternoon. Although I had at that time little contact with him, he insisted that I come along. That afternoon we were ushered into his home-study, of which I remember little. On looking at him one realized that he might not have much more time on this earth; in fact, he died some weeks later. On that occasion he seemed as self-controlled as ever, and as polite. His speech was a little slow though clearly articulated; but I presume that under such conditions all conversation is much more symbolic than related to the specifics of ordinary life. I excused myself after a few minutes; Charlotte remained for another half-hour or so.

I have by now spoken of a number of people who had flocked to Göttingen in this period to be close to a major event in the history of science: the discovery of quantum mechanics. As one of the most significant scientific discoveries ever made, it deserves some brief discussion apart from the personalities involved. It seems to me that I should point out how this discovery fits into the broader pattern of human thought for which I shall use the term "philosophical," although it may, indeed, be broader than whatever is being taught in an academic "department of philosophy."

In his book, *A System of Logic* the nineteenth-century philosopher John Stuart Mill speaks of the "uniformity of nature," a term not often used by physicists. But it perfectly characterizes what is most impressive about modern atomic and molecular science. The world of the physical scientist is of an overpoweringly uniform structure. It consists of three particles, the electron, the proton, and the neutron. Protons and neutrons form nuclei; nuclei combine with electrons to form atoms; and atoms combine with each other to form molecules. The way in which these structures are built is regulated by simple and precise laws, the laws of quantum mechanics, discovered and formulated in this period. For most of the processes in atomic physics, chemistry, and astronomy, these laws not only describe what happens, they do so in a most quantitative manner, to a great many decimal places.

There exists a habit of careless talk among some popularizers of science, to the effect that the laws of nature are provisional, that, for instance, Einstein has superseded Newton. This puts Einstein in the same category as a Latin-American strong man who has replaced the strong man before him. It would be more realistic to say that Newton's mechanics holds true in 99.9 percent of the cases that the physicist and astronomer encounters in a certain field of practice; in the remaining 0.1 percent, a small correction to be obtained from Einstein's theory must be applied. Of course, this should not make us deny that Einstein's work is of great mathematical elegance and of the most profound philosophical importance.

When quantum mechanics is applied to atoms and molecules, it also holds for some 99.9 percent of the cases that physicists and astronomers encounter in their work. This is not to denigrate the activities of those who labor at the frontiers of knowledge. But within the area of "ordinary" phenomena, under conditions found both inside and outside the laboratory, the chemist's as well as the physicist's, quantum mechanics does hold. At the same time there is overwhelming evidence for the fact that all electrons are exactly alike: No differences among them have ever been discovered even in the most refined of observations. One can go one step further if one explains chemical bonding by means of quantum mechanics. This was first done by W. Heitler and F. London in 1927, and was then elaborated by London in a series of subsequent papers. One of the results is that chemical bonding is critically dependent on the exact equality among the electrons which do the bonding: Otherwise, the chemical bonds which we observe couldn't exist. If, for instance, two electrons differed in their mass by, say, one part in ten thousand, then a chemical double bond which could be maintained indefinitely if the two electrons were identical would last only a very short time and would then break apart.

These early successes in applying quantum mechanics to molecules raised hopes: Could not chemistry be explained or, as the ordinary terminology goes, be "reduced" to the application of quantum mechanics in the understanding of molecules? This would be a vast task; but it is made difficult by two circumstances: First, molecules are often complicated structures, so the mathematical techniques to achieve the reduction would have to be complicated. Even in a very simple case, that of, say, the water molecule consisting of an oxygen atom with two hydrogen atoms attached, the amount of labor needed to build a mathematical model of the molecule is large. Second, there are so many species of molecules, hundreds of thousands of inorganic ones, and even more organic ones that contain carbon atoms—how would one ever get through with the theoretical analysis of such a catalogue. Then, there is an extremely serious economic handicap to such a program of "reduction": To carry out such a program would require highly trained theoretical specialists. But it is much easier to be satisfied with the results of careful chemical experiments. In other words, there is no economic incentive to the expensive job of proving that chemical data can be derived from a unified and basically simple theory.

But there are always minds who find such tasks attractive. In 1927, when Heitler and London first expressed chemical bonding in quantum-mechanical terms, the prospects that this could be continued and elaborated already seemed bright; these prospects improved as time went by. Now, we can look back on fifty years of steady progress. There has never been any moment when the ideal of theoretical chemistry could be questioned: This ideal is the calculation, by increasingly theoretical means, of the chemical properties of a molecule, if to begin with one knows only its chemical formula, that is one knows only how atoms of diverse kinds enter into its composition. The voices of the sceptics, those who like to question whatever is not proved beyond the slightest doubt, have become dimmer and dimmer. Reductionism, the view that all details of chemical observation can, "in principle," be derived mathematically from simple premises, has been victorious in chemistry.

There had been a prologue to this played in the second part of the nineteenth century. At that time much of scientific interest centered on the so-called "kinetic theory" of matter which sought to explain the phenomena of heat in terms of the motions of molecules. These are usually invisible but can on occasion be observed, for instance in the so-called "Brownian motion" which is an incessant trembling of fine particles that can be seen, for example, when one looks through a microscope at cigarette smoke. The kinetic theory has been eminently successful: All observations on heat have been "reduced" in a quantitative manner to molecular motions. This is of some importance philosophically because we happen to have separate sense organs that are specialized in the perception of hot-and-cold. Before the mid-nineteenth century, most physicists believed, therefore, in a separate heat-substance, the "caloric"; but the progress of kinetic theory completely destroyed this belief.

This is, however, not the sense in which the term "reductionism" is taken among most contemporary scientists. With the successful advances of reduction in the physics of heat and in all of chemistry, the great question was whether the phenomenon of organic life could also be treated in this manner: Can biology also be "reduced" to physics and chemistry? Those who believe that this last ideal is meaningful call themselves reductionists. It is the most significant open problem in the philosophical aspects of modern science. The question absorbed more and more of my own thinking and energy as I grew older, and I shall return to it later.

One branch of physics, spectroscopy, the analysis of light emitted by atoms and molecules, provides much detailed insight into their structure. Astrophysics amounts essentially to applying spectroscopy to objects in the depth of the universe, most of them far outside the solar system. The experience of astrophysics is remarkably uniform and specific: The atomic and molecular building blocks of matter are exactly the same everywhere and the laws by which they move and combine into higher structures are also exactly the same everywhere. Modern atomic-molecular physics, including astrophysics, has given the broadest possible meaning to the "uniformity of nature." Nature lets us know inescapably that in our universe billions of billions of billions of billions of electrons, protons, and neutrons are exactly identical to each other.

When Descartes wrote *cogito ergo sum* (I think hence I am) he was clearly answering questions of a type characteristic of adolescents:

"How do I know things are real? How do I know I am real? How do I know the world is not a dream?" It seems that Nature has given us an answer to the question concerning "reality," at least in the domain of inorganic matter, with a power such as no previous maker of religious mythology or cosmology, let alone philosophy, had ever imagined. The size of the known universe exceeds all the dreams of poets, and the regularity and quantitative order expressed in all of its parts puts to shame the most extravagantly rational ideas of any rationalist. There are, of course, premonitions of this universal regularity in the regularities known to everybody, such as the experience that, say, ordinary objects do not just vanish some day. But this earlier insight is like nothing compared to the universal, broad, and utterly pervasive type of regularity that atomic physics had revealed.

These aspects of the physical universe appeared with the greatest clarity during the years that saw the birth of quantum mechanics; they have been endlessly strengthened by all scientific research undertaken in the half-century that has passed into history since. There is also little that could be called obscure and inaccessible about the technical aspects of quantum mechanics: I think it is altogether fair to say that the amount of mathematical technique required in this field is, while different, comparable in difficulty and complexity to the mathematical techniques that the majority of engineers on the university level will have learned before they complete their studies. But the unification of our intellectual "world view" which this has produced is something unique in history.

In Göttingen, there was, of course, no lack of interesting lectures on physics, especially theoretical physics. One course was a seminar that had existed for many years under the title "The Structure of Matter." It played a germinal role in the development of quantum mechanics. It was listed under the name of David Hilbert, the famous mathematician who had long since set out to bring atomic physics closer to his fellow mathematicians. Since Hilbert was getting older and was not in good health, he made only occasional appearances; the conduct and guidance of the seminar was left to Max Born. I was one of its regular attendants during all of my stay in Göttingen.

I distinctly remember one of the earliest presentations in this seminar, by a student of Born's named Friedrich Hund. Later on Hund made major contributions to the interpretation of atomic spectra and eventually became a professor at the University of Leipzig where he remained for much of his life; after the war he concluded his teaching days in Göttingen. The subject of that particular seminar was an experiment by two Americans, Davisson and Kunsman, that had been reported in the *Physical Review* of 1923. Davisson was then the leading scientist of the Bell Telephone Laboratories, at that time a newly established, extremely small group of physicists and engineers who worked in a commercial loft near the south end of Manhattan.

These two experimenters had discovered a rather remarkable phenomenon. They had shot electrons with moderate voltages at a polished plate of platinum in a high vacuum; then they had observed how these electrons were scattered back from the plate, that is to say, how the intensity of their distribution varied with the angle of scattering. It was an experiment of major difficulty carried through with great skill — and the results were extraordinary: They found that the distribution of the electrons in angle showed maxima and minima, a surprising and quite mysterious result. But coming from what was even then considered an unimpeachable source, one could not simply shrug it off as a product of careless technique; what then was it? Hund told us that Max Born had developed some ideas to explain the phenomenon and that Born had asked him, Hund, to study the matter more closely, along the following lines: An atom with many electrons has its electrons arranged in "shells." Just what was meant by a shell of electrons was not clear in all details at that time; but there were enough data to show that shells existed. One could presume that there were spherical layers at regular distances from the nucleus which is at the atom's center, and that the electrons were concentrated in denser layers that alternated with less dense ones. An extraneous electron passing through such a structure may then be deflected more or less depending on which layer it would hit. It was conceivable that on combining such effects one would get maxima and minima, as measured. But this was by no means certain; as every physicist realizes, such effects must be calculated, not just guessed at. Hund had not carried through such calculations, he merely presented the ideas and left the impression that something rather significant for atomic structure might be hidden behind these intriguing experiments. It was impossible to know whether this suggestion was correct. I filed the story away in my mind, not suspecting that it would recur a few months later.

One day, in May, 1925, I found in the library two recent papers by Einstein on the effect of quantum theory upon gases. They had appeared in the winter of 1924–1925 and were, by the way, the last work that Einstein published on atomic physics; he kept on writing about the theory of relativity for many years. Einstein had shown that certain gases did not behave like assemblies of particles, the way most gases do, but that they did in other respects behave like assemblies of waves; these additional effects might yet be observed. Coming from Einstein—who, twenty years earlier, had remarked that light, of which everyone thought as a wave motion, had also particle properties and that light energy was emitted and absorbed in packages called quanta—this was significant news indeed. Einstein then quoted a thesis of Louis de Broglie that had just been published.

It occurred to me to look for de Broglie's thesis in the university library. It was unlikely that a French thesis would be found in a provincial German library, but there it was and I took it home. I later speculated on how it got there but only one idea came to my mind: It was that de Broglie sent it to Born, who, being a busy man, had only glanced at it before sending it to the library. I found no difficulty in reading the first few sections of the thesis that contained de Broglie's basic idea that all primary components of matter have wave properties. There was also the now famous, simple formula that connected the wavelength with a particle's velocity. I could also not help recalling Hund's seminar. What if Davisson and Kunsman's maxima and minima were diffraction phenomena similar to those produced when X-rays, also waves, go through crystals? In this case, the electrons would not go through the platinum plate but would penetrate ever so slightly and then return; but the diffraction pattern, if such it was, should be similar. I could readily calculate the energy of the electrons required for the maxima; this needed no more than an ordinary slide rule. To my surprise it came out just right. Of course, the experiments were still crude, so this was only a guess, but it was clearly an exceptionally interesting and promising guess.

The next day I went to talk about this problem to James Franck who was open-minded and quite helpful. A number of times before he had said: "Now you seem to get dangerously close to wild speculation," which I, of course, invariably took as a signal that it was wise to rein in my imagination—but not this time. He thought this was a most interesting though still highly speculative idea, and that I should go through it carefully again and then write to *Die Naturwissenschaften* (a weekly, the German counterpart of the ancient British journal *Nature*). I let the matter rest for a couple of weeks; then wrote it up. In print it became a note of about half a page in the large (folio-size) volume of the journal. After showing the manuscript briefly to Franck, who had no objections, I sent it off. I did make one mistake—I should have also shown it to Max Born.[2]

I discovered the fate of my little manuscript from stories told me later. It seems that the paper was first sent to a distinguished physicist, P. Pringsheim, but he declined to review it, saying it should be sent to Einstein. The latter, in turn, indicated that he was not quite sure how literally the idea of waves associated with electrons could be taken, but he thought that the paper should certainly be published, and it appeared shortly thereafter. It was my first venture into print; it was also premature, since I lacked the skill to exploit its contents. I didn't even know enough of the conventions of research to send a copy with a suitable letter to Davisson. Later, when I was in the United States, I met the distinguished physicist and historian of physics Karl K. Darrow. I became well acquainted with him, and he told me that at that earlier period he had shared an office with Davisson at the Bell Telephone Laboratories. He was inscrutably silent as to just when they had first learned about my little note. In 1927, when the decisive publication of Davisson, with Germer, appeared, where the wave character of electrons was experimentally demonstrated without a doubt, and the de Broglie wavelength had been measured, also without a doubt, the authors referred to Schrödinger's papers of 1926 which were by then generally known. In retrospect, I feel that since I was then so young, the stream of scientific history had bypassed me, which, I think, was in the long run all to my good. But it was not entirely forgotten. In 1944, the theoretical physicist Max von Laue reproduced the text of my little paper in a book dealing with matter-waves (the same as de Broglie waves).

In the first half of 1926, with the appearance of Schrödinger's work, the attention of theoreticians centered on the relationship of particles and waves, two aspects of the constitution of matter that seem at first sight to have little in common. One of the first stabs in the dark, was Max Born's article on collision processes that appeared in the summer of 1926, in which he treated the collision of an electron with an atom as the scattering of a de Broglie wave by an obstacle. This permitted him to develop a whole mathematical machinery for wave scattering, extending over a good many pages of formulas. In the introductory paragraphs of this paper, the notion of probability appeared for the first time in quantum mechanics; Born proposed that the wave function was a "statistical" guide for the particles, in the sense that the amplitude of the wave specifies a probability for the particles to travel in certain ways.

The whole procedure was typical of Born: He introduced a novel and altogether revolutionary idea, that the fundamental laws of motion themselves are statistical, in a very casual way, associated with pages of mathematical formulas whose technical validity could not be doubted. This was Born's style: If the physical idea proposed was wrong, his method of calculation would stand nonetheless. The notion of probability meant that in the new physics one could no longer follow the path of a single particle as in Newton's physics; instead, the laws of quantum mechanics refer to "classes." Classes of phenomena are so important in this new physics because the several members of the class, the individual electrons, are indistinguishable. Dirac was perhaps the first to recognize that mathematical symbols, which in Newton's physics described attributes of specific objects, were now representing classes, although he may not have formulated it in these terms. This made the appearance of probabilities altogether natural. From there, the way was open for the systematization of quantum theory. Heisenberg himself had given much of the initial momentum to this whole development, only a few months after de Broglie, but in a completely independent and superficially even unrelated manner; now, Heisenberg put a capstone on this development in his famous paper on the uncertainty relations, that also appeared in 1927. No basically novel ideas were introduced to achieve a synthesis, but the synthesis was there, carried out in a technically flawless manner, and draped into most appealing intuitive imagery.

Toward the end of his paper on collision theory, Born had quoted my little note of 1925, which was then less than a year old. But the reference is only factual—that I had correctly interpreted the experimental results of Davisson and Kunsman; there is no evidence to show whether Born himself had benefited from reading it. Born's statement to an interviewer, nearly forty years later, that he had "suggested" my note, is no doubt a lapse of memory in old age. As a young student in Born's classes, I hardly knew him personally, and I had talked with Franck, whom I knew well. I had not even consulted Born before publishing. All this, however, came too late for Max Born. Early in 1926 Schrödinger's series of papers appeared; Born's work on collision supplemented it and gave the interpretation in terms of probabilities. The spectacular results that could be compared to observational data were all Schrödinger's; Heisenberg and Schrödinger were both awarded Nobel prizes in 1933, whereas Max Born had to wait until he was seventy-two, twenty-one years later, for his prize.

In the summer of 1925 the publication of the little note had "turned my head." I felt that I could not afford to forego such an opportunity of making a major discovery. I asked Franck whether he would allow me to study through experiments the scattering of electrons by metal surfaces. This was quite foolish because that type of experiment is technically most difficult, and my exhibition of experimental skill had so far been less than adequate. Franck's answer was characteristic of him: I was free to do so, but I would have to do it on my own, I could not expect assistance from members of his laboratory. While he tried to maintain a certain flexibility, he could not allow his group to engage in extremely speculative enterprises no matter how great the hoped-for rewards. I should have understood him and stopped, but I was young and foolish. My unaided efforts lasted for about three months; by then I understood how silly it was for an inexperienced young man on his own to try formidably difficult experiments. I ruefully asked Franck for another subject, one in harmony with his general plan of research. He obliged and gave me another problem, which was probably a little easier than the one I had had before, but still required a lengthy effort and some experimental skill, as did all of Franck's theses.

After I had abandoned these experiments, there was still one pleasure that I could procure without much difficulty. It was a personal interview with Albert Einstein, who was already as celebrated as he ever would be. He lived in Berlin, and by 1925 my parents had also moved there. I found that I could walk to Einstein's apartment from my parents' in a few minutes. So, one day late in 1925, perhaps during the Christmas vacation, I entered Einstein's study. His apartment was at a street corner in one of the endless rows of six-story apartment houses. The corner rooms of the upper floors had been built out to form a sort of tower, with a view to three sides, detached from the rest of the building. The interior was comfortably but simply furnished, and Einstein received me with that simplicity of which all his biographers have spoken. Nothing startling happened during our conversation. Since his impact on science has been so often described, I will not give a feeble imitation of my own, but will, instead, add one comment of a psychological nature: How did Einstein's sudden appearance in the scientific world act upon Einstein himself? His youth has been well enough described; he was an intelligent young man, but there seem to be no stories, even apocryphal ones, about an older scientist having recognized his genius or, in terms of an older tradition, a prophet saying: Here comes a prophet greater than I. Einstein was a promising youngster among other promising youngsters that had congregated in

Zürich. Before he finished his studies he had, in order to make a living, become a minor patent examiner in the Swiss Patent Office in Bern. He continued to work on his thesis and obtained a Ph.D. in physics at the Swiss Federal Polytechnic School of Zürich in 1904. Then he dived into theoretical physics in total earnest. In 1905, when he was twenty-six, the chief German-language journal, *Annalen der Physik,* carried in the course of a few months three fairly lengthy articles by Einstein about three subjects that were not connected with each other. To describe each as a masterpiece would be an understatement. The first contained the theory of relativity, a total conceptual novelty, in a most elegant, classic presentation that has survived and is still read. The second gave the theory of the photoelectric effect; this article is a seed from which much of quantum mechanics was to develop. The photoelectric effect is the capability of light of short wavelength to eject electrons from a piece of metal into a vacuum. Einstein pointed out that this could only be understood provided light, then thought of as a wave motion, was also a set of packages of energy called quanta. Each quantum carried energy inversely proportional to the light's wavelength, and each energy package was used to speed up an electron. All the quandaries that later led to the development of quantum mechanics are implied in this work. There can be little doubt that each of these two papers by itself would have deserved a Nobel prize for its author; actually, the Nobel committee was ultraconservative and only gave Einstein the prize in 1921 for his work on the photoelectric effect which was considered "less theoretical" than relativity. The third of the three articles—on the theory of the Brownian motion—was not a novel, physical idea but still as spectacular as the two others; its brilliance was in the method of treatment. It showed how an exceedingly complicated technical subject could be treated with an incredible simplicity and elegance.

In less than a year, Einstein had made revolutionary contributions to the three most significant preoccupations of physicists of that time—to electromagnetism (in relativity), to atomic physics (in reopening the wave-particle controversy that had lain dormant since Newton's day), and to kinetic theory, of which Brownian motion is one chapter. Moreover, many of his new ideas were accepted by the leading minds of physics in a very short time, within a year or two. There has never been anything quite like it in the history of science. I believe that Einstein's serenity and a seemingly acquired (rather than inherited) spiritual quality, to which everyone who met him has attested, must have grown out of a conviction drawn from his own early achievements that he was a "messenger of the gods" in a manner of speaking. This produced a deep humility in him, which made him so much the hero of our century.

Einstein was not particularly fond of teaching. Except for the earliest years of his scientific career, where on occasion it was necessary, he taught almost no classes. But in his younger years he was extremely active among his colleagues. During the first third of the century, the German-language journals of physics were full of Einstein's contributions, often notes, comments, replies to other people's comments, and so on. It was only in the late 1920s that he began to fall more silent. I believe that this was mostly because he saw almost all physicists accept quantum mechanics, which he himself could not. He believed in full determinism, whereas it had become the accepted interpretation of quantum mechanics that strict determinism could be expected only of averages over classes, but that the individual events are indeterminate. But Einstein never forgot that his view of determinism, or any such philosophical view, was a hypothesis; he never even intimated that one might conceive of it as a self-evident Truth, as many other thinkers might have done. This, I feel, is one of the true signs of his greatness.

There was one thing I noticed in my talk with Einstein in 1925, and also on a second occasion nearly a quarter-century later when I had a discussion with him in Princeton. His conversation was totally down-to-earth and practical; he spoke exactly as an engineer would have spoken about the design of a machine. There was no rhetoric, no verbalization of vague concepts. When I was about to leave, he said: "Young man, you are sitting on a gold-mine." But I was not yet ready to exploit the mine. Such exploitation requires a commitment, for practical purposes a total and very probably life-long commitment. I was only twenty-one and not yet prepared to commit myself so completely.[3]

Meanwhile, I was still an experimentalist battling with technical difficulties. When I first joined Franck's laboratory, I took some instruction in the machinist's techniques and in those of glass blowing. This was normal practice. But it did not repair my deficiency in manual skill or what may better be called that mental skill which is related to manual activities. I had always felt that a man must have mastered some skill thoroughly if he wants to be successful as an equal among his fellows, but here I found that I was hardly able to acquire the basic skill that would be needed in my chosen profession. The number of research students working toward a Ph.D. in Franck's Institute was small, perhaps six or eight; among these I was no doubt the one most passionately interested in, and also the most knowledgeable of, theory; I was also by far the clumsiest and least successful when it came to building apparatus.

This situation was made a little more difficult because James Franck, brilliant scientist that he was, had no deeper interest in devices or instruments. He was a thinker, but he was not also what is called a tinkerer. Not until some ten years later when I came to the United States, did I find an almost universal preoccupation with instruments and devices, and then it became much easier for me to learn to handle devices. I believe that in this respect the American attitude to science as a branch of the "useful arts" is unique except for some British precursors; it had no counterpart in the older developments of science on the European continent where the scholastic tradition, dating in effect back to the ancient Greeks, had dominated. I remember one experience I had fairly early during my stay in Göttingen that illustrates this. I took a course called "Astronomical Exercises" from an elderly professor of astronomy. This course evidently sought to teach one how to use one's ingenuity and mathematical skill to get results from utterly inadequate measuring devices that involved shaky suspensions, wobbly screws, and so on. It made me aware of the fact that technical proficiency based on manual dexterity is not native to man but must be cultivated. There is always the danger that a high level of technical proficiency will relapse into a primitive state. Thus, a high level of perfection in science and engineering can no more be taken for granted than a high level in art, say, where every well-informed person knows that a very high level has been repeatedly lost in the course of history.

But to return to the situation in Franck's Institute, it had by then become clear to me that Franck's generation had seen the transition from low-technology science to high-technology science. Equipment that now can be bought from commercial suppliers had earlier to be hand-made by the student of experimental physics. My own inadequacy in this respect caused me constant, deep frustration. It ended unexpectedly. In the summer of 1926, Max Born approached me to say: It was obvious that my interests were very theoretical; so, he could presume, were my talents. Would I consider becoming a theoretical physicist and doing a thesis with him? I was, of course, attracted by this offer but told him at first the obvious: I would have to think this over and discuss it with James Franck. Born then told me that he thought I had been sitting around long enough; he would give me a thesis that was not too difficult technically and would allow me to get a Ph.D. in a relatively short time. Born's argument impressed me greatly, as it would any young man struggling to get a degree; this argument was, however, rather distorted because I had been in Franck's Institute less than two years whereas it ordinarily required three or more years to finish an experimental thesis, a fact which Born knew. Sometimes the period was even longer; it took Houtermans five years to complete his experimental thesis. But I finally decided to accept Born's offer after talking it over with Franck who, as I had expected, was the perfect gentleman. I was unable to tell whether he had any positive or negative feelings in the matter; he said it was a personal decision that I must make for myself. Also, I was never able to ascertain whether Born had spoken to Franck previously to obtain the latter's agreement before offering to take me on.

Thereafter, I saw Franck now and then casually, and more formally at my Ph.D. examination in 1927. I then lost personal contact with him for many years. I happened to meet him by sheer accident again on Cape Cod around 1962 when he was eighty and seemed altogether unchanged except for slight signs of aging. He died two years later. In that summer I was working at the Woods Hole Oceanographic Institution and he was living nearby on the Cape. He invited me at once to lunch. We had hardly sat down when he told me how glad he was that I had finally "made good"; then we discussed old times and the long stretch of the history of science we had both witnessed.

Max Born kept his word: He gave me an uncomplicated thesis. It was an application of his collision theory to the simplest case that could be devised: the collison of an electron with a hydrogen atom. This required working out a big pile of formulas by rather straightforward mathematical techniques. I rarely ran into difficulties, but in the few cases when I did, I tried to contact Born. This offered some technical obstacles because Born always worked at home. He had certain hours set aside when he would receive collaborators and students. To get an appointment, one first had to reach his home by phone, which was usually answered by a female member of the household. One made an appointment a day or two in advance. But I found him very hard to deal with; he always seemed distracted and to be only half-listening. He did not show the slightest interest in me as a scientist or as a person; I seemed to be just another one of the nuisances that students sometimes

Max Born with Friedrich Hund

represent for professors. Fortunately, during this period, in the fall of 1926, I had become acquainted with Robert Oppenheimer who had no difficulty in answering my questions. He would not try to tell me how to solve this or that specific problem, but drawing on his vast memory he would say: You will find this in the seventh chapter of such-and-such a mathematical book. I looked it up and there it was. When Oppenheimer first appeared in Göttingen early in 1926, he had already published several articles on quantum mechanics. I made a major effort to read and digest these, but with very meager results. His mind seemed to be roaming when he wrote these papers, and there was no simple order or logic in them. I am sure that he knew this, and after his return to the United States he concentrated largely on teaching and supervising graduate students, tasks in which he gradually acquired a remarkable proficiency. I mention these facts because mankind is still very far from understanding the complex problem of mental "creativity"; centuries may pass before men will gain an inkling of how this capability functions. After securing Oppenheimer's assistance, I soon ceased to visit Born, and did not meet him again after leaving Göttingen in 1927.

No doubt Max Born was a complex personality. He was first and foremost a virtuoso in mathematical analysis, having cultivated the special variety necessary for theoretical physics. He began his career with a long article that ultimately became a book, entitled *The Dynamics of Crystal Lattices*. It is certainly one of the most elaborate efforts ever made to apply mathematical analysis in the greatest detail to a specific field of pure physics; certainly, it was an extraordinary monument to Born's industry. After this youthful exertion which trained him in virtuosity, Born turned to atomic theory proper. His book, *Lectures on Atomic Mechanics*, came out in 1925, just before quantum mechanics assumed its present form. It was, therefore, mostly an application of older, more traditional techniques of theoretical physics to the problems of the atom; but it was, nevertheless, done with fabulous skill and elegance and a gold mine of information.

For some reason that I never fully understood myself, I could not find it in me to be angry at Max Born for the mildly shabby way he had treated me, attracting me and, indeed, giving me my degree in rather short order, but otherwise completely ignoring me. About ten years later, I once discussed Born with Robert Oppenheimer. He was evidently quite angry with Born for reasons of his own. He criticized me sharply for being too idealistic about Born, who was, he said, a terrible egotist. This was quite unusual for Oppenheimer, who while capable of being very unpleasant to one's face, would almost never criticize a man behind his back. But Max Born was a virtuoso, and like many other virtuosos he was a primadonna. It took the accomplished psychological skill of a James Franck to handle him. For those interested in Born's accomplishments and personality, his extensive correspondence with Einstein, which has also been translated into English, is now available.

There was one conversation I had with Born at that period that I remember in detail and which gave me fuel for thought for years thereafter. Born told me that I was not outstanding in mathematics but that my main strength was in conceptual thinking. I feel inclined to elaborate, first on not being a very good mathematician. This seems somewhat absurd to nonmathematicians. I may explain this in terms of an example: A man might be an excellent violinist, good enough to play in a small-town musical event, but were he to play in a major concert, say on the stage of Carnegie Hall, he might flop. There is in this sense, of course, a difference between a competent mathematician and one who wants to be a professional. I felt that while I was a competent enough mathematician, I was not ready, and might never be, for a Carnegie-Hall standard of theoretical physics. I am sure that Max Born was thoroughly aware of his virtuosity in mathematical analysis, but that he felt less certain in conceptual thought. By the time he arrived in Göttingen he had gone as far, externally, as he could expect to go. He was hardly one to work out other people's ideas although he had made an exception for Heisenberg's great idea on the nature of quantum-mechanical mathematics, which he recognized as matrix mathematics. For this work he secured the help of Pascual Jordan who had started as a mathematician. Jordan was a very quiet, extremely hard-working and diligent man who, while I was in Göttingen, performed a great deal of theoretical analysis with Born as well as with Franck. There was never any doubt about Jordan's superior mathematical abilities and his keen understanding of physics. Later Jordan was for many years professor of theoretical physics at the University of Hamburg.

About the time I came to the end of my thesis, Born acquired a new research student, Maria Goeppert, with whom at that time I had little contact. Her father was professor at the university and a well-known physician. She seemed to stand out as the best-dressed woman on the streets of Göttingen. I suspected that she was not subject to the severe economic constraints with which we other young people had to contend. But this did not keep her from progressing in theoretical physics and developing a high degree of expertise in calculations that must have been very useful to Max Born. Later on she married Joseph Mayer, an American who became a distinguished theoretical chemist.

Let me now return to the question of conceptual thought. Just what is meant by this term? I was aware, even then, of my own capabilities in conceptual thinking and my self-confidence grew stronger as I grew older; I was also not afraid of anybody's competition in this field. Concepts have existed for a long time, in Europe since the days of the Greeks and in the Far East for even longer, though not as precisely chiseled. Everybody who works in quantitative science knows the difference between mathematical analysis and conceptual thought, but while the former is relatively easy to define, the latter is not. I was deeply interested in this question, not just for reasons of egotism, but because I wanted to know more clearly the nature of the area in which I expected to be active. Since I considered my talent for conceptual thought as the main gift with which nature had endowed me, it appeared important to me to gain insight into the nature of such thought. A common idea is that conceptual thought precedes precise, mathematical analysis, and the history of physical science offers some splendid examples of this: Models and patterns have emerged out of the primal chaos of data and thoughts of general human experience, and in many cases the result could not have been forecast on superficial scrutiny. The development of the Copernican and Newtonian system of the Heavens took millenia and could surely not have been predicted by one of the ancient Babylonians who so assiduously observed the motion of the stars. It seemed to me, therefore, that the maturing of my thinking about natural philosophy and the understanding of the nature of conceptual thought were closely connected problems.

By the spring of 1927 my thesis was completed; then I had only an oral examination which lasted an afternoon. By a coincidence I got my degree about two weeks after Robert Oppenheimer. I remember the last conversation we had before he left. Robert told me that he had six offers of professorships from the United States, of which he had decided to accept two: His mainstay would be Berkeley, but he had agreed to spend two to three months every year in Pasadena at the California Institute of Technology. Robert, who was usually the soul of discretion, had made me feel very jealous indeed. My prospects for a future in Germany were limited by political circumstances. They pointed to a career as a high-school science teacher, not, of course, in itself a bad prospect. I did not receive any encouragement from Oppenheimer to come to America. He once told me that he was sure that the simpler American atmosphere would dissolve some of my psychological complexities; but he never concretely encouraged me to try my luck in the United States. This was, I am sure, not any lack of trust in me, but a juvenile lack of confidence in his own place and in the growth of American science.

During the two and a half years I spent in Göttingen, I was deeply absorbed in science and was mainly in the company of scientists, with the exception of one adventure of a different type that I will describe later. The Ph.D. program of Göttingen did require that a student have two minor fields in addition to his major. As minors I chose astronomy and mathematics. There is little I need say here about astronomy. The professor of astronomy was a young, very capable and active astrophysicist named Kienle; his classes and seminars all tended to confirm the ideas of the uniformity of atomic physics and its laws, of which I have already spoken.

I cannot deal that briefly, however, with my interest in mathematics and with what the university had to offer in that respect. Mathematics at Göttingen had been established by Carl Friedrich Gauss who is generally considered one of the most remarkable and versatile mathematicians who ever lived. He was professor at Göttingen for nearly half a century until his death in 1855, and director of an astronomical observatory that had been built for him. In the latter capacity he was also in charge of the geodetic survey of the then kingdom of Hanover. He saw to it that an extremely accurate triangulation be made between three mountains that could just be seen from each other by telescopes; he wanted to ascertain whether the sum of the angles was exactly 180°, trying to make use of ideas on non-Euclidean geometry which had by then become fashionable among some mathematicians. But of course he was unsuccessful; one century later such effects could be specified by relativity theory, where one finds that these effects arise only in vast cosmic expanses, compared to which a triangle on the earth is as small as a pinhead.

The observatory building had also served as Gauss' private residence. In my time it was no longer inhabited, but was kept in exactly the condition Gauss had left it, serving as an unofficial museum. As a student I had easy access to this building that then housed the offices of the astronomy department; the walls of the former large living room on the ground floor were covered with bookshelves that contained the huge non-mathematical part of the library that Gauss had assembled in his long life. On occasion I browsed among this very varied collection of books, all dating from the first half of the nineteenth century.

There had been other distinguished men in the history of science in Göttingen. Wilhelm Weber was one of the leading physicists in Germany during the middle years of the century and had often collaborated with Gauss in his younger years. His main interest was in electric and magnetic phenomena; he not only advanced substantially the mathematical theory, but also made measurements of unprecedented precision, and the whole of his work greatly clarified the understanding of electromagnetism. This is the same Weber of whom I have spoken above in connection with Philipp Lenard.

A meteor in the sky of mathematics was Bernhard Riemann who was professor of mathematics in Göttingen before he died at age forty from what was then called consumption. He generalized geometry nearly beyond recognition, and what became known as Riemannian geometry later formed the mathematical foundation of the theory of relativity. From among a whole series of other mathematical stars, I shall only mention two, closer to our own time: Felix Klein and David Hilbert. Klein possessed a remarkable combination of talents: He was a brilliant mathematician as well as a superb organizer. In his efforts to re-structure existing mathematical thought, he developed a number of ideas that did show much of mathematics in a new and more brilliant light. In his later years Klein was very much involved in the development of applied mathematics. He established close relations with some of the political powers of the day and succeeded in having the government of the State of Prussia establish a string of research institutes in applied science. This was a revolutionary novelty in the nineteenth century, when, on the European continent at least, the official purchase of a lathe by a university professor would have been a major and rather suspect undertaking. Universities existed for culture, and lathes belonged in crude and uncultured engineering schools. Several of the research institutes were located in Göttingen; the most famous was the Fluid Mechanics Institute directed by L. Prandtl, which for many years played a seminal role in the development of German aviation and later even rocketry.

In my time, Felix Klein was no longer alive. The dominating figure in mathematics was David Hilbert[4] who had been professor in Göttingen for some thirty years, but was now aging and ill. Sometimes, when I saw him in lectures or seminars he looked very ill indeed. I remember being told that a medication for his illness had just been invented in the United States. It was not yet on the market, but through the efforts of American admirers it was shipped to him and allowed him to live until 1943. Hilbert was an altogeher different type from Klein; he was an extremely "pure" mathematician. This is illustrated by the following anecdote often told at the time and which, if not literally true, is characteristic: Klein was in the habit of taking his seminar once a year to visit a major industrial enterprise or factory. This was usually followed by a banquet. One day Klein fell ill after everything had been arranged, but since the industrialists involved were very important people, another celebrity had to be found as the banquet speaker. Hilbert agreed to prepare a speech and was carefully coached to say kind words on the close relations between mathematics and technology. When the time came, he delivered himself of a speech sounding, roughly telescoped, something like this: "Gentlemen," he said (ladies being almost totally absent at that time from both mathematics and technology), "gentlemen, mathematics and technology, mathematics and technology are on the best possible terms with each other. They are so now and they are likely to remain on the friendliest of terms in the future. For a simple reason, gentlemen; they have nothing to do with each other."

Hilbert was generally thought of as the Grand Old Man of Mathematics, and there was an air of hushed silence whenever he appeared. I also met some of the galaxy of brilliant mathematicians that then enlivened the university, but I will just mention some whom I encountered again later in my life. What I learned from these contacts with mathematicians was that I, myself, although able to learn and to apply mathematics, am primarily an empiricist. I believe that some descriptions of nature will never be fully replaced by mathematical analysis. Hilbert, now and then, when he was in good health, used to come to the "Structure of Matter" seminar and berate mathematicians for their lack of imagination, as he put it, usually in very blunt terms. Mathematicians, he said, should have discovered relativity on their own but they didn't; it took this physicist, Einstein, to find it. On another occasion he told us that in the early years of the century, he had applied great effort to developing a mathematical theory of spectral lines but had failed completely to match his results with observations. It took physicists like Heisenberg and Born to achieve this. Pessimistic as this kind of sermon may appear to mathematicians, I found it rather reassuring because it showed that progress had indeed been achieved even though by physicists.

The major mathematician who was closest to the Franck-Born group of physicists was Richard Courant. He was a short, slender, and very agile man whose agility of mind matched his physique. His genius for organizing mathematical material was expressed in the tremendous success of his books. This should have made him an excellent teacher, but he always seemed too busy to prepare himself for the classroom, , with corresponding results. Courant, with his organized mind and his ease in dealing with people, was an excellent businessman; he used this capacity later to found an Institute of Applied Mathematics in New York with the funds he was so successful in collecting. This institute, a branch of New York University, eventually acquired its own building near Washington Square; it was, after Courant's retirement, appropriately renamed the Courant Institute and is still flourishing.

Since Göttingen was a world center of mathematics, there were many visitors. Most of these were outside my horizon, but there was one visitor whom I remember vividly. This was an American, Norbert Wiener, who must have stayed some weeks. He was then a young man in his early thirties. His activity was far from the things I knew then, so I had not previously encountered his name, but from the way the mathematics department treated him, one could infer that he was already a mathematical celebrity. At a social occasion, I had some small conversation with him and he seemed none too happy and balanced a person. He later wrote an autobiography which revealed the sources of his unhappiness: His father, apparently, was a man of no mean intellectual endowment, who had grown up in Russia and had come to the United States in his early youth; he had eventually become professor of Russian at Harvard University. He was the first man to translate Tolstoy's works into English. But in the too rapid process of change, father Wiener had become something of a rationalist, the preferred religion-substitute of that age. When he discovered unusual intellectual abilities in his young son, he began to "train" the boy systematically into a genius with rather unfortunate psychological results.

Later, I very occasionally encountered Norbert Wiener in the United States. But I was greatly taken when his book *Cybernetics* came out in 1948. In it Wiener succeeded in familiarizing the scientific and engineering community with the concept of "feedback" whose recognition was long overdue. If the magnitude of a discovery is measured by the time elapsed between the moment it could first have been made and the time it actually was made, then Wiener must certainly be given first prize. Circuits that involve feedback had been discovered by nerve physiologists a century or more before Wiener's book, but the generality of the abstract concept of feedback had escaped the research workers in both the physical and the life sciences. The subject dealt with by Wiener, in the wake of the then rising tide of computer technology, is now commonly called systems theory. The term "system" is equivalent to what more concretely is called a machine; thus, systems theory is the general mathematical theory of machines that operate in a causal manner, also called automata.

By the time I read Wiener's book after World War II, my own ideas had crystallized in a manner that I will sketch now and explain in more detail later. I felt by then that quantum mechanics, a subject in which I could claim a reasonable competence, had led to a broad confidence in the "uniformity of nature," and that from there one could attack and penetrate a central problem in the philosophy of science: the relationship of inorganic science to organic life. In the early days of modern science, the age of the "clockwork universe," Descartes had followed a very ancient dualism in declaring that while there were two substances, matter and mind, the body—the organism as we would say today—pertained to matter and hence was a machine pure and simple, an automaton. But to decide whether or not the organism is simply an automaton, one must first have a sufficiently general theory of automata; one must find out what machines can and cannot achieve. This is exactly what modern systems theory claims to do. And Norbert Wiener has the unquestionable merit of having given the subject its greatest single push forward.

I have left to the end of this chapter my first encounter with the man who probably influenced my scientific thought as much as any other individual: the mathematician John von Neumann. But I felt most of his influence long after I had left Göttingen. As one of Hilbert's assistants he was specifically charged with keeping Hilbert abreast of the new developments in quantum mechanics in which Hilbert maintained a passionate interest since it impinged on a branch of mathematics that he himself had helped develop in earlier years. I saw von Neumann in seminars and lectures but had no other contact with him. When we both left Göttingen in 1927, I lost sight of him until around 1946 when he was living in Princeton. From 1946 to 1949 I visited him in Princeton at the rate of about once a month. Our common interest then was hydrodynamics, in which he was a dedicated specialist, and I had acquired an interest through geophysics.

Von Neumann, born 1903, was the son of a wealthy banker in Budapest. He early showed an unusual talent for mathematics, and his father hired a professional mathematician as his tutor, at an age when others learn elementary arithmetic. This early training gave him a skill in the manipulation of formulas that sometimes frightened people less gifted. I once heard Dirac say that his chief shortcoming lay in not having learned mathematics at a very early age, so that later he painstakingly had to construct his mathematical arguments. I wonder whether this is not, in the long run, an advantage. John von Neumann was at the other extreme. His tremendous ease in computation made it almost too simple for him to carry through any argument, and it sometimes led to his leaving a rather baroque demonstration in a form where with a little effort at polishing the result could have been much simpler and easier to understand. He was, however, able to simplify when the subject seemed sufficiently important.

None of his early training seemed in any way to have disturbed his psychological balance. During the years that I heard about him from one source or another, or knew him myself, he was invariably a sane, sensible, and well-balanced individual. He was certainly less given than almost anybody I have known to that unconscious expression of his own superiority that is so common among highly talented people, to what is called primadonna behavior. Due to this engaging aspect of his personality everybody who knew him, up to his later years at least, called him "Johnny." It is almost impossible for me to think of him otherwise than as Johnny. In 1927 he moved to the University of Berlin; later on, he was one of the first men to be appointed to the newly opened Institute for Advanced Study in Princeton, in 1933. In his later years he became deeply immersed in the design of electronic computers and, in fact, acquired a vast knowledge of electronic devices worthy of a first-rate engineer. At that time numerous stories circulated in scientific circles about how Johnny had scandalized the sedate world of mathematics which had always worked with pencil and paper, by doing mathematics with electric wires and assorted gadgetry. In fact, after his early death from cancer in 1956, all electronic equipment rapidly disappeared from the Institute for Advanced Study and only the grating of pencils on paper remained.

One of Johnny's capabilities was often mentioned when I first knew him in Göttingen: his photographic memory, or what some specialists call "eidetic" memory. This is the rare ability to look for a few seconds at, say, a page of a book and thereafter "read off" the entire text of the page from the detailed image retained in memory. Since I never saw a demonstration of this capability, I am only repeating hearsay. But the stories were so persistent that I have little doubt of their truth.

Von Neumann continued his studies of the mathematical aspects of quantum mechanics for several years. They culminated in a book, *The Mathematical Foundations of Quantum Mechanics*, that appeared in 1932. Its contents are now so widely spread in the literature that practitioners rarely read it. For me, at that time, it was a revelation. First, one could be sure with a man like von Neumann that one dealt with unimpeachable mathematics contrasting favorably with the crude, home-made techniques used by many physicists. Second, von Neumann eschewed any specializations, for instance to chemistry, but gave general principles and theorems to which one could attach a philosophical analysis if one wanted to, as I later did myself. It became particularly clear in von Neumann's analysis that the introduction of probabilities into basic physics, perhaps the most distinguishing feature of quantum mechanics, did not "loosen up" the framework of the theory; hence, quantum theory appeared more mechanistic, deterministic in-the-mean, or else suitable for reducing everything to physics, than traditional Newtonian mechanics ever had been. This was a valuable lesson but also one that dissatisfied me deeply because I distrusted reductionism. I struggled with von Neumann's book for some years, not only to absorb all the technical details, but more to exhaust all its philosophical implications. It was nearly twenty years later that I found an escape from the philosophical impasse: The escape consisted in comparing the infinite sets of symbols underlying the mathematical description with the finite sets of observations that experience offers. But this is a technical matter that I have dealt with in my books.

I had learned a most useful lesson from von Neumann: Any model of organic life that was based only on the existence of statistical features in physics was likely to be false. Among those who tried to proceed along that treacherous path, one of the fathers of quantum mechanics, Pascual Jordan, was prominent. His book *Physics and the Secret of Organic Life* came out early in World War II and for that reason, apparently, was never translated into English, although the German original went through several editions. In it, Jordan proposes what he himself calls an "amplifier theory" of organisms. The amplifiers are, however, not those of ordinary electronics but are exemplified by Geiger counters and similar devices of atomic or nuclear physics that convert an atomic event into one on a much larger scale. I felt that this amounted basically to harnessing strictly statistical phenomena for what may crudely be called an "explanation" of organic life. Considered from the viewpoint of von Neumann's mathematical scheme, I decided that such ideas were barely distinguishable from straight reductionism and that a deeper, more philosophical analysis would eventually be required.

These remarks give an idea of the kind of "philosophical" thinking that engaged me in the years after I had left Göttingen. Most of those who were involved in the early development of quantum mechanics sooner or later abandoned such philosophical speculations to return to physics proper; but I continued to belabor these problems for many years to come.

4

The Troubled Years

Shortly after I had received my degree and before I had thought much about the future, an unexpected letter arrived from Paul Ehrenfest, professor of theoretical physics at Leiden, Holland. He said that his assistant was leaving for America; would I be interested in the job? He added that at first he could appoint me for only one semester, but this could be extended. Of course, I accepted. It was by then common knowledge among physicists that George Uhlenbeck, Ehrenfest's assistant, as well as Samuel Goudsmit, the two inventors of the "spinning electron," had both been offered positions at the University of Michigan in Ann Arbor. But who had recommended me to Ehrenfest? It seemed unlikely that it was anyone of the men in Göttingen. The more I thought the more I focussed on Robert Oppenheimer, although he had never mentioned any specific contact with Ehrenfest. Later, I learned that Oppenheimer had, indeed, been in Leiden and was personally well known to several of the physicists there. But I did not solve the puzzle decisively, although I was never able to doubt that it was Oppenheimer's doing.

I had once encountered Ehrenfest during a meeting of the "Structure-of-Matter" seminar. The speaker of the day had already started when the door opened and a short, dark-haired gentleman of middle years entered with a travelling bag in his left hand and a cape flowing loosely about his shoulders. He motioned to the speaker to continue, but later took an active part in the discussion. He must have disappeared as suddenly as he arrived for I did not see him again, but the exhibit had been too flamboyant to be readily forgotten. Then, in August of 1927, some weeks before I was to leave for Leiden, there came another letter. This one was quite long, six pages in a tight, rather convoluted scrawl, and it was definitely not about physics. It dealt, instead, with some of Ehrenfest's psychological problems whose exact nature was unintelligible to me. I read the letter again, and then a third time, but was still unable to extract any clear sense from it. At the end of the letter, he had said I should let him know the time of my arrival, as he would be sure to receive me at the railroad station. So I wrote in reply that I felt his letter could best be discussed orally when we met. I was somewhat worried about this strange development, since, although I had run into many peculiar human beings, I had not yet met a man who tried to explain the complexities of his soul to a total stranger half his age whom he had hired to be his future assistant but had never met.

But this problem could wait. I was going to celebrate my new freedom by going to Paris. I had enough money with me to stay there a little over two weeks. And although I didn't know a soul in Paris, I had a glorious time. I went from the Halles, best seen in the early morning, to the museums where I spent part of each day, to the boulevards with their colorful evening crowds. This was the much-touted civilization, but it was ever so much better than literature. It was truly a many-splendored thing.

When I arrived in Leiden, I found that Ehrenfest had kept his word and was waiting at the station. He at once took me on a walk that lasted for an hour and a half, during which he did most of the talking and again about the psychological problems that he had discussed in his letter, and that did not become any clearer to me. When at the end of this lengthy talk his attitude became almost pleading, like that of a drowning man who asks for help, I tried to assure him that I would be of as much help as I could—but this was not to be, as the subsequent events showed.

Meanwhile, I tried to settle down in Holland. I found an agreeable sitting-bedroom in a small lodging house run by a pleasant and kindly middleaged lady. I soon learned something about the Dutch style of life: Whenever I stayed in my room for long, the landlady would gingerly knock at my door, enter, and say, "Would you like a cup of tea?," hand me a cup of pleasant-smelling hot tea, and withdraw again. I was pleased with the tea, but at first I was uncomfortable—what did the good lady want? It took me some time to discover that she wanted absolutely nothing, certainly not money, and not even an occasion to gossip, which would have been very difficult, given my very limited knowledge of Dutch.

I began to explore Leiden by walking around town. It is typically Dutch: Many streets are not ordinary streets, but canals bordered on both sides by roads. The Dutch houses were brick and usually of two stories. As a rule there was a very big front window that came to within three feet of the ground, so that one could overlook a large, placid-looking living room. Sometimes a lady would sit there reading a book. Being a life-long lover of paintings I soon recognized scenes that Vermeer had immortalized. I had seen numbers of Vermeer paintings in various European museums and was to see more of them in Holland. Vermeer was born in Delft, a city not far from Leiden; he lived there all the years of his short life. There was a wonderful feeling of peace about this Dutch scenery, but it was not the peace of raw, uninhabited nature; it was a man-made peace, but no less impressive. To savor genuine Dutch country scenery, one must, of course, leave the city for the flatlands. Often they are as flat as an ironing board with an occasional tree or windmill close to the horizon, overarched by a limpid sky like a gigantic crystal bowl. I have seen such scenery in many other parts of the world but, for reasons unknown to me, never accompanied by the same emotional impact. Perhaps this is because by then I had already seen so many Dutch landscape paintings.

On my perambulations through Leiden, I noticed that the living-room windows all had their curtains wide open during daylight hours—only occasionally did one see a half-closed curtain. This seemed an unwritten convention; it certainly gave the whole town a wonderful look of openness. It was also in sharp contrast to Ehrenfest's house into which he took me shortly after my arrival. Ehrenfest had come as a professor to Leiden in 1912, and a few years later had built a house. It stood at the end of a short street not far from his office. It struck the visitor at once because there were no windows at all on the front side. It was the first such house I had seen and, it seemed to me, it must have been unique in Holland. As I readily ascertained, there were windows at the sides and many windows looking to the garden in the rear, but the front was a two-story blank wall with a little opening at one place that was closed by a solid wooden door. One entered a large room with white-washed walls that covered most of the first-floor area of the house. Along one side a wide black ribbon ran between the front and rear corners. On closer inspection it turned out to be a blackboard fastened to the wall.

At that time Ehrenfest was living there with some of his children. His wife was a Russian mathematician who had returned to live in Russia and teach mathematics. He told me that he and his wife saw each other occasionally, but given the distance it could not have been too often. There was, it seems, a cruel fate looming over the Ehrenfest family. One of the younger children, I was told, was mentally retarded; the very gifted older son perished in a skiing accident; and some time later, in 1933, Paul Ehrenfest committed suicide at age fifty-three.

But I was occupied by a much more personal question which concerned my survival in the competitive world of science. I could see that I would hardly last longer in Leiden than the promised semester. I first had to settle on a temporary course of action, and I decided that I must keep total control of myself, be casual, and not let myself be provoked into saying or doing anything temperamental. This did not seem to suit Ehrenfest; in fact, it became increasingly clear that he was an intellectual pugilist: If he could not argue, he felt stymied. Later, after I had been in Leiden for some weeks and had come to know several people, I began to make remarks about the difficulties in dealing with Ehrenfest, hoping that the answers would give me useful clues. They did after a fashion: The surprising thing was that the replies were utterly stereotyped and ran like this: We Dutchmen are the most peaceful people on earth. This man Ehrenfest is too difficult to last for more than a short time among any other people. But now, since he is here, we must endure him.

By that time I had learned enough to be able to interpet that language. Ehrenfest had been brought to Holland by H. A. Lorentz to be his successor, when the latter retired from Leiden in 1912. Lorentz was widely considered the greatest mind Holland had produced in the quantitative sciences since Christian Huyghens, a contemporary of Newton. Lorentz, in spite of his formidable reputation, had to overcome great social as well as technical difficulties to get Ehrenfest appointed. So what these people were telling me was understandable enough: They were quite aware of the problems raised by Ehrenfest's personality; they were also determined not to let these problems come into the open. This would have been embarrassing to the great Lorentz; it could also be bad for the reputation of Dutch science, since Ehrenfest's name was very well known in a number of neighboring countries. So I decided to drop such resistance or reaction as would have been conceivable otherwise.

I wanted, then, to get the most out of my stay in Holland with whose scenery, spirit, and culture I was profoundly taken. I had the weekends to travel to cities, leaving out the countryside since it was autumn. Holland proper is the strip of lowlands close to the coast where all the major cities, with the exception of Utrecht, lie along a railroad line on which a rapid train runs about every half hour from Rotterdam to

Amsterdam, stopping at Delft, the Hague, Leiden, and Haarlem. One day I went to Haarlem to pay a visit to a colleague, the theoretical physicist A. D. Fokker. He was at that time the director of the Teyler Foundation, a privately endowed institution whose directorship was not very burdensome and was, therefore, given to distinguished scientists who could thus find time for research. I was told before going that the Foundation's museum had one of the largest collections of Rembrandt drawings and etchings in the world. I had written to Dr. Fokker that I would be grateful if I were permitted to see some of their famous Rembrandts. After my talk with him I was led into a small room draped with heavy, old-fashioned curtains, the table in the middle covered by a rich damask cloth; an attendant brought in a huge, booklike item, so heavy that he could hardly carry it, and said: "This is a selection of our best Rembrandt etchings." He then handed me a big magnifying glass and said: "I shall now close this door. When you've seen enough, just ring the bell and I shall let you out." For a long time I feasted my eyes on the best of Rembrandt's etchings.

Fokker's predecessor as director had been the famous H. A. Lorentz himself who had resigned his professorship in Leiden at the age of nearly sixty. Lorentz's merit may be summed up by saying that he achieved the transition from the nineteenth-century physics of the electrical continuum to the twentieth-century physics of corpuscular electricity, the physics of electrons. Maxwell, the founder of modern electromagnetic theory, had developed his models by basing himself strictly on the analogy with the theory of elasticity. In elasticity, one studies continuously distributed forces and the displacements they produce. But after experimentalists had established the existence of electrons, there was an entire new field for theoreticians—to reformulate physics in terms of electrons as basic constituents. This posed major conceptual and mathematical puzzles. Lorentz was one of the most successful of those who addressed these questions; he solved many of them with extraordinary elegance and impressive simplicity, thus preparing the ground for the rise of both relativity theory and quantum mechanics. Lorentz became so famous among physicists that he was the second man, after W. C. Röntgen, discoverer of X-rays, to receive the Nobel prize for physics, in 1902. He shared the prize with Pieter Zeeman of Amsterdam, an experimentalist who had found the effect of magnetism upon spectral lines, while Lorentz had provided the analysis and understanding of Zeeman's results in terms of his then novel model of electrons bound in atoms.

Hendrick Antoon Lorentz

My Dutch friends told me that later in life A. H. Lorentz became a member of the Zuider Sea Commission, the body in charge of the huge engineering works that reclaim land from the ocean. A large part of Holland proper lies below sea level and had become inundated by the turbulent North Sea largely in historical times. With modern technical means, such works can, of course, be carried out on a big scale and can comprise extended areas. I was told that for some years Lorentz had been in charge of the preliminary theoretical calculations that are required if such an undertaking is to be reasonably efficient. A few years after my visit, in 1932, a gigantic enclosing dam, some twenty-seven kilometers long, was put across the mouth of the Zuider Sea. Since then, a vast area, over 1500 square kilometers, not quite half of the water surface, has been drained of salt water and reclaimed as arable land.

Shortly after my arrival in Leiden, I had the good luck to assist at a series of lectures on the electron that Lorentz presented. He was then in his mid-seventies with snow white hair and beard, and he had the most spiritualized face I had ever seen. This may have been his last public appearance since he died in the following year.

At first, Lorentz's lectures were utterly strange to me; I could not make any sense of them. He would first discuss general propositions in a pleasantly undulating voice that seemed to have an almost hypnotic effect; then after some ten minutes or so, one would suddenly mentally perceive the precise image of an electron as a little, charged ball; one would begin to understand how it moved under the influence of electric forces. He would write down a few simple equations that expressed his ideas in quantitative terms. This style was radically different from that in German universities, where a lecturer began by stating in a clear and precise manner his assumptions and then proceeded to develop the logical consequences of the assumptions, also precisely, step by step. I felt at first uncomfortable with Lorentz's manner until, after a couple of hours of this, it suddenly occurred to me that Lorentz was really presenting the scientific counterpart of what I knew so well from Dutch painting, especially Rembrandt's: the clair-obscure style, an undulating variety of shades of brown from which there emerges now and then a face, or some object, intensely illuminated. In terms of this visual simile I could understand the difference between Lorentz's method of presentation and the one I had been accustomed to. Thereafter, I enjoyed Lorentz's lectures immensely.

When I remember those early experiences, I wonder how much of my later thinking originated in these lectures of Lorentz. There are certainly roots here of thoughts that loomed large in my later thinking: Mainly, that the scientist should imitate Nature in discovering how order can be created out of chaos. There was much in the clair-obscure technique of Lorentz that first gave me a glimpse of this way of approaching science. But on continuing this kind of philosophical musing, one could soon recognize that Nature herself had thrown great difficulties in our way: If the scientist starts to think about creation, he soon recognizes two quite different types. First, there is the creation of raw, inorganic matter in the depth of the universe, by a "big bang" or by whatever other cosmic device the astronomer can conceive. But then, anyone who admits that living things are not just automata, must somehow also assume that there is an ongoing creative process in organic life. This process is presently as unexplored as the cosmic process, but it is so much closer at hand, and so much material is available for its study, that this study is utterly challenging to the scientific mind.

But back to the reality of Holland: I formed pleasant friendships and felt very much at home. But the period was so short and so somber personally that I was unable to develop longer-lasting attachments. I mostly met physicists, of course. In Leiden, experimental work in physics had long centered on the study of low temperatures. Techniques at that time were not, of course, what they are today. Extremely low temperatures were produced once a week, on Wednesdays, if I remember right. The refrigerating machinery was started early in the day, and toward noon the first drops of liquid helium would appear. Anyone who had prepared an experiment at low temperatures would have his apparatus set up in the neighborhood, and after waiting long enough he would receive his ration of liquid helium that he used immediately before it could evaporate. During all this procedure, tea was served, and every physicist was invited to assist at the ceremony. This genius of the Dutch for smoothing the jagged edges of existence by serving tea at the proper time!

Meanwhile, my relations with Ehrenfest had not become regularized. The first few days I felt simply paralyzed from the shock his reception had administered. Within a very few weeks, his attitude changed from aggressiveness over indifference to downright hostility. I was well aware of my own shortcomings in theoretical physics, a field in which I was still almost an apprentice. In a few weeks Ehrenfest had discovered that too; he asked me in his seminar, in front of the students, questions about his own field, statistical mechanics, to which I should have known the correct answers but didn't. Then he would comment most sarcastically.

Although I had only been in Leiden since the beginning of the semester in early October, it was clear that something would break soon, and it did. One morning in November, Ehrenfest walked into my office and the following conversation ensued:

E: (sniffing the air) I smell something here, what is it?
I: Sorry, I don't smell anything.
E: Now I smell it more distincly; it is perfume.
I: I don't use any perfume, never used the stuff in my life.
E: (agitated) I am quite sure there is perfume here, how does perfume get into this office?
I: Now I remember: Earlier this morning I had a haircut, and you know how these barbers douse your head with vile-smelling pomade.
E: (now very agitated, shouting and gesticulating) I cannot stand perfume, I will not tolerate perfume here. Get out. Go home, get out. Get out. Get out.

Short of being prepared to engage in a fist fight, I had to disappear. I returned to my office the next day and kept on working and studying quietly. I expected that he would come and apologize but he didn't. After a few days he suddenly appeared in my office and without introduction said: "I have been able to make arrangements with the finance officer of the university, so that the salary checks for the remainder of this semester will be sent to your home. Please leave your home address with the proper official. You may leave any time." Two days later I was on the train to Berlin.

I have preferred not to speak about Ehrenfest's scientific work since I may be considered biased, and since there exists a biography of Ehrenfest going up to the end of World War I, by the historian of science, Martin J. Klein.[1] Professor Klein describes Ehrenfest's scientific accomplishments in some detail. One thing I learned, however, and learned for good from this particular experience: If I had ever thought, in the style of Hitler, that any one group or race of people had a monopoly on rawness, or mishandling of their fellow creatures, then the encounter with Ehrenfest disabused me of such ideas. In manner and attitudes he seemed to me still close to the Jewish ghetto. I realized, of course, that he could not have risen to his level of prominence without having some outstanding personal characteristics. In my case, clearly, he felt safe in yielding to his less glorious instincts; to get rid of me would be a simple matter.

When I arrived in Berlin, I could sense the contrast between the gentleness of the Dutch and the harshness of the Prussians. At that stage in national development, my father's contention that one's antecedents such as Jewishness were irrelevant in the face of Progress had become very false indeed.

Berlin was still a flourishing cosmopolitan center, but this seemed very much a hot-house growth, not just a natural development. I never took to the town. But if I had had dreams of escaping to the United States, it was clear that the Ehrenfest episode would greatly reduce my chances. I realized that both Oppenheimer and Uhlenbeck, who were great admirers of Ehrenfest's intellect, had not seen the same side of this man's complex personality, or not as violently, as I had; and in trying to get a job in a new environment, one cannot afford to deal with such psychological complexities. Disregarding emigration at that time, my more immediate prospects seemed to be as a high school teacher of science and mathematics. In itself, this seemed a reasonable enough career, but, given the mood in Germany, I could see myself spending most of my future existence defending myself against gangs of anti-Semitic hoodlums. I found this the more difficult as the growing alienation from the majority of my fellow-citizens was not compensated in turn by any strong positive feeling of my own, of being Jewish. My parents had never provided any opportunity for that kind of association, and later I was too old for it to form. In psychological terms, it is much easier to transfer an existing attachment from one group as well as from one individual to another, than to create it anew, after a certain age.

Feeling completely blocked in, I became severely depressed. It was not an out-and-out "nervous breakdown," but it approached one. I could function with some effort in ordinary life, but I lacked enough initiative to formulate and carry through scientific research. In addition, I had been spoiled by my two and a half years in Göttingen. I recalled an old saying that a youngster from the country should avoid the company of the great of this world since it would bring him only grief. My full forces did not return until some five to six years later when three events occurred almost simultaneously: I underwent some

Wolfgang Pauli

psychoanalysis, as I will describe in Chapter 6, I moved from Germany to France; and in France for the first time in my life I was given a steady research position that was likely to continue if I produced results and that would not vanish as the outcome of somebody's whim or of political pressure.

Fortunately, my parents seemed to be aware of my precarious condition. Nothing much was discussed, but they gave me to understand that I could stay in their home until I had gotten back upon my feet again. They also agreed to let me spend another post-doctoral semester away from home; I chose to study with Wolfgang Pauli in Zürich, Switzerland.

Pauli had just been installed as the professor of theoretical physics at the Federal Polytechnical School; he was then twenty-eight and had previously been in Hamburg for some years; he remained in Zürich for the rest of his life. I attended his lectures on quantum mechanics and tried to work more closely with him, but he did not seem very interested. It was only five years later, in 1933, that he told me the reason for his reserve: "You seemed so weak and shaken-up at that time," he said, "I was worried that you would faint and keel over if I breathed hard at you." I tried to learn as much as I could about quantum mechanics from his lectures which were both powerful and elegant.

Wolfgang Pauli had entered the world of science as a prodigy. At the age of nineteen he had written a comprehensive review article on the theory of relativity for the *Encyclopedia of Mathematical Sciences*.[2] This was a multi-volume collective work whose contributors were all top-level scientists. Pauli's article was soon recognized not only as an altogether comprehensive review of the subject, but also as unsurpassed in power and conciseness. It established him as one of the leaders of theoretical physics. In thinking of Pauli's skill, I am reminded of an ancient story: In the days of the Renaissance there was once a friendly contest among a group of artists to see who was the most skillful. Giotto, when his turn came, dipped his brush into paint and with one stroke drew an absolutely perfect circle. He was given the prize. Pauli's mastery was based on his penetrating power to simplify and on concentrating his knowledge and memory on what was essential. With his ability to assimilate the significant and to eliminate everything else, he became the conscience of physics during the critical growth period of quantum mechanics. I once had a glimpse of what this meant when I lived in Paris and was writing many scientific papers. Usually, I thought they were tolerably good, but once I slipped: I concocted some bad piece of nonsense. Promptly, about two or three weeks after my little note had appeared in print, I received a brief letter from Pauli. It said that if I ever published any similar goddamn nonsense again, he would withdraw his good-will from me. This implied that Pauli not only took notice of any piece of new literature in the field of atomic theory, but actually read everything critically. He corresponded whenever he thought his comments would do some good, his note to me being only one very small example; and I believe that in this resided a large part of his importance for modern physics, quite apart from his own monumental contributions.

The most important of his discoveries concerned the evaluation and exploitation of the "rotating electron," or "electron spin" as it is more usually called, invented by Uhlenbeck and Goudsmit. This model turned out to be unusually difficult to treat by known mathematical techniques, but Pauli showed that on using some techniques of quantum theory, the mathematics could be turned into utter simplicity. Then there was the question of how an atom, provided it consisted of a number of electrons, could maintain itself without contracting steadily. Pauli showed that if one included the spin as part of the motion of an electron, then the electrons in any atom were arranged so that no two electrons carried out exactly equivalent motions. This insight, known as the Pauli exclusion principle, is now an integral part, and one of the most essential, of modern atomic theory.

Wolfgang Pauli was a short, rather rotund man. He had a well-developed sense of humor. His mainstay in that respect was the so-called Pauli effect. This was a phenomenon thoroughly known to every physicist of the 1920s: Whenever Pauli (a pure theoretician) entered a laboratory, all kinds of things would go wrong. Meter needles would dance wildly, delicate glassware would crack, electric wires would suddenly spark, and so on. Pauli himself was very good in entertaining an audience with tales of his past exploits in this field. Once, however, I saw him wax really furious. This was when a professor at a smaller German university forbade Pauli to enter his laboratory because the man was afraid of the "Pauli effect." This was too direct and too blunt even for Wolfgang Pauli's sense of humor, and it took him many months to get over it.

As he grew older, Pauli's interests broadened. One might say that he then allowed himself the time to look beyond quantum mechanics. A witness to this period is a book, jointly written with Carl Gustav Jung,

From l. to r.: R. Oppenheimer, I. I. Rabi, L. Mott-Smith, and W. Pauli, in a boat on the Zürchersee, 1927

the psychologist, also living in Zürich. Pauli wrote about the psychological development of Johannes Kepler; Jung wrote about an abortive attempt of his to deal with astrology by means of statistics.

Much later, in the spring of 1958, when my first book on "philosophical biology" appeared, Wolfgang Pauli was the only colleague who read it. He wrote and asked me several questions about it which I tried to answer in my reply. Early in the fall of that year, Pauli visited Berkeley. Since I lived then in San Diego, I managed to go there and meet him. We had a pleasant visit; Pauli told me that he had resumed contact with Heisenberg after the end of World War II, and that they corresponded extensively about the problems of quantum field theory. Pauli had not lost his decisiveness which sometimes bordered on sarcasm. He said that Heisenberg was extravagantly optimistic about constructing a theory in a field that was still mostly unexplored, and that he, Pauli, did his best, sometimes by rough means, to convince Heisenberg of this.

After his return to Zürich that fall he was suddenly stricken by cancer. It developed so rapidly that the doctors could do nothing, and two months later he was dead. More than any other person I ever met, he seemed an incarnation of the great forces of nature, whatever their ultimate character may be.

There was one other man with whom I became acquainted at the Federal Polytechnic School, the famous Swiss mathematician Hermann Weyl, who taught a course in the theory of relativity. He had also written a book on the subject that was "all the rage" at the time. It was entitled *Space, Time, Matter* and has been translated into several languages. At first I studied it ravenously. Then, I began to have second thoughts. While it was a fabulous and wholly admirable exhibition of the prodigious technical skill of a mathematician, it made only tenuous contact with physical reality, the domain of the observer. I began to be aware, for the first time, and as yet dimly, that one cannot grasp reality by a commitment to any one technique or one procedure. I perceived, albeit still dimly, that any man who depicted nature in a manner that seemed utterly comprehensible, ought to be approached with the greatest scepticism. It was only many years later that I realized how difficult it is to be truly sceptical about the comprehensibility of scientific description. As soon as one raises any such question, one is at the boundary of scientific thought; many otherwise sound scientists become uncomfortable, with the result that they instantly freeze into dogma, and all reasoning then becomes utterly fruitless.

In all fairness to Hermann Weyl, I should say that the preceding
digression was triggered by only one of his books. I am not familiar
enough with his great work in pure mathematics to discuss him in that
context.

While in Zürich I became acquainted with some local people and
eventually succeeded in feeling quite comfortable there. But a semester
is soon gone, and at its end I returned to my parents' apartment in
Berlin. There still was no prospect of any gainful employment, and my
depression continued. In the early fall of 1928, Fritz Houtermans
moved to Berlin; he had finished his Ph.D. under Franck and had
obtained a post of assistant in experimental physics at the Polytechnic
School in Berlin-Charlottenburg. This was a big institution, and since
every engineering student must pass through almost the entire physics
laboratory, the latter was a large-scale undertaking of the school.
Houtermans was kind enough to procure for me a small position as an
auxiliary laboratory assistant paid by the hour. I kept this small place
for two academic years, from the fall of 1928 to the spring of 1930, and
while the pay was barely enough to live on, I had in this way at least
some income of my own. Since my parents uncomplainingly continued to provide room and board, this arrangement gave me enough
independence to lead at least a limited life of my own. I saw rather little
thereafter of Houtermans who lived in an easy-going, highly cosmopolitan, and often left-wing crowd with which I had only a limited
affinity.

There was one man in Berlin who impressed me deeply: the theoretical physicist Max von Laue, at that time a professor at the university.
From our first contact, he showed a more than average interest in me for
an obvious reason: Von Laue was responsible for the discovery of X-ray
diffraction by crystals, and he had been struck by the little note I had
written in Göttingen about the interpretation of the first experiments of
Davisson, with Kunsman, as demonstrating diffraction of de Broglie
waves. Later on, during the Second World War, von Laue wrote a book
on the *Diffraction of Matter Waves*, and this must have kept him from
dwelling on the devastations of Hitler for whom he had no sympathy
whatsoever. I have gathered a little information about his personal life,
especially from Vol. 3 of his collected works.[3]

Max von Laue was a distinguished-looking man, rather reserved
in his dealings with others. He was the best product of a Prussian
upbringing with its total concentration on duty and the public interest.
His father, apparently, was an official of the Prussian administration,

and young Max had to move around a good deal, but he still managed to get an excellent education in the "gymnasium." He started his study of theoretical physics at the University of Berlin where the leading theorist was Max Planck, the father of the "quantum of action," the initiator of quantum theory. Both men, Planck and von Laue, seemingly at once recognized the overwhelming importance of Einstein's work on relativity, so that, perhaps for the only time in the history of science, a novel and revolutionary idea was recognized without first having been held back for years by established sceptics. It was one of the several historical events that gave the first third of the twentieth century the particular character which made the American physicist K. K. Darrow describe it as the "renaissance of physics." Von Laue wrote the first textbook of relativity theory, which appeared in 1911. The book is unique in that, starting from general principles, it proceeds ultimately to formulas for specific events that can be verified by specific experimental observations. It is only too true that the majority of books on the subject, if they are not monographs such as Pauli's that are only accessible to the specialists, are broad treatises typified by Weyl's book where a magnificent but purely mathematical structure supports a verdant *Naturphilosophie.*

The discovery that made Max von Laue famous is perhaps the best scientific example of that combination of luck and the prepared mind for which English writers use the delightful term "serendipity." In 1912 von Laue was teaching at the University of Munich, where the senior professor of theoretical physics was Sommerfeld. One day a student named P. P. Ewald consulted him about his thesis subject, which was the study of the effect that the molecular lattice structure of crystals could have on light going through it. Von Laue reports that it occurred to him that X-rays would be much better than light for studying such a relationship, and he mentioned this idea to Ewald. At the time, X-rays, discovered by W. C. Röntgen, had been known for over sixteen years and had been thoroughly investigated from many angles. The accumulated evidence left little doubt that X-rays were electromagnetic radiations that were not basically different from light except for their wavelength, which was much smaller, perhaps a thousand times smaller than that of ordinary light. To study crystals by X-rays was not farfetched for von Laue since he had just completed a major review article on crystal optics for the *Encyclopedia of Mathematical Sciences.* Ewald in turn discussed the idea with his younger experimental colleagues. It was only a few days later that two young experimentalists, Friedrich and Knipping, asked von Laue to agree to their carrying out an experiment on the diffraction of X-rays by crystals. The experiment was simple enough: A cathode-ray tube served as a source of X-rays; a piece of crystal was placed at some distance; and farther away stood a photographic plate, wrapped so that it was not exposed to ordinary light. The crystal consisted of copper sulfate, which was chosen simply because this material is readily obtained in large single crystals. The second exposure was already a success: It showed that, in addition to the direct X-ray beam, there were secondary, deflected beams. The pattern was irregular, but this arose solely because the crystal had not been aligned along its axis. When this was remedied, one very soon obtained those beautiful symmetrical patterns of spots that have become known as Laue patterns. Not much later, Peter Debye developed the method of exploring the structure of materials that are aggregates of many small crystals oriented in random directions, as most ordinary materials are. This results in a set of rings rather than in a pattern of spots. From these beginnings there rapidly developed the science of crystal analysis by X-rays, which more recently has succeeded even in determining the structure of molecules as complex as proteins, provided only they can be crystallized.

Those of a later generation can hardly imagine the tremendous impact of this discovery on the world. Atoms had been a stock article of philosophical speculation since the ancient Greeks, but they were not yet "real." In the last years of the nineteenth century, a school of scientific thought called "energetics" emphasized the still largely symbolic and hypothetical nature of the term "atom." The discovery of radioactivity, where one could see under the microscope the scintillations produced by individual atoms, convinced quite a few experts that atoms were real objects, not just symbolic abstractions. But given the mysterious nature of radioactivity, this was not suitable for impressing a broader public. But in the case of Laue patterns, one merely had to understand the trick of nature which lined up many atoms in a regular array called a crystal, a trick that had been endlessly discussed since R. Haüy in the eighteenth century had founded crystallography on this basis. Here it was for everyone to see, an easy experiment whose outcome could be photographed. The theory was simple to understand; it involved only the principles of the optical diffraction grating, which could be made clear to almost every high-school student. I still remember the reverberation of this sense of a radical scientific revolution in the semi-popular literature I read in high school.

Phot.: Lotte Meitner-Graf, London

Max von Laue

Some twenty years after this discovery, when Hitler rose to power in Germany, von Laue was horrified. In 1937 he sent his only son to the United States to escape conscription by Hitler. The son remained there after the war. The father decided to stay in Germany, although he had occasions to escape; he wanted to be ready to re-build German science after the conflagration had burnt itself out, and he later did so with the extreme dedication and singlemindedness that characterized all his actions.

It was a sign of my psychological difficulties in that period that I could not utilize the presence of von Laue, who was clearly very favorably disposed toward me, to start over again in theoretical physics with emphasis on the study of crystals, a field in which I had already made a small but spectacular start. P. P. Ewald carved a successful academic career out of just such an activity. For most of his later years, he edited the *Strukturbericht* (Report on structures), a periodical appearing at irregular intervals in which, on a comprehensive, world-wide scale, the experimental work on the analysis of crystal structures by X-rays was reviewed and systematized, an activity of immense value for structural chemistry. This field was still young and actively growing. But I could not organize myself to participate in this activity or to ask von Laue to serve as my mentor, a task which, I am sure, he would have gladly accepted.

One event of these days has remained vividly in my memory. From the proceeds of his Nobel prize, von Laue had bought what was then in Europe an article of high luxury, usually inaccessible to members of the middle class such as professors: an automobile. One day he invited me and another young colleague to accompany him on a two-day tour through the "Mark Brandenburg," the country surrounding Berlin. The German word *Mark* is a medieval term that designates frontier-land and dates from the time when the boundary between the Germans and the Slavs ran there. Our general direction was toward the Elbe River, which flows about one hundred kilometers to the west of Berlin. What I saw on this trip was quite different from the fertile, hilly countryside where I had spent my youth, and, in fact, different from any parts of Europe I had seen so far. It was a perfectly flat country with sandy soil, mostly covered by pine forests. Correspondingly, there being no stone available, all the houses were built of brick. There were the older, more well-built edifices that are found in any European countryside: castles, manor houses, churches, monasteries; but here they were different—not only the old castles, but all the more permanent buildings had a warlike appearance. Their walls were heavy, with just a few small windows on the upper floors, surmounted always by impressive parapets: One had the feeling that this was a country of perpetual warfare, where the inhabitants were prepared to withdraw behind their bulwarks at any sign of danger. The villages, the habitations of the peasants, were also different. They were typically Slavic houses such as one finds all over Eastern Europe: circular clusters of one-story houses with thick thatched roofs, easily distinguished from the German type of houses.

There are, I believe, few things so perfectly suited to demonstrate a man's strengths and limitations than his becoming immersed in a completely foreign ambiance. This happened to me during that period. The externals of the story are quickly told: Some time late in 1929 the telephone rang: "This is Obreimov, I am in Berlin and would like to see you." Obreimov was an experimental physicist who had been in Leiden at the same time as I; and since we stayed at the same rooming house, we had become well acquainted. He now told me that he had been made director of the Ukrainian Physico-Technical Institute in Kharkov, a large industrial town in the Ukraine. The Institute, still new, was devoted almost exclusively to research in physics. Would I be interested in coming to Kharkov for a year as a "technical specialist" under a suitable contract. Half of my salary would be paid in rubles that could not be taken out of Russia, the other half in marks or any other currency convertible on the world market. The sum he mentioned would have been generous for a reaonably experienced practical engineer; for me it was princely. He also informed me that I was the first non-Russian to be associated with this Institute, so it was a thoroughly experimental and challenging undertaking. Also, on Obreimov's suggestion the start of my contract was set for the early summer of 1930. Then, he explained, the country would be at its most attractive.

After only a short hesitation I agreed. Although it might not be beneficial to my career as a scientist—and ultimately it wasn't—it offered both a new possibility of escaping from Germany and a great adventure. By then, with the large American stock market crash which everybody had heard of, the employment situation in the Western world was bound to deteriorate. Here was an opportunity to try the East, and with a one-year contract this step was not final.

The trip on the railroad from Berlin to Kharkov took two days. The Institute was a new building that included living quarters for the professional people with ample-sized rooms. I was given accommodations and was made to inscribe myself on the list of people who had the privilege of buying at a store reserved for foreign specialists. There was a need for this store, since numerous engineers, British, American, and German had begun to work in the factories and other industrial enterprises of the Ukraine. At first I tried to ignore this special store whose stock was rather limited anyway, but I found out soon enough that the food served in the Institute's cafeteria and the articles my colleagues could buy in the Russian stores were of poor quality and very limited quantity. I soon discovered that I had fallen into the middle of a vast famine; everyone starved, although it seemed accepted practice never to speak about it. After a while I began to go to the specialists' store now and then, buy a few things such as eggs, butter, and white bread and consume them by myself in my quarters. I found that it was quite impossible to invite any of my colleagues to share such a meal with me; they politely but very firmly refused.

At no time during my months in Kharkov did I gain the remotest impression that there was a secret police in the background. It is easy after all, or so it seemed to me, to tell the difference between a man who refrains from speaking out of discipline and personal pride, and one who keeps quiet because he is afraid of police stool-pigeons. Both might say the same things, but there is a vast difference in numberless nuances. Here my isolated position as a single representative of the West in the Institute turned to my advantage as an observer.

My colleagues were very young, many of them about my own age, which was then twenty-six. They were clearly the very children of the workers and peasants who had made the revolution, a selected group with the talent and the stamina to finish the educational process successfully. There were only a very few representatives of the old bourgeoisie. It was difficult to forget that Russia had been a class society of the most extreme kind for centuries, and I saw many sights that bore witness to this condition. Westerners frequently overlook that Russia had been radically isolated for many centuries. This attribute is usually assigned to Japan. The error in perspective arises in the West because Russia was christianized around 1000 A.D., whereas "heathen" Japan had introduced Buddhism as its official religion 400 years earlier; and while the Japanese kept close contact with their neighbors, the Chinese and Koreans, during most of their history, the very vastness and monotony of the countryside acted as an impediment for Russians. In central Russia a man can walk for weeks on end in any desired direction without noticing a significant change in the type of his surroundings. In Europe, even during the deep Middle Ages, an alert young man who had mastered a trade could wander for some years from one end of the continent to the other while earning his keep and seeing the world; but nothing of the sort is reported from the regions of Russia. The Mongols with their disciplined cavalry trained for the kill, managed to conquer and govern most of Asia for a stretch of time, but then they merged with the local populations and the old, melancholy existence began again. One can believe that before the advent of modern technology, the flatlands of Eastern Europe and Northern Asia were only marginally fit—perhaps quite unfit—for the establishment of a settled civilized community. For centuries on end the forebears of the present Russians had lived in the lowest of conditions, often closer to that of domestic animals than of humans.

One thing that was perfectly clear during my visit to Kharkov was the transformation of society then occurring. An example brought this home to me: My large quarters were in the charge of a young girl, obviously a peasant girl who had been raised and trained by a Communist youth organization; she had an open face, was perfectly clean, and turned out to be altogether reliable and honest. Almost from the beginning, she tried to convince me that I should engage her mother, a peasant woman, to wash my laundry. I could see no objection to this, so I agreed. My colleagues warned me at once that I should never let that woman out of my sight, since in her presence everything movable would promptly disappear. The woman wore the traditional old-fashioned garb of the Russian peasant, several skirts on top of each other slung around her hips, and anything smaller than a locomotive could, and did, readily disappear there. My experience soon showed that I had received good advice. The discontinuity between generations, mothers and daughter, was spectacular.

But let me speak of the work of the Institute and my own involvement in it. I found soon that everything was still very raw; the government had ordered a new and very fancy machine for producing low temperatures from Britain, but this did not arrive for many months. Much of the local activity consisted in marking time, since in Russia, where there is no free market for technical implements, any technical undertaking of this kind can only begin to function after a certain "critical mass" is achieved.

I talked to people as best I could. I had, of course, tried to learn Russian. But Russian is not a simple language and has a rich vocabulary; my inadequacy in any but the most elementary conversations was obvious. Fortunately, Obreimov and the few older people there knew enough German to converse with me. I learned from them that this Institute was an offshoot of the famous Röntgen Institute in Leningrad, an extremely large research establishment in pure and applied physics. The latter's existence and growth to large dimensions during the perilous post-revolutionary years were due primarily to one man, its current director, Abraham Joffe. He must have had a strong paternal streak for he was worshipped by the workers in his Institute. There was one story about Joffe that I heard, and, in fact, heard repeatedly, that has never ceased to puzzle me. It seems that Joffe had some subterranean connections with the secret police, and as a result, on the days when the police were making a raid, Joffe was invariably away on an important business trip. The secret police came and went, and one or two people left with them, never to be seen again. When Joffe returned it was, of course, too late to search for people that had vanished without trace. Here was a psychological problem that was beyond me. I had read some of Joffe's scientific papers and had judged him a highly articulate and perceptive man. How could he behave like a savage on the war-path? I have no doubt that his behavior was rational from his viewpoint and was designed to serve the best interests of the Institute. It was the first time that I saw bluntly demonstrated the relativity of moral judgment. Generalization of moral judgment, as if moral judgment were on the same level as the law of gravity, is, of course, one of the most deep-seated and universal of human vices. Here I saw how it could come into being.

The band of young scientists whose life I shared were clearly an elite. They had not been selected solely on technical grounds. They were proud; they had great dignity; they never complained in spite of conspicuous hardships. The revolution, 13 years in the past, was still sufficiently near for these young people to feel that they themselves were the new society. There was no authority above them, only some bureaucratic machinery; there was even less a tradition that could sustain them, a perspective in time that had given Western aristocrats the strength to govern their countries for centuries. If they wanted a tradition, they had to create it themselves.

This was brought home to me very clearly in a conversation with Obreimov. The name of a scientist came up about whom we both had heard. I mentioned that this man had had a psychotic episode—which in the Victorian age had been called a "nervous breakdown"—had been in a sanatorium for some years, but had then recovered and been productive again. "Oh," said Obreimov, "do they have that in the West too? I thought that kind of thing was a typically Russian phenomenon." Thereupon, I began to look at my Russian colleagues with more critical eyes. I began to see that they carried in them a perfectly natural insecurity, almost an inferiority complex, produced by the lack of the time-dimension in their outlook on the world. Most likely, the vast majority of their forebears had been peasants living in a state of material and social degradation. I decided that the best I could do for these people was less to teach them a few mathematical formulas than to express clearly that I felt comfortable while living among them, as indeed I did. Most of them had probably never had day-to-day contact with a Westerner; they must have thought of a Westerner more as a plaster-figure than as flesh and blood. I was rewarded now and then by a glimpse of that most precious of their features, the "great Russian soul," so much touted in literature, that ability for creating a unique degree of social warmth which is possessed to such an extraordinary degree by the Russians. It seems nature's gift to help them cope with their otherwise near unbearable existence.

In August, 1930, there was to be a large congress of physicists in Odessa, a town located on the north shore of the Black Sea. Many people were coming from the West, and some of them came by way of Kharkov, so that I met a number of familiar faces. I had decided not to attend, for a strange reason: I had accumulated too much money on my ruble account, and since expensive objects were unavailable as well as useless, the only way to spend money was by travel. Paul Dirac appeared suddenly, and we travelled together by train to the east coast of the Black Sea, stopping at a town called Suchumi that used to be a resort for Czarist nobles and now was a resort for proletarian workers. We explored the region and found it intriguing. It is the center of a local tribe, the Abkhasians. One could recognize them by a surprising uniform that many of the men wore. It looked like something that a fanciful fashion designer had invented a century or two back, consisting of long, dark blue pantaloons and a matching jacket with black cuffs and collar. Two leather cartridge-belts crossed over their breast and were filled with resplendent brass cartridges. Since no horses and no arms were in evidence, it looked like so much opera. This is the region, by the way, so often described in newspapers and magazines where the inhabitants live on yogurt and are healthy enough to reach ages over one hundred years. In Sukhumi, Dirac and I separated, he to go in the direction of Odessa, I to the south, by train to Batumi. It is one of the most beautiful places I have ever seen. The old town was then paved with cobblestones on which one could hear the cloppety-clop of little donkeys. But the main marvel of Batumi is its vast botanical garden which climbs up the high hills behind the town. From what I saw, it seemed largely devoted to the breeding and acclimation of tea plants. I climbed as high as I could and enjoyed the view of the green city far down and the deep blue sea beyond. In the evening I took a train to Tiflis. Not having prepared myself for this ancient town, and tourist services being non-existent, I got little benefit from my visit and proceeded to take a bus line to the north that crosses the Caucasus on a very ancient highway, the Grusinian Road. This goes through valleys bordered by high mountains, and the views were not only spectacular, but sometimes strange: High up on the moun-tainsides one saw numerous black holes that gave the impression of inhabited caves. Whether these were ancient or had been dug as refuges during the civil war, I do not know. After two days the bus delivered me to the railroad that runs north of the Caucasus from Baku to Rostov. In Rostov I changed to the train to Kharkov.

I had come in extensive contact during this trip with a singular phenomenon left over from the revolution: I still remember the Russian name—*bjesprisorni*, in English, the neglected children. They were children that had become lost or separated from their parents at an early age during the revolution or the civil war and had grown up truly wild. There were a number of them at every railroad station. One was emphatically warned to close all windows before the train stopped because any garment hanging there would be immediately stolen. These children, mostly in their early teens, looked hardly human: With their incredible agility, their small, pointed eyes, and their weather-hardened faces they resembled a cross between a fox and a monkey. At one time there were many hundreds of thousands or even millions of them in Russia. The government spent vast sums on a program of re-education, but this effort was an utter failure. They were all infected with venereal disease, and being apparently unable to outgrow the mental level of street urchins, they all died early in their twenties. Seeing these creatures at one railroad station after another left an indelible impression on me.

One conviction that I brought back with me from Russia and have not changed since, is that the Russian revolution was primarily a social and educational upheaval and only rather secondarily a politico-economical affair. Confronted with a harsh environment that they could not subdue, these people had sunk lower and lower, century after century, and they were now thirsting for the rudiments of a human existence, for simple cleanliness and orderliness, for elementary decency and honesty, for all the things that Western children learn before they are six. To understand how bad things had been in the old Russia, one need only recall that in those times a peasant who owned a pair of shoes was all but unknown. In spite of the harsh climate, the normal footgear of the peasant in winter was a bundle of straw wrapped around the feet and held together by some rags and strings. This was still common in 1930, and I saw it many times that fall.

I was impressed by the much greater enthusiasm and dedication for the educational rather than the political aims of the revolution. Americans in particular should be well enough informed to understand this. They know that the legal emancipation of the slaves did not make them citizens except in a purely formal sense, and that it takes endless decades of education to bridge the gap. The instigators of the Russian revolution, Lenin at their head, had to find an ideology that could carry along a vast, rather primitive, very conservative population of peasants that on the whole is none too imaginative. They searched and they found Marxism, an ideology evolved in Western Europe to fit politico-economic conditions in the middle of the nineteenth century. To think that the Russians are Marxists because of a desire to break the power of "international capitalism" is a simplification that ignores the primacy of their internal problems, of which the greatest and most overriding is the desire to give the majority of their citizens a life of dignity and decency based on a minimum of material sufficiency.

I remember an incident that occurred after I had been in Kharkov for some time and had learned to carry on a simple conversation. One day I met outside the Institute an elderly man, simply but very cleanly dressed, who was quite articulate; he explained to me that he was self-taught, that he had been a factory worker before retiring two years ago because of age and health. Since he had no other skills and no family, he was forced to live on the pension the government paid him. But this was just not enough to feed him adequately, so he was very, very slowly starving to death. I presume that if a secret police agent had overheard this conversation, the poor fellow would have been arrested and executed as a counter-revolutionary; but this, of course, does not preclude that his report might have been factually true, in part at least.

It became clear to me that a country that cannot feed a retired worker is none too likely to stay at peace.

The summer in Russia had done me much good, psychically speaking. When I returned to Kharkov, there was little disturbance for a while, and I succeeded in completing a scientific article. But in October, with the cold season coming on, I fell ill: Soon my skin became as yellow as that of a ripe lemon; I had contracted infectious jaundice, then endemic in the Ukraine. I tried to have myself admitted to a hospital, but all hospitals were overfilled and had waiting lists for critical cases. I could not see myself as a critical case yet, but I continued to get weaker by the day. Finally, I decided that the sensible thing was to take a leave of absence and to go to my parents' home to recover. From this decision to my arrival in Berlin, there passed almost a week of dismal adventures—first, struggles with the bureaucrats to get a permit to leave Russia, and a Polish transit visa; then trying to use railroads that had become badly disorganized, so that the trains were many hours late. But eventually I arrived in Berlin. At home, the doctor kept me in bed for two months.

By the time I had recovered, it was 1931, and I clearly had to make a final decision for or against remaining in Russia for the rest of my life. Staying there would certainly imply not seeing my family again, or almost never. I also thought about the life of a theoretical physicist apart from teaching, and I suddenly remembered that in Kharkov by accident I had failed to meet a Russian physicist whom I had previously known: J. Frenkel, the chief theoretician of the Röntgen Institute. In 1925–1926, he had spent several months in Göttingen. He spoke and wrote German rather fluently; but I had assisted him by correcting a manuscript so that his German became even more understandable. As we became acquainted, he told me something of his earlier days. He was a young adult during the revolution, after which everything had to be reconstructed. There was one young man, a mediocre scientist, but a party affiliate, who conceived the idea that Einstein's theory of relativity was part of the "bourgeois" ideology; by lecturing and writing on this, the man had drawn a good deal of attention. Some senior people such as Joffe were seriously concerned with the effect that this might have on professional activity in physical science and the possibility that it might keep out young, talented people (as happened later with Lysenko in biology). Frenkel decided to go on the lecture circuit to put things aright; he prepared a lecture in which it was demonstrated that the theory of relativity was a clear logical consequence of the doctrines enunciated by Marx, Engels, and Lenin. He presented an impassioned talk before any suitable technical audience that he could gather in the U.S.S.R. and eventually won his case. His opponent was ignored and forgotten after a time.

While I was thus musing over my future, I began to doubt whether I could really adapt to this strange world. I felt myself to be a Westerner with an individuality to lose, and I might have to sacrifice more of my Western notions than I was prepared to do. Slowly, I came to the decision that Russia was not to be the scene of my future activities. Since it was only some three months to the end of my contract, I decided there was no point in going back at all, and I wrote to Kharkov in this sense. They promptly sent back all the luggage I had left there, with not one item missing, which I took as a sign that we had parted in good faith.

The half-year I spent in Russia amounted to the most profound external experience of my entire life. Simply by displacing myself some 1600 kilometers (say as from Boston to Kansas City), I had not just entered another country, but another universe. None or almost none of the concepts I had grown up with were applicable there. Earlier in these pages I have pointed out the tremendous uniformity that governs the behavior of matter and that enables us to predict safely the behavior of atoms and molecules in distant galaxies. Nothing of the sort, clearly, was true of human behavior, especially of the conditions of social existence. Many years later I read a statement by Aldous Huxley that restates the same observation in different terms: Mankind, he says, is so heterogeneous that any ideas of its unification are just illusions. But this, one should add, is not the same as denying that peace can be achieved. In order to have peace one does not need either the organizational or intellectual unification of all men. One does need a small amount of the moral courage that a missionary has who goes unarmed among savages. I believe that it is possible to communicate that kind of mentality to a sufficiently large number of people, so that it can be put to use. If we have to wait until our politicians have really understood the mind or soul of the Russians, it will be too late to avoid a nuclear holocaust. The Russians have certainly during recent decades shown an amazing proficiency in the development of great technology; the net product is extraordinary. But to conclude from this that we now can begin to "understand" the Russians is just as certainly illogical.

After I had recovered from my illness, I remained in Berlin for several more months. In the summer of 1931, I received a letter from Erwin Madelung, professor of theoretical physics at the University of Frankfurt, asking me to join him that fall as his assistant. Already before, Schrödinger of whom I will speak later, had spoken to me about this possibility and had written a letter of recommendation. Frankfurt, some eighty kilometers north of Heidelberg, was, of course, the nearest thing to home-ground for me. An aunt, a sister of my father's, who lived there, told me when I arrived that Frankfurt was an ancient mercantile town where Jews had always lived, prospered, and been respected, so I need have no fear of discrimination. Six months later she was proved wrong, the racist disease had spread there.

Professor Madelung was, in a manner of speaking a victim of the German university system. He had written an excellent Ph.D. thesis about the electrical interactions of atoms in crystals, which was quoted many times in the pertinent literature. He also had a father who was a famous medical man and professor at a major university. This combination resulted in his being offered the newly founded chair of theoretical physics at the University of Frankfurt three or four years after his Ph.D. But Madelung did not have much drive, and he did not publish another original piece of research in his life. Instead, he wrote a book entitled *The Mathematical Tools of the Physicist* which was just what its title said—a reference collection of formulas with explanatory text. He felt uneasy about his place in the profession but was very honest about it; he told me this whole story in the first few days of my presence. Otherwise, Madelung was a very sensible man, who also had shown character in dealing with the nationalist extremists when he had to fulfill administrative functions for the university. Very early after my arrival in Frankfurt, however, the political situation had developed so that there was not much hope of a person of Jewish descent remaining in a university position. After a year and a half, in the spring of 1933, I left there and left Germany, under circumstances that I will describe later in more detail.

Among the people whom I met during this period, one stands out, and I will limit myself to describing him. His name was Friedrich Dessauer, the director of an Institute for Medical Physics and one of the great pioneers in the application of X-rays to medical practice. Having started as an engineer, he had gradually moved into physics and had since 1924 been professor of what we would now call biophysics and director of a sizable research laboratory that he had founded. In his early days, he had been instrumental in developing X-ray tubes to the level of reliability where they could be applied in medical work. Nothing was then known about the physiological effects of X-rays, and, not too surprisingly, Dessauer eventually developed radiation sickness. A few years before I arrived in Frankfurt, he had started a regular routine: Each spring he went to Switzerland where a plastic surgeon transplanted some skin from his arms or other parts of his body to his face. But one did not notice too much of the details of his face because his wonderful eyes were so expressive and penetrating that one saw little else. I did not feel close enough to the concrete aspects of biophysics that I would have tried to make more contacts with his collaborators. But I recognized that they were a brilliant lot and I learned that they had done some of the earliest work on the effect of "hard" radiation on living tissue, especially on the selective character of "hits" whereby individual molecules in the chromosomes were broken apart, yielding evidence about their genetic significance.

Dessauer was unusually active and versatile. Being an active Catholic, he had extremely close ties with the large Catholic political party of the German Republic. When Hitler came to power, he had to leave, or at least left, and spent the war years at the Catholic university in Fribourg, Switzerland. I had befriended his son, who was a few years younger than I and a student of physics, and who later emigrated to the United States. Through him I was able to keep informed at least to some extent about the fate of this remarkable group.

5

Sketches from Berlin

Between the time I obtained my Ph.D. and my leaving Germany, about six years passed. I spent almost half of this period in Berlin. At that time Berlin was a cosmopolitan center with a tremendous, almost feverish activity. When I lived there the city was at its apex; far more cosmopolitan then the rest of Germany, it had become the gathering place of numerous groups, especially from Eastern and Southeastern Europe. These regions had long looked to Germany as a leader and to Berlin as a cultural capital. Many of the countries of Eastern Europe had German-speaking minorities who cultivated their relations with the mother-country which their ancestors might have left centuries ago. There were many talented people among these East-European Germans and, since even apart from speaking the language they were almost all Protestants, they were readily accepted in the professions and in the universities of Germany proper. One could not fail to meet such people also among scientists. All these scattered German groups were relocated, dispersed, or otherwise disappeared during or in the aftermath of the Second World War.

During these years in Berlin I developed the habit of exploring the town on foot. It was so large that it took a good many hours to walk from one end to the other. As in all large cities there were districts. In the west and southwest there were well-appointed modern buildings where the bourgeoisie resided; the east was given over to proletarian quarters, Prussian style: The tree-lined streets had been laid out in a grandiose manner, wide, perfectly straight and rectangular with vast blocks between them. There were no gardens. The apartments facing the street were occupied by doctors, dentists, shopkeepers, and other members of the middle class; through the main door one had access to the back courts, commonly three in succession, each a rectangular box with a paved floor and four sides filled with windows, four or five stories high. There was never a tree in these courts and they were so narrow as to admit little of the sun's rays except to the top levels. It was in these stone cages, called *Mietskasernen* (rental barracks), that the industrial workers of Berlin lived. Eastern Berlin was easy to reach by subway, and from occasional visits I received a liberal education in social problems superior to what I could have learned from purely literary social critics like Dickens or Zola. I also began to realize that the people living there or their ancestors might have escaped from a lot that had been no better, as the serfs of a landed gentry, in fact if not in law, living on poor soil. But I also recognized that nothing had been done yet, officially, to lead people out of their desperate situation.

One day, on such an excursion I found an older, somewhat decrepit, and less well organized quarter which, as I readily recognized, had become an eastern Jewish ghetto. There were a few older men wearing beards and kaftans, but most people were young and did not wear traditional garb. One day I came into this region in the early evening and found the streets thronged with literally thousands of young people, men and women, who all were poorly but diligently dressed and seemed engaged in a sort of evening promenade, the only sort of exercise available in those cramped quarters. There was still a slight air of the ghetto's melancholy about them, but on the whole they looked healthy and self-confident, quite different from the downtrodden native proletarians of adjacent quarters. I never found out where this large group came from, but I presume that for them Berlin was only a way station from the open spaces of eastern Poland or Russia to the New World. My main impression was that they were not only a lively and vigorous group, but also rather homogeneous, resembling what I had seen in Russia although more refined. On the few occasions I visited there, it seemed like a vision of history in process. I can only hope, however, that most of this crowd escaped before Hitler began to carry out his extermination policies.

There was quite a difference between the spectacle in eastern Berlin and the people whom I met on the western side, in the middle-class quarters where everything seemed individualized and competitive. Most memorable was a group of talented Hungarians, all of them entirely or partially of Jewish descent, but all far from any Jewish tradition. Many appear in the history of physics: von Neumann, Wigner, Szilard, Orowan, and Polanyi, the first four almost contemporaries, the last a few years older. I met most of them at the Kaiser-Wilhelm Research Institute at Dahlem, a charming suburb in the southwest of Berlin, at the end of a long subway line. Such research laboratories as then existed in Germany, were not so loaded with tradition and less under the public's eye than universities, and hence they could more readily attract capable people from other countries. Polanyi had established himself at the research institute in Dahlem which was devoted to physical chemistry, and he served as a center of a group that met in a weekly seminar. I found the discusssions so lively and stimulating that I often went there although the trip was lengthy. Of the group mentioned I will now only speak of Eugene Wigner and of Egon Orowan, with both of whose work I later became well acquainted.

Eugene Wigner was born and grew up in Budapest where he must have become acquainted with John von Neumann while still in high school. He then became a student of chemical engineering at the Polytechnic School in Berlin-Charlottenburg. This was certainly a wise choice of subject for a prospective theoretical physicist since among all the branches of engineering certainly chemical engineering is the one in which complicated theoretical aspects are most prominent. Wigner soon switched to theoretical physics; after a Ph.D. and a stay in Göttingen, where I first met him, he became a member of the faculty at the Polytechnic School, teaching theoretical physics. In 1930 he was invited as a guest lecturer to Princeton University, undoubtedly with some support from John von Neumann, but I am unacquainted with the details. The association with Princeton soon became permanent and he remained there until his retirement a few years before these memoirs were written.

Among his colleagues Wigner was famous for his extreme politeness even under conditions that would have provoked an unpleasant reaction from others. There is one famous story about a man coming to Wigner's office on a rather irrelevant matter and refusing to leave in spite of several rather explicit hints. Wigner's irritation mounted, but he did not yield to it. Finally, it became too much and he blurted out: "Go to hell, please." Just what psychological cauldrons smouldered underneath this more than exemplary courtesy, I cannot say because although quite familiar with much of his work in my younger years, I did not get to know him well socially.

Wigner was one of the great pioneers of quantum mechanics. Although he has no monumental "breakthrough" to his credit as do Heisenberg and de Broglie, the literature of the twenties and thirties is full of brilliant and profoundly original articles by him. He was a hard worker, of phenomenal patience and consistency. There is one encounter I had with him in these days which I remember vividly. I must have been somewhat too easy with my imagination, and Wigner no doubt wanted to convey some quasi-fatherly advice. (I say quasi- because he is only two years older than I). He said: "One should tackle a problem only when its solution seems trivially easy, it will then turn out to be just at the limits of the manageable; when it appears more difficult, trying to solve it is usually a hopeless undertaking." I have always taken this to be as good a description of Eugene Wigner the scientist as I could find; it contains his method in a nutshell. And with this method, joined to remarkable will power and drive, Wigner blazed a trail in modern physics. In quantum mechanics as in any other branch of science, one acquires mastery only by working through a large number of special cases which show the nooks and crannies; one does not attain the same level by absorbing general principles. In quantum mechanics, the mathematical calculations involved in special examples while not hopelessly involved are often quite lengthy so that they must, if possible, be executed and interpreted by a master craftsman. In many instances this task was taken up by Eugene Wigner. In his earlier years he was best known for introducing group theory as the mathematical tool of choice for atomic physics; but since the technique had been elaborated by mathematicians, this was essentially an adaptation which required more labor than originality. Far more original are Wigner's smaller articles about specific problems of atomic physics. During the war Wigner went to Chicago where he worked with the group dealing with isotope separation and later on reactor construction. He spent years of his later life designing nuclear reactors; although I know next to nothing about this subject myself, I remember one expert telling me that Wigner was the most skillful and most ingenious of all the designers of nuclear reactors. A fitting climax indeed for a former student of chemical engineering.

Finally, I shall discuss Wigner's role in the development of solid-state physics. It goes without saying that the physics of solid materials is the basis of a very large part of engineering, in fact, of a nearly overwhelming part. In the 1930s a number of theoretical physicists, Wigner among them, began to apply the theory of quantum mechanics as it had by then developed to the understanding of the structure of crystals and, more generally, of solid substances. Years later, I obtained and studied an early set of Wigner's lecture notes on solid-state physics whose exact date I do not remember, but it must have been around the mid-thirties. The scientific literature then contained a vast number of older articles on crystal physics and related subjects, predating quantum mechanics; the first task was to cull these in a discriminating

Eugene Wigner

manner, so that an intelligible text for the future researcher could be made from them. Wigner's unpublished notes showed that he had been very successful in this. In 1933–1934 Frederick Seitz was a student of Wigner's; they published jointly a couple of papers on the electronic structure of a simple solid, in this case of a monatomic metal. So far as I know, it was the first major effort to treat a simplified but still realistic mathematical model of a solid by the scheme of quantum mechanics. It led to Seitz' Ph.D.; a year later Seitz left Princeton and went on to a distinguished career of his own. He continued gathering material for his book *The Modern Theory of Solids*, which appeared in 1940 and was an immediate success. Together with John C. Slater's book *Introduction to Chemical Physics*, that had appeared a year earlier, it inaugurated a period in which quantum mechanics began to lead to pragmatic results, that is to a quantitative understanding and prediction of matters of engineering significance. Fairly soon thereafter the theoretical physicist became a respectable and even a respected member of the industrial research laboratory. Seitz' book was the beginning of solid state physics; now, a whole shelf of similar books is available. Seitz already touched on many of the properties of solids that were henceforth to be at the center of interest: the chemical structure of crystals, the ability of metals to conduct electricity, the cohesion of solid matter, the conditions under which a hot metal is effective as an emitter of electrons, the magnetic properties of some solids, and the variegated optical properties of others. The physics of semi-conductors was not yet in existence; it was only after the end of the war that various groups, prominent among them one in the Bell Telephone Laboratories, began the exhaustive study of the properties of semi-conductors which culminated in the discovery of transistor action by William Shockley in 1949. Since that time the so-called "solid-state" techniques, in which transistors replace the old-fashioned vacuum tubes, have conquered electronics.

Another man who had come from Hungary to the Polytechnic School in Berlin-Charlottenburg was Egon Orowan. When I knew him in Berlin he was the assistant of Richard Becker, the professor of theoretical physics, a distinguished researcher in his own right. Orowan straddled physics and engineering all his life; he was predisposed to this, as his father was an industrial engineer in Budapest. Apart from a broad knowledge and a considerable ease in engineering matters, Egon had a wide-ranging philosophical mind that appealed to me. We became close friends and saw much of each other during my years in

Berlin. Later, when Hitler came to power, Egon managed to move to England and spent the war at Cambridge. In 1950 he was appointed professor of mechanical engineering at the Massachusetts Institute of Technology where he remained for the rest of his active life. Egon and I had little contact with each other during these years, but when, in 1962, I moved from California to Princeton to teach geophysics, we resumed our friendship.

In 1934 three men independently published articles on the significance of "dislocations" in the mechanical motions of solids: Egon. Orowan, Michael Polanyi, and Geoffrey I. Taylor, the British hydrodynamicist. The last two abandoned the subject of dislocations almost at once, but Orowan continued to do research in the deformation of solids all his life. I find it a little difficult to explain dislocations in other than graphical form, so I have reproduced a diagram (Fig. 1)[1] that conveys at least some idea. As Fig. 1 shows, a dislocation is a disturbance in an otherwise regular crystalline array. The heavy dots are meant to describe atoms, and the straight lines indicate chemical bonds between them. Note that this is an 8 × 9 array; one can readily verify that each horizontal row has 9 atoms and all but two of the vertical rows have 8 atoms, the two short rows adding up to 8 again. The pattern shown may arise as an accident in the natural growth of a crystal. If now one single bond (the one between the two ⊥ symbols) is shifted from one of the atoms to an adjacent one, the crystal assumes the configuration shown by the dashed lines. The net effect of this is to shift the dislocation by one unit, that is one row, to the left (as indicated by the dashed ⊥). It is easily found that this process requires no net energy and can be repeated, and by a series of such steps the dislocation can migrate through the crystal. As the figure shows, a dislocation corresponds to an abrupt ending of one vertical row of atoms in the middle of the crystal. This model is two-dimensional; one obtains a three-dimensional model by taking a large number of copies of the pattern of Fig. 1 and stacking them on top of each other along a line perpendicular to the plane of Fig. 1.

The discovery of dislocations and of their role in the deformation of solids turned out to be of the utmost significance. Before this, it often seemed as if solid materials did not behave according to the inferences drawn from atomic physics and chemistry. The atomic physicist knows the forces that attract atoms to each other, so he can calculate the forces needed to break a piece of solid material apart. The observations never fitted these results; it commonly turned out that the breaking strength of crystalline solids was many times, often hundreds of times, smaller than had been foreseen. This was an utterly obscure fact, until in 1920 an Englishman, A. A. Griffith, showed that small cracks which always exist near the surface of a solid, will widen and grow when one tries to pull a solid apart. The Russian physicist Abraham Joffe was one of the men who studied experimentally this effect of cracks. Orowan made the following simple experiment: Taking a sheet of mica he modified the usual breaking-strength experiment. Instead of clamping a strip at its ends, he took a larger sheet and put the clamps near the middle, far away from any edges. The breaking strength increased tremendously. Modern technology has made such things familiar to everybody—think of how much harder it is to tear a nylon string apart as compared with a hempen one. Clearly, one can make nylon string without any surface

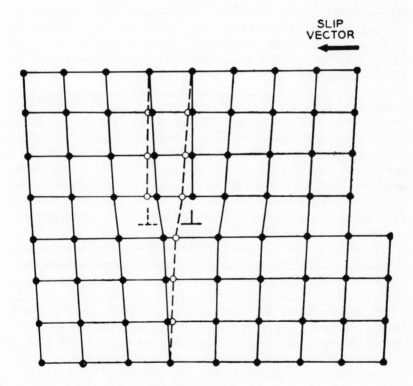

Fig. 1. A dislocation in a simple lattice

cracks. It is reasonably true that dislocations and cracks together account for almost all modes of the mechanical behavior of crystalline solids, which are the overwhelming majority of all solids.

The modern science of materials underlies much of present-day engineering; it relates engineering practice closely to the concepts of atomic physics. In electrical engineering the layman knows that solid-state electronics has replaced the older, more clumsy state of the art in radio and television. A similar situation exists in mechanical engineering. One utilizes there the ability of crystalline solids to deform permanently, mainly through the microscopic action of dislocations; this property of solids is called their plasticity. Since almost all solids of practical importance, especially all metals, are micro-crystalline, the study of dislocations and of their effect upon the properties of materials, especially metals but also, for instance, ceramics, is a challenging and active field pursued in numerous laboratories of applied physics and engineering throughout the world. The forging of metals, the shaping of plastics, the drawing of wires through an orifice, and innumerable other technical processes can be studied in great detail and often improved by present-day scientific methods that were totally unknown even fifty years ago. But one must admit that only a few technically educated people are aware of the scientific background of these everyday technical matters. Everyone knows that when a wire or a strip of metal is repeatedly bent, it becomes hard and brittle, a phenomenon known as strain hardening. On the atomic scale this is based on the creation of numerous, mutually interfering dislocations. Again, the material is made soft by heating, known as annealing. And while many such processes have been known and used by craftsmen for thousands of years all of this knowledge was merely a disorderly heap of crude observations until quite recently.

But let me return to Egon Orowan who made the study of solid materials his life's work. He was one of the few persons whom I have met whose visual and auditory sensitivities were equally highly developed. He is an indefatigable piano player, and I can also recall his forever playing with some beautiful object, a crystal, a fossil, and so on. He had acquired a thorough mastery of mathematical theory which he combined with a skill for doing simple experiments that made a visit to his laboratory interesting and challenging, even to one like myself who does not claim any advanced knowledge of experimental technique. One of the applications of the physics of plasticity to which Egon had long paid much attention is the deformation of rocks. There is a

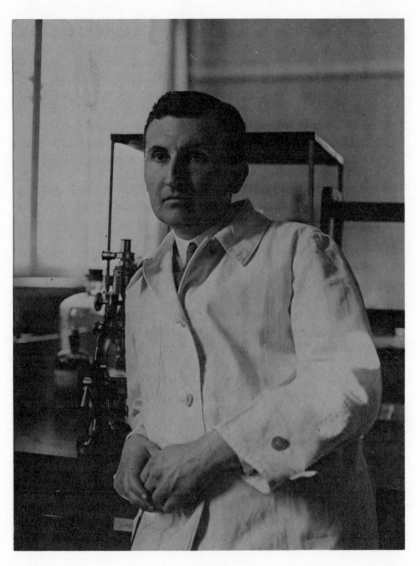

Egon Orowan

branch of geology that deals with such deformation, often simply referred to as mountain-building. It is known technically under the name of tectonics. The processes involved in geology, resulting in deformation at speeds of a few centimeters per year, are many billions of times slower than those used to deform metals in a workshop. But no doubt has ever been voiced that the basic underlying processes are the same.

Since most geology is field-work, successful geologists have as a rule little time to acquire knowledge in the quantitative sciences. To put this fact in another context: What in physics has been a revolution taking place in a dozen years, say, becomes a very slow evolutionary process requiring a few generations as it spills over into other fields. I mention geology here because in this field I have acquired sufficient personal experience to allow me to judge on a practical and personal basis. I feel quite confident that similar conditions prevail in many other fields of science into which the ideas and methods of modern physics penetrate but slowly, as time goes on. Among these fields is, I believe, most of technology and also much of the bio-medical sciences.

Let me say a few more words on the impact of modern scientific thought upon technology. So far as my experience goes, this historical process has simply failed to impress the general public, that is to say that part of the public which has not much of an engineering background. How many people would understand at once if they were told that the hot forging of iron and the flowing of a glacier are basically similar phenomena but on two different time scales? Both represent an expression of the physical processes of plasticity. This penetration of scientific thought and scientific methods into technology is frequently ignored. To take just one small example, such products of modern industry as, say, stainless steel or the heat-resistant linings of jet engines are the outcome of highly advanced studies in materials science. To think that the difference between the ancient artisans and modern industry can be exhausted in terms of social relationships, a view one sometimes hears, is an exercise in self-deception. No doubt, views will change, but in the meantime great damage is done by ignorance. Since the foundation of modern technology is in basic science, the evolutionary change from a society whose existence rests on the activity of artisans and peasants to one that rests on the modern type of industrial activity is irreversible. This is troublesome on the social level primarily because the contempt for techniques, and technology, including its more intellectual, scientific aspects seems an almost universal tradition of mankind that has powerfully survived. From the historical viewpoint, it seems clear that this one-sidedness has arisen because all past societies were "elitist"; even the few republics in history reserved full freedom only to a very limited minority.

Everybody knows and many people tell us that we are living through a period of unprecedented social crisis and revolution. Perhaps the most reactionary and obscurantist notion that puts our society on the rack, so to speak, is one held by so many supposedly educated people that the nitty-gritty of technology is beneath them, and that the clever manipulation of verbiage is enough. This state of affairs is perhaps what Robert Oppenheimer had in mind when in his public addresses he so often insisted that the study of science leads to humility. I do not propose that one give scientists and engineers a bigger role in the councils of government, that would just be a way of jumping from the frying pan into the fire; I do propose that the more talented of the younger generation should concern themselves with the concrete aspects of scientific technology and present the matter to the public in a form sufficiently interesting to be assimilated into the general patrimony of human thought. This has been done in the Communist countries, but it seems clear enough that the coupling of this mode of thought with Marxism is incidental and can one day be broken.

To return now to Berlin: One of the great men of physics whom I came to know rather well in the period after my return from Russia, was Erwin Schrödinger. I believe him to have had a profound influence on me, touching on many of the notes that reverberated later in my life and thought, hence I shall speak of him at some length. He was born in 1887 in Vienna, the only son of a fairly prosperous merchant. His extraordinary talents seemed to have been recognized early at the University of Vienna; this was no doubt helped by his having all the right credentials: He was a distinguished-looking man, of Austrian descent, with a Catholic background, and his maternal grandfather was a professor of engineering. His mastery of English, so useful to him in later life, can be traced to this man's wife, Schrödinger's grandmother, who came from England. He obtained his Ph.D., made an easy entrance into Viennese academic circles, and stayed on as assistant in physics; after the First World War, where he served uneventfully as an artillery officer, he taught in succession at three German universities, before going to Zürich as professor of theoretical physics. He stayed there for six years during which, in a sudden burst of creativity, he contributed a major share to the foundations of the new science of

Erwin Schrödinger

quantum mechanics. In 1927 he was called to Berlin as the successor to Max Planck, the man who in 1900 had first introduced the idea of quanta into physics. He stayed in Berlin for another six years. I am not convinced that he ever felt at home there. When Hitler came to power, he chose to leave quietly, this being his style; he became a fellow at a college of Oxford University, until in 1936 he was again offered a professorship, this time in Graz, Austria. But when two years later Hitler occupied Austria, Schrödinger and his wife, although not explicitly threatened, decided to flee with only a few pieces of baggage. Taking refuge in Rome he found help through his membership in the Papal Academy. At that time Eamon de Valera, the hero of Irish independence and originally a mathematician, wanted to establish an Institute for Advanced Study in Dublin. De Valera consulted with Schrödinger, and when in 1940 this Institute was founded, Schrödinger together with Walter Heitler moved there to form its section of theoretical physics. After fifteen years in Dublin, Schrödinger retired and returned to his native Austria where he died in 1961.[2]

I have no precise recollection of my first encounter with Schrödinger. All I remember is that it must have been at an occasion such as a seminar, and that at the end I asked him whether he would some time have a few minutes, so that I could ask him questions. He replied: "Please come to see me at home, not at my office in the university; I dislike this office very much. Please give me a ring on the telephone." The university was located in a big stone palace in the old center of town at the eastern end of the boulevard *Unter den Linden*; Schrödinger lived in an apartment house in a southwestern suburb easily reached by subway. From there he could commute to his office when his presence was required. At my first visit to his home, there sprang up an easy mutual understanding, and he asked me to come back. In this way I visited him a number of times, and our conversations would often extend well into the night. I felt like a Boswell to this remarkable genius. We did not, however, work jointly on a scientific program but simply conversed. When the evening wore on, he would say: "Why don't you stay here for a little longer, let's look what there is in the refrigerator." It was invariably well stocked, and we made some sandwiches and kept on talking. At that time Schrödinger's marriage must have been passing through a crisis; Mrs. Schrödinger was usually absent, and when she came in, she stayed only for a moment before retiring to her own section of the apartment. They did not have any children. The dedication of a book by Schrödinger to his wife many years later indicates that the rift was eventually healed.

When I try to analyze what drew me to Schrödinger and seemed to make me agreeable company to him, two explanations occur. First, he was quite preponderantly a visual type as I also am; this in a field, mathematics or theoretical physics, where the majority of practitioners are passionate musicians. Secondly, Schrödinger's conception of science appealed to me very much: He thought of science almost exclusively as what British writers have called "natural philosophy." To quote an analogue, Clausewitz, the military writer, defines in the beginning of his book, *On War*, what war is. He says that war is "the continuation of politics by other means." Similarly, one could well say that for Schrödinger, science was the continuation of philosophy by other means. I never discovered any trace, in Schrödinger, of a low opinion of pragmatic or applied science. His was very much an aristocratic personality, and he simply felt that he possessed the talent and never had lacked the opportunity of being a "pure" scientist, so he simply left the practical and engineering aspects of science to others. The last thing that would have occurred to him would have been to "look down" on people who concern themselves with the practicalities and technical applications of scientific research. Some of this attitude must be strange to Americans because the American tradition has been totally different in this respect from that of Europe. The early inhabitants of this country, even at the foundation of the republic, were confronted with an unconquered continent; even when there was no longer danger from Indians, nature had to be subdued. Their mind was concentrated on immediate, practical things, so that science in the New World came to be an adjunct of the skills of the "artificer." This attitude is still widespread in the United States. I have never been quite sure (not having grown up in America) whether this attitude, in college students for instance, had been drilled into them in high school, or whether they absorb it unconsciously from their ambiance, or both. Since those who have not had a scientific education are quite naturally inclined to confound science with one of its end products, most commonly modern scientifically-based technology, semantic confusion is widespread, and it would be foolish to sermonize about this. I need hardly say that in these pages I call science what others may call "pure" science, and most of what in the newspapers is called "science," I would describe as technology.

To understand Schrödinger one has to appreciate that he was very much an Austrian, that is to say, steeped in the European tradition. He returned to Austria on two occasions from English-speaking countries, first from Oxford to Graz in 1936, having refused at that time a chair in Edinburgh, and then from Dublin to Vienna in 1955. What I remember most about him is his great serenity and his playfulness. He has even said in his later, philosophical writings that science develops from the play of a civilized society. His own life testifies that in this he had deep-seated feelings. Schrödinger's serenity was not the exuberant vitality of a healthy, uncomplicated person; one could perceive without too much difficulty that it had been gained and established across a high degree of sensitivity and hidden suffering. The ancient Austrian society to which Schrödinger belonged was the complex end product of endless compromises: The old Austrian monarchy consisted essentially of what is now Austria together with what is now Czechoslovakia, and the northern tip of Yugoslavia. There were about two Slavs for every German. To this were added the Hungarians whose country was connected with Austria by a common monarch. But for centuries the Habsburgs had been ruling this mixture of people in relative peace, with eminent success. This has given the native Austrians a certain skill in the art of living and letting live, and a facility for compromise that was very well represented by Schrödinger. I had difficulty seeing him assimilate among rigid and dogmatic Prussians.

Even before I had met Schrödinger in person, I had by an accident become acquainted with a sideline of his: a series of articles he had published in the early 1920s about the mathematical theory of physiological colors. He has said himself that this was a brief vacation he took from the severe demands of atomic physics. Physiological colors, that is those a human being sees, can be described in advance of any analysis as combinations of three base colors, blue, yellow, and red, mixed in various proportions. Besides these primary colors, any color has what is called a "hue" which can be expressed by mixing pure colors with various amounts of black. This manifold of colors depends on three variables, the proportions of the primary colors and the hue, and can be represented in a spatial diagram. But the space is curved; the details of the space structure are found by letting human experimental subjects find the point at which two neighboring colors can no longer be distinguished. By doing this for all colors, one finds a "metric" in color space. This was not a new result, and Schrödinger made no claims for originality although his terminology and his point of view might have been novel. Schrödinger showed that this way of dealing with the variety of colors could be put into close parallel with the way Einstein had used curved spaces in the theory of relativity. I still remember the extreme esthetic delight I experienced when I read these papers for the first time as a very young man.

Starting at an early age, Schrödinger produced scientific articles of significance, but in later life devoted more of his energy to writing books. There was a tremendous spurt of creativity which carried him to unexpected heights in 1925 and 1926, when he became acquainted with the ideas of Louis de Broglie on the wave nature of matter. De Broglie had proposed that every material particle was associated with a wave, leaving unspecified what "associated" means, except for giving an equation that connects the wavelength with the velocity of a moving particle. This was, in a manner of speaking, an extension of Einstein's paper of 1905 in which the latter had shown that every wave of light could also, with respect to some other properties, be considered a quantum, that is a particle. De Broglie's theory was only semi-quantitative, and Schrödinger saw his chance: He succeeded in setting up a differential equation whose solutions are the matter-waves; this is now universally known as the Schrödinger equation. These waves, electron waves for instance, are bent by forces that are ordinarily said to be acting on the electron. He showed that the energy levels of atoms can be described as "standing" electron waves. This whole abstract machinery, mathematically formulated, is extremely similar to the way physicists had long since treated sound waves. Schrödinger eventually could explain in quantitative detail the spectrum of the hydrogen atom by means of the model of standing waves. This, of course, was a tremendous success and assured his theory immediate attention.

I vividly remember the quandary that arose among physicists in 1926 when both Heisenberg and Schrödinger had developed mathematical schemes of atomic physics which led the same numbers to be compared with the observations while their mutual theoretical connection was totally obscure. The puzzle was solved, still in 1926, by two men working independently of each other, Schrödinger and the American theoretical physicist, Carl Eckart. They both obtained the same results and, as Eckart expressed it at the end of his paper, they showed that one kind of quantum mechanics can be mathematically transformed into the other. Schrödinger's article appeared two months before Eckart's which was in the printing stage. Eckart introduced for the first time a mathematical technique called "operator calculus," which is now universally used in quantum mechanics. For a young man then only twenty-four years old, this achievement was altogether extraordinary. But since Schrödinger was very famous and Eckart young and unknown, and since the former also had a nominal priority in time, everybody quoted Schrödinger, and Eckart was forgotten. Around 1939 Eckart moved to the Scripps Institution of Oceanography in La Jolla, California, where he directed underwater war research work, and remained there until his death in 1973. I came to know him very well in later years and know how deeply this early neglect hurt him. He was a rather reserved man and would not have desired to make an issue out of this. But he did abandon atomic physics and went into hydrodynamics where he produced major mathematical masterpieces in the physics of the ocean and atmosphere.

Schrödinger maintained his scientific productivity for many years after becoming a celebrity. But he gradually supplemented his research by a series of small books, thirteen in all. Several of these deal with fields of theoretical physics: relativity theory, statistical thermodynamics; they are pearls of the art of exposition. Others are frankly philosophical. Their pervasive theme is best described by the title of one of them: *Science and Humanism*. Schrödinger clearly was a traditionalist who drew his spiritual nourishment from the society in which he had grown up. The straight line of development which Europeans had constructed as their cultural pedigree goes from the ancient Greeks through the medieval Church to modern times. This sequence had been drilled into me with considerable force when I was still in the Gymnasium. But Schrödinger came from a more balanced social background where these things were not just formal traditions but were still alive. In his little books he asks the significant questions of the philosopher: Who am I? Why am I here? Where am I going? His answers came out of traditional philosophy, from the Upanishads to Spinoza. Although a great man, he was very much a child of his time. He was twenty-one when the Habsburg monarchy fell; so he still knew the *ancien regime*. I cannot help remembering here the famous words of Talleyrand: "He who has not known the *ancien regime* does not know the sweetness of living." I sometimes had a glimpse of the more tragic aspects of Schrödinger's life carefully hidden below a sweet and gentle serenity. Not only was he childless, which must have been hard on a man who loved life so much, he also saw the total collapse, through two gigantic wars, both ending in defeat, of his homeland, the ancient Austria that had been an essential part of Europe for so many centuries. There had been no such cataclysmic upheaval in Europe since the days of the Migrations some 1500 years ago. In the intervening centuries the Austrians had guarded the southeastern borders of Europe against the Turks and had built up a resplendent center of European culture, perhaps not quite equal to Florence or Paris, but not too far behind. Vienna became the music capital of the world, not to speak of countless other cultural achievements. By 1940, say, it was clear to everyone that this was the end—history would go on, but Old Austria had disappeared.

Schrödinger's strong sense of humor kept him on an even keel, which was very helpful after he became a celebrity and had to undergo the buffetting that this often involves. I remember one scene: I had come to visit Schrödinger and found that a noted philosopher on a visit to Berlin was about to arrive to talk to him. This man was supposed to see him in the afternoon but had been detained, and they had agreed by telephone on a meeting at Schrödinger's home in the early evening. Schrödinger insisted that I must not leave but wait at some distance until this conference was over. When the noted philosopher appeared, I was introduced and then retired to a corner of the room with a book. I could see the two arguing, the philosopher being very intense, all business. Now and then he would pull out a book from a big briefcase, open it and point to a passage. In the short moments when the philosopher looked down, Schrödinger would look in my direction and wink, with a gently humorous expression in his face. It was as if he were saying: See here what a celebrity has to bear, but I am not about to let it get me down. Eventually, the philosopher left, and we continued our conversation.

Schrödinger's commitment to historical continuity in his philosophical thought must have been very strong. This is the only way I can explain why, as he grew older, he began to doubt the statistical interpretation of quantum theory again and seemed to suggest that a statistical theory is only preliminary and must, at the fundamental level, ultimately be replaced by a strictly causal theory. This was also the view of Einstein and de Broglie. I have the greatest difficulty in commenting on this since I do not understand how one acquires those particular predilections. For me, scientific theory consists in finding all the order that can be detected by observations of nature, and in representing it by suitable means, mathematical, logical, or other.[3] I cannot understand any preference for the traditional physical causality which is so clearly patterned after the behavior of machines. This, I believe, is not an innate direction of man's mind; one can make a good point that it dates from the seventeenth century, the age of Galileo and

Descartes, and if it was born in history it can disappear in history. But in philosophically inclined scientists, this often appears as a "gut-feeling," not entirely scientific and hence not fully capable of rational analysis.

This brings me to one book of Schrödinger's that has become more widely known than the others: *What is Life?* which appeared in 1944. I read it, of course, and read it many times. It is clearly an effort at reconciling Schrödinger's humanistic philosophy with the results of biochemistry, now often called "molecular biology." But for all I can see, the reconciliation fails. I think Schrödinger must have been aware of this, at least unconsciously. How else could one explain the strange pompous title of a minuscule book of 96 pages written by a physicist who flatly lets you know that his knowledge of biology is second-hand. Here was Schrödinger's highly developed sense of humor in action. There is, in this book, merely a juxtaposition of a short account of his philosophy with the then current results of biochemistry which concern the storage of information in the DNA molecule, by way of the well known "genetic code." This is done with Schrödinger's usual superior skill, but it does not congeal into a whole. The "philosophy," if I may use this term, on which the overwhelming majority of biochemists operate is strictly rationalistic. It ultimately goes back to Descartes in the seventeenth century, and his "two substances" which form the world, matter on the one side and mind-soul on the other. The body belongs to matter and is therefore basically a machine obeying causal laws. This is a "paradigm" in the sense of Thomas Kuhn, and before this paradigm has been replaced by a better one, any advance in life science will be problematical. I believe that the division between body and soul that has come down to us through history has been so weakened by the advances of science that it is about to crumble. The experience of modern life science clearly suggests that man and beast are very similar and are not to be distinguished by assuming that man has a rational soul which the brutes lack. Instead, there seems to exist a much more powerful dividing line between the inanimate and the living. As Schrödinger makes very clear, the contrivances of the vitalists will not do this; there is no reason to think that this difficult philosophical problem can be advanced by assuming against our better knowledge that the laws of quantum mechanics are unsatisfactory and have to be altered or supplemented in the organism. These are just flimsy substitutes for a real criticism of the nature of the still accepted paradigm. It was my meeting with Schrödinger that first brought out my hitherto somewhat latent passion for "natural philosophy" which has inspired much of my later life.

On closing this gallery of remarkable scientists, I wish to add some remarks about a man with whom I did not work myself and whom I never came to know on a very personal basis, but with whom I could not help getting acquainted in these and later years on numerous occasions, scientific meetings, and the like: Hans Bethe. Born in 1906, he was already a distinguished man, even externally, in his younger years. With his high, domed forehead, his deep, sonorous voice, and a somewhat reserved demeanor, he would draw the attention of any company. His father was a professor, a physiologist very distinguished in research, who must have provided his son with many opportunities to develop scientific pursuits. While Hans was young, his father was teaching at the University of Frankfurt; the son studied physics there, went to Sommerfeld to get his Ph.D., and then was an assistant at Frankfurt and other universities. Leaving Germany in 1933, he spent two years in England, before going to Cornell University for the rest of his active life.

When I came to Frankfurt to take the position that Bethe had held some years earlier, I heard stories about him before I ever knew him, from those who had been in contact with him. What struck people most was the incredibly regular and unemotional way Bethe used to work. One witness described it like this: Hans Bethe would arrive in his office at nine o'clock in the morning, would open his notebook and start writing. He would go on steadily with this until it was noon. At noon he would close his book after having written equation 37, say, and go to lunch. At one o'clock he would return to his office, open his book and start working on equation 38; and so on. With such a system it is understandable that Bethe was fabulously prolific during much of his life. He first concentrated on calculations that applied to atomic shells and crystals and never abandoned this interest completely, but his greatest work was done in the mathematical analysis of nuclear structure and nuclear transformations. This had for long been a very limited field of research since it had begun with the discovery of radioactivity. Rutherford's model of the atom (1911) with the heavy nucleus in the center and the electrons surrounding it, either predated or at least paralleled the meteoric development of the physics of atoms. The latter started with Bohr's atomic model (1913) and culminated in the discovery of quantum mechanics in 1926 and the fundamental discoveries that followed in its wake such as the theory of chemical

Hans Bethe

bonding and the theoretical elucidation of the constitution of solid bodies, especially crystals. Nuclear physics came into its own when Chadwick, working in Rutherford's laboratory at Cambridge, discovered the neutron in 1932. The neutron is a particle without electric charge. Although Rutherford had hypothesized years earlier that neutrons must exist and must be building blocks of the nucleus, Chadwick put this idea on the solid foundation of experiment, which enabled modern nuclear science to develop. This led only six years later to the discovery by Hahn and Meitner that when a neutron falls upon a very heavy nucleus, especially certain varieties (isotopes) of the uranium nucleus, such nuclei tend to break apart (fission) with a great release of energy, used in nuclear bombs for warlike purposes and in nuclear reactors for peaceful purposes.

Bethe turned to the innumerable mathematical problems required in this new field. There are hundreds of different nuclei. The number of electric charges of a nucleus is equal to its number of protons; the number of neutrons is equal to the number of protons for light nuclei and is somewhat larger than the number of protons for heavier nuclei. Nuclei of the same proton number but different neutron numbers represent the same chemical elements and are called isotopes of that element. In nuclear transformation, or reactions, a nucleus is bombarded with either protons or neutrons, and during the transformation it emits other protons or neutrons. There are numerous regularities in nuclear structures and in nuclear reactions, and the number of special problems of interest, often both from the viewpoint of fundamental understanding as well as from that of engineering application, is very large indeed.

Bethe's most significant work concerned the understanding of the energy production in stars due to nuclear reactions. This must seem highly speculative to the nonphysicist and to the layman in astronomy, but it is actually far more sound than a layman can appreciate. The famous Giordano Bruno, a visionary burned in the year 1600 at the stake (for his religion, not his science) was perhaps the first man to conceive of the heavens as an endless expanse of space filled with innumerable stars similar to the sun. But it was not until late in the nineteenth and early in the twentieth centuries that astronomers who based themselves on a vast edifice of interlocking observations and calculations confirmed these visions. Again, it was not until around 1920 that Edwin Hubble, using the relatively large telescope of the Mount Wilson Observatory then available, surveyed innumerable galaxies and found that the more distant they are the faster they fly away from us. This soon led to the concept of the "big bang," of a universe created at a given moment in time, expanding and "running down." The time-scale of this universe is of the order of magnitude of some billions of years. When toward the end of the last century physicists first succeeded in making radiation a quantitative subject, a tremendous gap had become visible: Stars radiate and their radiation cools their insides. The calculations were quite simple and showed that the sun must become cold and cease to radiate in a very few millions of years at the most. Two men almost single-handedly closed this gap: the great British astronomer Arthur Eddington and Hans Bethe. Eddington proposed in the 1920s an extraordinarily simple theoretical model of the constitution of stars based on the assumption that the laws of physics in stars are exactly the same as those observed in the laboratory. The model is so simple because stars are composed of hot gases, predominantly hydrogen gas, and of radiation which at these high temperatures is so powerful as to have many mechanical effects which in the laboratory can be found only with the finest of instruments. On this model the temperature near the center of a star turns out to be tens of millions of degrees. At these high temperatures the atoms move very fast, and nuclei hitting each other can produce nuclear transformations. The question was then whether the energy released in such transformations can provide enough heat to keep the stars alive and shining for billions of years. Bethe went one by one through all the nuclear reactions that could possibly arise through the high temperatures in the center of stars. By a systematic exploration he succeeded in eliminating all but two of these; the most significant by far is the so-called carbon cycle in which a carbon nucleus absorbs four protons successively over a very lengthy period of time. Two of the protons in the nucleus are converted into neutrons by so-called beta emissions, and the end product emits an alpha particle consisting of two protons and two neutrons, the nucleus returning thereby to its initial state, so that it can repeat the same cycle again. Bethe's theory explains in quantitative detail why and how stars live. Although the details have lately been somewhat improved upon, the basic ideas have had a most profound effect on astrophysics.

Bethe's mastery of nuclear physics led to his appointment as head of the Theoretical Division of the Los Alamos Laboratory soon after the inception of Los Alamos. He stayed there for three years, then returned to Cornell University, and has since become one of the most respected elder statesmen in the dark and labyrinthine field of nuclear public policy.

6

The Conversion of a Rationalist

While I lived through the experiences described in the previous chapters, a series of events occurred whose import was far from apparent at their start but which decisively influenced my later activities. The entire process extended over a period of years, from 1926, when I first had decided to become a theoretical physicist, until I finally settled in the United States; and it had its effects years later. In view of these later turns, I am interrupting the story of my professional career to describe these events.

The story begins innocently enough. One day in the late summer or early fall of 1926, while I was still a student in Göttingen, I happened to meet a girl whom I will call Dora. She was perhaps a few years older than I, fairly good-looking and intelligent, and seemingly rather spirited. In a small university town overrun with male students, such a girl was at a premium. Moreover, there seemed to be a mutual attraction between us. Dora said that she was from the Rhineland and lived as a free-lance typist, but her general style of life belied the idea that typing was her main source of income. I had a couple of pleasant evenings with Dora, but there seemed to be some strange reticence in her behavior that I could not pin down. I suspected, of course, that there was a man in her background, but this idea turned out to be false. At our third meeting she asked me an unexpected question: Had I ever heard of Lou Andreas-Salomé, then living in Göttingen? Yes, of course, I had, as many people had heard of the age's best known hunter, or collector of celebrities. But I had never met this lady since our social circles did not intersect. Then Dora informed me that Lou was a practicing psychoanalyst and that she, Dora, was one of her patients. Although I did not much enjoy discussing this particular subject with a girl, Dora talked at great length about psychoanalysis, making it appear not as the therapeutic technique I had assumed it was, but as a sort of secret society into which one had to be initiated. Eventually, she came around to what seemed to be her main point, to convince me that I myself needed to be psychoanalyzed. She ended by telling me that she would arrange for me to visit Lou, so that I could learn what it was all about.

Lou Salomé had been born in 1861 in St. Petersburg, now Leningrad, the daughter of a czarist general. She early showed literary talent and later published some books. But her main achievement was her ability to befriend famous men and then hold on to them. There were three great names; Friedrich Nietzsche, scholar and philosopher; Rainer Maria Rilke, the great lyrical poet; and Sigmund Freud, the father of psychoanalysis. She went about the business of gaining the friendship of these men with the greatest diligence and circumspection; thus, I once read that when she first approached Freud in 1912, she read every word that he had written. She acquired some skill in psychoanalysis, and after marrying Mr. Andreas, who was a professor of history at the University of Göttingen, settled down there.

My visit a few days later was set for the late afternoon. Lou's house was one of several villas standing in gardens that had been cut into the wooded flank of a mountain to the east of the town. One entered her garden through a gate of hewn stone, on top of which I could discern the word *Loufried*. Overcoming my discomfort at this Wagnerian display (*Friede* means peace), I walked in and was ushered into a very large room that seemed to serve as combined living room and study. Lou greeted me; she was very tall, imposing, and slender, her fine somewhat aged features showing traces of former beauty. Almost an entire wall of the room was taken up by a huge picture window. Through it one saw a gorgeous spectacle: The entire sweep of the broad valley in which Göttingen lies was bathed in the rays of a late-afternoon sun, mellow and colorful. The time had been perfectly chosen—it was evidently the best view of the day. We sat down and Lou, who was an animated conversationalist, told me about her experiences with her celebrity friends. I was so captivated that I asked for more, and there were four more such one-hour sessions, always at exactly the same hour. She told me about her friendship with Nietzsche, which was quite an achievement since he was well known as an extreme woman-hater, and there is no record of any other female ever having penetrated his armor. Gradually, in speaking to me she worked her way around to her other great friend, the poet Rilke. I knew that he was quite another type, very fond of women. He was idolized, surrounded, and pursued by them except when he forcibly isolated himself to write poetry. She described how she introduced Rilke to

Russia, and how the two of them travelled down the Volga on a large pleasure-steamer. It was during the Victorian age and it was considered a major scandal when two unmarried people travelled together, and even more so when they shared adjacent staterooms, as she explained. But Lou had certainly succeeded in becoming one of his intimates of many years' standing. Rilke had died just a few months earlier after a long, terrible agony, but had apparently kept up his correspondence with Lou to the very end. She spoke about his sufferings. All this was heady stuff for a young man of twenty-two; but I realized that the purpose of my visits to Lou was to be introduced to psychoanalysis. I tried to bring her round to this subject but had little success. She only spoke vaguely about psychoanalysis and never about Freud. Finally, at the fifth meeting I told Lou that I would go back to Berlin to ask my parents to finance an analysis. It was late August or September; I was working on my thesis under Max Born, but the university was not in session, and Berlin was only a few hours away by train. Meanwhile, Dora had made it clear that she preferred to bestow her favors only on fellow-conspirators in the game of psychoanalysis. When I returned to Göttingen some two weeks later and told Dora that my father had refused the money, she said that our relations would have to terminate totally and at once; in fact, I never saw either Dora or Lou again. There was an aftermath: Some time later my father received a rather substantial bill from Lou for five hours of "therapy." I told him he was silly to pay for this, but he did nonetheless. Years later I read in a book on the history of psychoanalysis that Lou's husband was dying or had died about that time and that she desperately needed money.

When I told my parents about my encounter with Lou and about my somewhat vague desire to be psychoanalyzed, my father, to my surprise, seemed not at all dumbfounded by such an idea. He told me that he had recently become acquainted with a psychiatrist of some distinction; I should make an appointment with this man and see what he had to say. The psychiatrist's name was J. H. (Johann Heinrich) Schultz. He was then about forty years of age; he had a private practice that he ran in his house located on a secluded street near the large park called the *Tiergarten*. I found him very urbane and also endowed with an extraordinarily high and well-trained intellect. Between us there was nothing of the usual doctor-patient relationship; instead, I was given the feeling of a junior colleague consulting with a wiser and older man. He told me about a book of his on psychosomatic medicine which, he claimed, was the first ever written on the subject. He also occasionally told me about a major problem of his: There were always the numerous and largely unoccupied middle-aged wives of wealthy men who insisted on psychiatric treatment. This was more of a problem then than it is now because the social status of such a lady required that she not work. Schultz dealt with these ladies in short sessions that always involved hypnosis but owing to their shortness did not preempt all his time. Schultz managed to survive Hitler and died at a ripe old age. He eventually became well known as the inventor of a psychological method which he called Autogenic Training and which seems to be widely used in Germany. So far as I see, it is a mixture of traditional yoga techniques with modern psychological conditioning.

At about my third session with Dr. Schultz, he tackled my personal question, saying: "Didn't you tell me that you are engaged in work for the Ph.D.? This is a situation where many people develop fears, and as a consequence they try other things. I strongly suggest that you do not change the order of these two programs. Get your Ph.D. first and then, if you still feel the need for being psychoanalyzed, we will see. But then, we'll have to find somebody better than Lou." I accepted this advice at once, considering my own experiences with Lou. Thereafter I made it a point to visit Dr. Schultz once or twice a year. He always seemed happy to chat with me but never made any suggestion about treatment by him. For this I was grateful since I thought of him more as a powerful analytical intellect than as a man endowed with that outgoing love of the patient that seems indispensable for the true healer. Then, when I visited him in the summer of 1931 and told him that in the fall I would go to the University of Frankfurt, he said: "That is just fine. If you still are interested in being psychoanalyzed, you will find there the perfect man for the purpose." Since Schultz, clearly, was not a party to any of the factional struggles that so often rage around psychoanalysis, I judged that this was high praise, indeed, and decided to take his advice. My father still had to supply a large amount of money, but I found him surprisingly accessible: "The way things are going with Hitler," he said, "nobody's money will be worth anything in a few years, so perhaps this is a good investment." Being a lifelong student of history and having by then lived through a good deal, my father seems to have become prescient, in 1931, of things to come, as I was not.

In the nearly five years between my first and last visit to Dr. Schultz, I had very little contact with scientific psychology and was not personally acquainted with any psychiatrists. I did encounter psychology in a slightly disguised form, by becoming an aficionado of Marcel Proust. I had heard about him first in Holland, had later read something of his and had become most enthusiastic. At that time no complete German translations of Proust existed, but that was no major obstacle for me since French was the one language I knew fairly well. Although I was never an avid reader of fiction, I made an exception for Proust, and over two or three years I bought and read in succession every one of the twenty-two volumes that made up the original edition of his great novel. I do believe that it is the best introduction to depth psychology for anyone who does not have a profound affinity for the great Russian novelists, which I never had. I certainly think that it made me sensitive to the process of psychoanalysis which followed.

But my extensive reading of Proust had still another, far more personal significance: Ever since I was a small boy I had learned from those surrounding me that I was nervous and oversensitive. When I attended high-school in Heidelberg, the family doctor, a distant relative, always referred to me as "a bundle of nerves." Such remarks and others gleaned during my boyhood years convinced me early on that I was a rather high-strung individual. Such personality features appear to a youngster only as deficiencies, especially if he grows up in an environment already pervaded by considerably brutalized, pre-Hitlerian feelings. But Proust had succeeded in putting his own oversensitivity to work, so to speak. He had used his thin-skinned constitution to help create a portrait of unequalled splendor, of a whole society. I began to think of myself as able to use my own weaknesses for constructive purposes, as Proust had so clearly and honestly used his. This idea has stayed with me for the rest of my life.

When I moved to Frankfurt in the fall of 1931, I met my future analyst, Karl Landauer. He is given a paragraph in the second volume of Ernest Jones' biography of Freud. Landauer had been a professional psychiatrist before he turned to psychoanalysis. He was a rather quiet, almost taciturn man, who was not given to telling his patients about himself. He was then in his forties and had gradually developed his own views about various aspects of psychology; he was not a man to be pushed or even persuaded into one of the numerous factions that seem to spring up constantly among the practitioners and their leaders, be their name Freud, Jung, Adler, or other.

Dr. Landauer's procedure followed the orthodox Freudian pattern. When he accepted me as his patient, he assigned to me the first hour of the day, from eight to nine, which very conveniently did not disrupt my day. I cannot recall details of the analysis, of course, but I remember that Dr. Landauer was always very quiet and unemotional. I can recall only one instance when he seemed to wax emotional: One day I remarked, not quite in earnest, that maybe I should have become a writer. I must have failed to convey a jocular tone because he became visibly upset and said: "How can you say such a totally silly thing? You don't have any of the internal pressures that a writer needs." But this incident was quite unusual; in general the analysis proceeded on an even keel.

Nevertheless, my emotional involvement must have been profound. For instance, one day I happened to stand before his desk when suddenly, for reasons not clear to me, I grabbed a big marble ashtray standing there and threw it in his direction. He flinched for a moment, then calmly pointed out that I had not thrown this heavy object at his face, but at an angle of about sixty degrees from where his head had been. The full measure of the strength of his analytical procedure dawned on me only after it had terminated. Then I felt like a man who has just left the dentist's chair, in the days before anesthetics were discovered. I had then for days on end, perhaps for weeks, the phantom feeling that someone was drilling in my innards although I consciously knew that he had already ceased to drill. There was one point at which I found conversation with Dr. Landauer most helpful. He indicated to me that I was a far stronger personality than I ever had perceived by self-observation. He pointed out that there was a core of violence submerged in my unconscious of which I was unaware. I fancied myself as a rather timid young man cowed into caution by years of Nazi bullying. But if he was right, then I had the material in me to develop, by the standard psychological technique of sublimation, into the kind of person who could eventually become a scientific innovator.

My last encounter with Dr. Landauer will remain in my memory as long as I live. It was the day, early in April, 1933, when the Nazis carried out their "seizure of power," long announced but without their giving the details beforehand. It was, in other words, the official death of the Weimar Republic with its constitutional guarantees of personal freedom and the official beginning of the Nazi Terror that was to last for twelve years. When I walked into his office a few minutes after eight that morning, Dr. Landauer was standing there, clearly somewhat agitated: "What in hell are you doing here," he said. "Why aren't you on the train out of the country? In three hours you could be in Switzerland. They might close the borders, you know, and then you would be caught." I was shocked and gave him some of the high-flown oratory that one produces on such occasions: "Should I let a gang of hoodlums throw me out of here? I have as much right as they do, etc." He said, now more quietly: "You are free and unattached, you can go wherever you want to go. I have a family to support, a wife and three daughters. I cannot leave. I wish I could go." He was clearly more perceptive than I. (Needless to say, he was of Jewish descent.) There was of course no possibility of analytical work that day. When I arrived at the university a gang of uniformed brown-shirts, each with a rifle slung over his shoulder, stood in front of the door. Their leader demanded my university identification card. When I handed it to him, he put it in his pocket and said: "Go home, you will be told about further arrangements." A few days later I left for Zürich: The borders had not yet been closed and my passport was still valid.

About half a year later when I was fairly settled in Paris, I felt the need to close the psychoanalytical procedure after that violent interruption. I wrote to Dr. Landauer to see whether he could recommend a German-speaking analyst then residing in Paris. He could indeed: It was an Austrian lady with all the correct credentials who was willing to take me on. But I found that making incantations in the right terminology was worthless unless the analyst could make true contact with the patient's unconscious, which just did not seem to occur. I ended the new treatment after three weeks, an action that seemed the more desirable since I was not sure how my financial sponsor, Mr. Kaufmann, would feel about paying money to Paris for such a purpose over more than a very short period. I concluded that a successful psychoanalyst had to be strong both in personality and in intellect, and such people are rare. It is not surprising, therefore, that the old-fashioned form of Freudian analysis requiring one hour every day has been replaced by psychotherapeutic methods that are less demanding on the analyst. I have never forgiven myself for not continuing to write to Dr. Landauer. A few years later it would have been of little use, since I would have been totally unable to assist him: He eventually fled with his family to Holland. The Nazis caught him when they invaded that country in 1940, and he perished. I do not know what happened to his family.

The term depth psychology, which has become widely accepted amonr English speakers, is defined in dictionaries as the psychology of the unconscious, so that the term is indeed appropriate. Dr. Landauer's interaction with me, for one hour every weekday, continued for some eighteen months until forcibly interrupted; this is, conservatively speaking, a total of about 400 one-hour sessions, a timespan that even a psychiatrist might not find negligible. My views about depth psychology, therefore, are based on what I think is a sizeable personal experience.

The word "conversion" in the title of this chapter is clearly a strong word. Within the Christian tradition it designates what may have happened to a man who was struck by a shaft of light midway on his life's journey and was converted from a persecutor to an apostle. While there is little that is spectacular in my recollection of these years, the cumulative effects of experiencing my own unconscious mind may well have been stronger than any sudden change. There never was any doubt about the overpowering role of my own unconscious which, under Dr. Landauer's apt guidance, confronted me at every step. I could not question the unconscious' reality, anymore than I could question the reality of the electrons, nuclei, etc., with which my profession confronted me. But it was a reality of a different and unexpected texture. I speak now of the elusiveness, the irregularity, the disorder, and often disharmony of the psychic phenomena I encountered in myself, in one brief word their irrationality (the term used by Jung). There was nothing in these experiences that indicated a well-designed, smooth-running piece of machinery such as the "cyberneticists" and others of their stripe would make me believe existed in my head. What I could observe was, speaking in the vernacular, "a can of worms," with none of the precise fit that exists, say, in sense physiology, and that a mechanistic view would induce us to find everywhere in the living organism.

In my forays into my own unconscious, I, of course, constantly encountered the well-known phenomenon of "resistance," that is the unconscious mind defending itself against being analyzed and being tampered with. Related to this resistance is the capability for rationalization possessed at the genius level even by simple and seemingly primitive souls: their ability to invent reasons, intelligible grounds for action, which camouflage the underlying, unconscious drives.

As I read literature on the psychology of the unconscious, I began to appreciate both its depth and its extraordinary breadth: Freud in his beginnings, when he dealt with psycho-sexual pathology, had clearly implied that the unconscious could not be sundered from its biological roots. With my curiosity aroused about depth psychology, I could not fail to discover Carl Gustav Jung. I do not see how one can doubt that next to Freud he is by far the greatest of the investigators of depth psychology. While I have not indulged in extensive reading as a specialist would have done, I can nevertheless say that I feel more comfortable with Jung's philosophy than with that of any of the other luminaries of depth psychology. Although clearly less incisive than Freud, he seems to be much broader. Freud appears, so to speak, as the Columbus of this new continent; to be successful in his endeavor, he needed very strong convictions bordering sometimes on the dogmatic. Jung, who was younger than Freud by nineteen years, was the only one with the strength not to succumb fully to Freud's intellectual influence; he had independently as a very young man first discovered the "complex" which he defined as an autonomous dynamical unit of the unconscious. Thereafter, Jung had, in his theory of types and in his concept of archetypes and their elaborations, laid the foundations of a broad psychology that branches into what one can only describe as the spiritual.

Such reading and corresponding musings filled a gap in my philosophical understanding, even of my science. Let me explain why I felt strongly about this: As a physical scientist, it was hard for me to think of the properties of the human psyche as purely abstract functionalities apart from any anchoring in the material substratum of the brain. An alternative approach would conceivably be through brain physiology. I felt that I was on my way toward an encounter with the most ancient of all philosophical problems, that of the dualism of body and soul. The philosophically inclined scientist cannot fail to encounter this question when he moves from physical science into biology. And perhaps the time is ripe for making such an encounter fruitful.

It is easy to see that the natural intersection of these two types of scientific thought, of the ideas of physics on the one hand, and those of depth psychology on the other, would occur in biology. Once I realized this, I began to acquire an interest in the philosophical basis of biological science, an interest that has not left me thereafter. My colleagues, somewhat baffled by this turn of my mind, spoke of my interest in "theoretical biology." This is not too apt a description because theoretical biology indicates mostly the application of mathematical techniques to biological questions. I developed a simple belief that I have never had any reason to alter: The methods of modern theoretical science are sufficiently advanced to allow removing a central

problem of philosophy, namely the body-soul dualism, from the
metaphysicians in order to treat it as a specifically scientific problem
with the methods of the theoretical scientist.

But this would no doubt have forever remained speculation, had it
not been for a personal encounter with a biologist that occurred about
half a year after I had left Frankfurt and Dr. Landauer's treatment. I
had moved by then to Paris where late in 1933 I became acquainted
with Theophile Kahn. We soon became close friends. During the three
years I lived in Paris, we saw much of each other; after I came to the
United States, we kept in looser contact.

Theo had been born and raised in Alsace. (The German equivalent
in Elsass, and one of my male ancestors who was born there had crossed
the Rhine eastward in the eighteenth century, at the time when the
Jews began to acquire family names.) This region, together with
Lorraine, had been part of France since the days of Louis XIV but had
been conquered in 1870 and annexed to the Reich. In the Peace of
Versailles, in 1919, it fell back to France and remained there except for
the occupation by the Nazis, 1940–1944. Thus Theo was for all his later
years a French citizen. He studied medicine but, with little interest to be
a practicing physician, he chose physiological research for his specialty. When I met Theo, he was a staff member of the Institute for
Physico-Chemical Biology located in a fairly new building in the Rue
Pierre Curie, right next door to where I myself had begun to work. This
Institute was private, belonging to the Rothschild Foundation; it still
exists, but is now run by the French Government; its present, well
known director is Dr. Pullman. Theo was working on the physiology
of digestion and used dogs as his test animals, studying their pancreas.
On the occasions when I visited him in his laboratory, I often had to
climb over a huge German Shepherd dog lying there with a bandage
across its abdomen.

Mostly, of course, we met, French fashion, in a cafe. Since it is
notoriously difficult to get acquainted with Frenchmen, Theo was a
godsend to me. Not infrequently, he would take me for lunch to one of
the bistros of the Latin Quarter. They usually have checkered table-
cloths and are frequented by bricklayers, carpenters, and similar
artisans who take there a leisurely lunch, accompanied by a bottle of
red wine. Theo also introduced me to a bachelor friend of his who
specialized in cooking and who now and then invited us. Those who
have watched Frenchmen when they exercise their ritual of savoring a
well-cooked meal will appreciate what I experienced. The French have,

or seem to have always had, an extraordinary genius for ritualizing mundane, everyday life. I have had no occasion, in my very limited experience, to see anything similar in other nations. It seems to me that the traditional attitude of the French upper classes toward sex was similarly ritualistic, though this did not extend to the lower middle class whose attitude toward sex was, as everywhere in Europe, based on procreation and property.

But to return to Theo Kahn's science: I failed to read his articles or his book on the regulation of animal metabolism, but I read with much delight his lively biography of Geoffroy Saint-Hilaire, the famous French naturalist. In discussion, Theo loved to indulge in philosophical perspectives about biology. He was the first "professional" of biology I ever encountered. It is difficult to say what exactly this term implies, since "biology" is much more a conglomeration of sciences than a single science. But I presume that Theo with his medical background, his vast curiosity, and his flexible mind might be called a professional biologist as well as any man could be. During three years of frequent and close contact with him, I acquired just the kind of slant on matters biological that one is very likely to miss if one is reduced to reading books. He also had a sufficiently well developed capacity for abstraction and generalization, so that even the naturally somewhat schematic mind of a physicist could follow him.

Theo's most impressive claim of a general nature was that biology was first and foremost the realm of utter complexity. This appealed to me because the idea was simple, abstract, and general, exactly the kind of notion that is so often constructed and used by theoretical physicists. It was only years later, however, that I found the most spectacular example of Theo's thesis: an atlas of human anatomy. Since every medical student must peruse such an atlas, excellent ones can be bought rather cheaply, and every medical library has them. There are few things more impressive for those who want to understand biological complexity than to study at leisure such an atlas. The presence of such formidable complexity in every one of billions of human beings cannot help but stir one deeply. Later, I made many efforts to compare this degree of complexity with that found in inorganic nature; my later work in geophysics offered me good opportunities to do this. I found that the complexity either in the fluid earth, say in turbulence, or in the solid earth, in the structure of minerals and rocks, cannot compare to the formidable complexity found in all higher organisms. From what was known of organic chemistry, one could easily surmise that there was chemical complexity of an extreme degree even in microbes, in fact, in lower organisms of all sorts. It was easy to think that the tendency toward complexity was a general principle underlying the structure and the dynamics of living things.

Years later I found that this idea of the utter complexity of organisms leads quite naturally to a second concept, that of individuality: An object as complex as an organism can vary its structural details in many ways. Calculations on which my later books are based show how vast this variety is. I want to give an example: A simple class of compounds of organic chemistry is that of saturated hydrocarbons, of formula $C_n H_{2n+2}$ where n is any integer. For $n = 6$, hexanes, there exist five different molecular structures obeying this formula, five isomers as the chemist says. For $n = 30$ the number of different isomers is already four billion.[1] Since organic molecules usually contain several other types of atoms besides carbon and hydrogen, especially oxygen and nitrogen, the number of possible different structures becomes incredibly large for any piece of organic tissue that contains as many as, say, a few thousand carbon atoms. One can safely say that any such piece of tissue has individuality in a narrow and precise technical sense: There are so many variants of any given arrangement of atoms that the chance that there is anywhere a precise duplicate of any one structure is negligibly small. Since individuality in this primitive but precise sense is to be found everywhere in large organic chemical structures, I have accustomed myself to use the word in the plural, individualities.

For present purposes I am using the phrase "complexity and individualities" mainly as a sort of slogan to point the way along which one ought to direct one's thinking when going from physical science to biology. The opposite would be "simplicity and universality." Years of acquaintance with these two pairs have convinced me that they are very well suited to bring out the difference, otherwise frequently hidden, between the ways of thinking needed on the one hand in physical science, and on the other in biological science.

Speaking specifically, philosophical concepts of the type characterized by simplicity and universality rose to paramount importance during the time of the Enlightenment (the seventeenth century) when both rationalistic philosophy and modern science were born. This age has left its traces on us: One must recognize the quite extreme, one might say extravagant, role that rationalistic philosophy still plays in the thinking of modern, contemporary scientists. This is not to deprecate rationalism; it has its unquestioned historical merits. It emphasized the capacity of men to think on their own and thereby emancipated the thought of that period from the tutelage of theology. But it did so within distinct limits: Descartes (1596–1650), the leading early figure, was a man who, as he changed his lodgings often, always carried two books with him, the Bible and the works of Thomas Aquinas. He was, then, clearly not a mechanist in the modern sense. In a later period, the role that enlightened rationalism played in leading toward that complete reorganization of society which culminated in the American and French Revolutions is familiar enough, but has little relation to science.

To me, the acquaintance with the new world of depth psychology had an overwhelming intellectual effect. Faced with this new world I recognized that there were two quite different and apparently incompatible ways of looking at life: that coming from physics and that arising out of depth psychology. I also realized that these two worlds could only be reconciled with each other if one of the groups involved yielded. But the psychologists merely presented what they saw in an orderly way. The physicists, in turn, if they wanted to encounter life had to leave their world of simplicity and universality and enter the world of complexity and individualities. I began to see that it is the man who is thinking in the traditional terms of physics who must change his ways and learn to accommodate complexity and individualities. This insight never left me and as later I became successful in my scientific activity in the United States, I became increasingly committed to such ideas. This led to many clashes with members of the biomedical establishment. Such drama as there is in the later years of my life arose mainly from this source.

Putting the matter into different terms, I had inferred from depth psychology that there was no point in dealing with biology, the science of life, unless one spoke of creativity as a basic property of all life. Did the transition from simplicity and universality toward complexity and individualities allow one to think of life as creative? If not, then there was little hope that a true science of life would ever come into being. As of now, my years of living and working with these problems have thoroughly convinced me that this is possible and that a genuine science of life can be developed. Of course, it will have to have a different complexion from our present-day "molecular biology," deeply mired as the latter is in purely rationalistic modes of thought.

It is clear that creative processes cannot be described scientifically in the way an astronomer describes the orbit of a planet. The scientist, then, must show that the complexity of life is of a broad enough character, so that the creativity of the organism can forever be hidden in it. That is far from a trivial issue. As I learned over the years, one needs no new and fanciful postulate: The enchainment of ever new and unpredictable individualities, which the organism creates by virtue of its complex structure, not only makes this creativity possible, it *is* this creativity. I am by now completly convinced that the physical and chemical structure and mechanics of the organism contain all the elements that allow one to develop a world of complexity and individualities leading to creativity. In such a world some matters can be explained by causality, by using the modes of thought of the physicist, but other questions may be asked to which no scientific answers can ever be expected.

I feel that I cannot leave the subject of this chapter without adding a few more philosophical remarks: I had the extraordinary good luck to be exposed, at an age when I was still receptive, to a new doctrine, a new philosophy as it were. It was depth psychology, the knowledge of the human unconscious. I soon understood that this was as much a scientific discovery of radical novelty as the discovery of atoms, molecules, and nuclei. There are some clever intellectuals who have spoken or written of the unconscious "before Freud." This is like speaking of gravity before Newton, correct but irrelevant. Newton did not discover gravity, he discovered the structure of its laws, and he was the first. Similarly, Freud, Jung, and their pupils did not discover the unconscious, but rather the structure of its modes of behavior, and they were the first.

From my rather extensive brush with depth psychology I had learned that nothing valuable ever came to pass in this world that did not have deep roots in the human unconscious. This does not mean that whatever the unconscious produces is "good." The unconscious is part of nature and as such resembles the sun that rises equally over the just and the unjust. It does not imply, however, that the unconscious is impervious to morality: It is well known that if one suggests a criminal action to a person under hypnosis, the suggestion is not generally carried out. For me at least, the collision with this new world had a tremendously liberating effect: It led me away from the sterilities of the rationalistic philosophy with which the society of my youth was saturated.

Here, I should say a word about the difference between rationalism and rationality. Man, of course, is made to be rational. He can no more desist from being rational than he can desist from being moral. In the jungle of life, one must make compromises between one's moral urges and the exigencies of a given situation, and there is no judge who will tell one whether the decision made was right. I mention such a platitude only because I want to apply the same kind of argument to the concept of rationality. Recognizing the limits of rationality, as the rationalist too often fails to do, does not mean being "irrational" or being an advocate of irrational behavior, any more than the sun's shining over both good and evil men is a license for immorality.

Such insights influenced my thinking in later years: I realized that of the two pairs of slogans I have quoted above, one pair, simplicity and universality, was the battle-cry of classical rationalism, whereas complexity and individualities are a slogan that if elaborated would lead one away from rationalism. If empirical complexity withstood exhaustive analysis, this meant that it did not yield to fully rational representation. The concept of individualities, in the sense that certain configurations existed only once in the world, negated the applicability of classes, an indispensable tool of rational analysis.

From such thoughts I was able to understand a remark that Max Born had made when I was still a student (Chapter 3): He had said that my strength was in conceptual thinking rather than in mathematics. This made no sense to me as long as I believed along extravagantly rationalistic lines that all thinking could ultimately be expressed in mathematical form. But if the utter complexity of living things, first structural, but then also logical, impeded the application of mathematical schemes, then conceptual thought was restored to a respected position as a valuable tool in the hierarchy of human mental endeavors.

I gradually began to perceive the mistake that rationalists consistently made: Because men have a powerful urge to think and to act according to ideas of rationality, they concluded that nature itself can be made intelligible by rational means. It is the basic prejudice of rationalism. Realizing this I saw that a new, radical distinction could be made between physical science and life science. Physical science had been utterly successful (in all but some very extreme endeavors, namely cosmology and high-energy physics) in its effort to represent nature by rational schemes through ordering it in terms of mathematical constructs, of which quantum mechanics was but the latest example. Such abstract constructs, based on relatively simple axioms, embodied rationality as thoroughly as one could demand, but now I doubted whether life science could ever be considered fully rational in the same sense. Of course, I did not know just what the precise meaning of this "irrationality" of organic life was; this would appear only at the end, not at the beginning of such inquiries.

The insight I have just discussed—that from the irrepressible urge of men to be rational one cannot conclude that nature itself is rational—constitutes, I believe, the chief fruit of my endeavors as a thinker in the philosophy of science. Certainly, ancient sages, Hindu, Hebrew, Greek, or medieval would not have had the least doubt about this, had they posed the problem in these terms. But at present, one can go much farther: One can identify the point where purely rational procedures in all likelihood cease to be sufficient; this point lies in the transition from physics to biology. If biology is the locus of utter and perhaps irreducible complexity, it can also be the locus of partial irrationality. It is exactly the utter complexity that makes the use of the term "partial" possible in place of the black-and-white, yes-or-no philosophy of the rationalist.

But while, of course, science cannot represent the irrational by rational means, I was now confronted with a challenging problem: It is clear that under these conditions organic structure serves as the vehicle of this irrationality, that is of our inability to order the phenomena exhaustively in terms of logico-mathematical schemes, and the study of the nature of this vehicle is strictly a scientific task. The preoccupation with this task filled many of my later years.

7

Rue Pierre Curie, Paris

When that spring of 1933, a few days after the Nazi's seizure of dictatorial power, I left Frankfurt and with it my homeland, Germany, I took the express train to Zürich. There, I went at once to the Physics Building of the Federal Polytechnic School which I well remembered from the semester I had spent there five years earlier. On entering the main door of this building one faces a broad and straight staircase leading directly to the second floor. Before I could take my first step on it, there appeared at the top of the stairs the moon-face of Wolfgang Pauli, who shouted down: "Elsasser," he said, "you are the first to come up these stairs; I can see how in the months to come there will be many, many more to climb up here." It was clearly not necessary to give Pauli further explanations, and after the exchange of a few courtesies, I proceeded to settle in Zürich for a stay of uncertain duration. But this time luck was on my side. A day or two later Pauli told me that he had just received a letter from Frederic Joliot, the son-in-law of Madame Curie, to the effect that the nuclear physicists in Paris would like to find a theoretical man. Pauli then added that he would propose me for the position. After a few days a letter from Joliot came back, saying that they would be happy to have me, but that it would take a little time to set the bureaucratic machinery in motion; he would write again later.

There was nothing to do but wait. During this period I met a young man who had just come to Zürich to study with Pauli, an Indian named Homi Bhabha. I saw him a number of times during this stay in Zürich; he was clearly a man of broad interests and wide culture. At that period, his most absorbing hobby was painting. Had he wanted to, he could undoubtedly have become a professional painter; his talents seemed substantial enough. The pictures he showed me were all characterized by an extraordinarily somber mood such as I had never seen before; they were dominated by the darkest colors and especially by black. I could not fathom the psychological background of the universal somber mood but it was profoundly impressive. I was less taken with Bhabha's efforts in theoretical physics. As I have seen many times, those who come from cultures far from the circle of modern Western rationalism seem to be impelled to plunge directly into the most profound problems of the Universe, of Matter, or of Life, never bothering about lesser, more accessible and more practical problems. Bhabha tried to model the properties of elementary particles in mathematical terms—but I had long since learned that manipulating mathematical symbols alone, no matter how ingeniously, is not a good way to approach the secrets of nature.

After I left Zürich I lost touch with Bhabha. I was able to piece his career together from notices in papers and magazines, and it was interesting enough: He was the offspring of a very old, wealthy, and powerful family of Mysore. I had suspected something of the kind from the way he skillfully evaded questions about his background. He was interested from youth in problems of basic physics, but his father persuaded him to go to England and study engineering at Cambridge. Having accomplished this successfully, he came to Zürich to work with Pauli. His family was connected by ties of marriage with the Tata family, possessors of a vast industrial empire, the largest in India. Later, Bhabha was able to convince those who directed the finances of the Tata enterprise that the industrialization of the country could be successfully accomplished only if accompanied by a sufficiently high level of fundamental research. In 1945 the Tata Institute for Fundamental Research was officially founded with Bhabha as its director, but it was not until seventeen years later that its workers could move into a building of their own in Bombay. I have little doubt that without the activities of this Institute the Indians would have been hard put to explode an atomic bomb of their own, as they did a few years ago—not, of course, that there is anything meritorious in a country's making an atomic bomb. Homi Bhabha died at a rather young age in 1966, in an airplane crash.

After having waited in Zürich for two or three months for another letter from Joliot, I finally decided that since I had nothing to lose I might as well wait in Paris. I went to the French consulate to obtain a visa. The office was not too crowded, and the clerk engaged me in a conversation, during which he drew me out about my background and intentions. This went on for quite a while, say ten or fifteen minutes, and it became clear to me that the clerk was doing his best to avoid giving me the visa without stating this intention in so many words.

Finally, I became impatient and said, "But I am Jewish;" whereupon the clerk said, "Why didn't you tell me that in the first place? Give me your passport." Down came his stamp; I paid and was ready to go to Paris.

I did not try to generalize from this about the French attitude toward the Jews. At that time there was almost universal sympathy for the Jews oppressed by Hitler; some years later when the Germans had conquered the country, all sympathy for Jews had to be practiced underground. But I dimly realized that here was a style of life with which I was not acquainted. This clerk was using his own judgment and methods, quite possibly on very general instructions from above, but he was certainly not an automaton who said either yes or no depending on which set of orders he had. He could not, of course, have inquired whether I was Jewish since this would have been incompatible with the secular character of the French Republic; on the other hand, at that time there began the infiltration of Hitler's agents into France which a few years later were so helpful in the formation of a fifth column. The French authorities were undoubtedly aware of this, but there was little they could do while the two countries were at peace; and the French, at least, hoped that they would remain at peace. I had had my first introduction to French individualism, of which I was to see a great deal more. The French military establishment, for instance, is pervaded by what is popularly called *Système D* (standing for *débrouille-toi*, roughly, disentangle yourself). This system is, of course, also known elsewhere, but it is not as highly developed and as carefully cultivated as it is in France.

When I arrived in Paris I went to Joliot's laboratory in the Radium Institute, located in the Rue Pierre Curie, a short street on the left bank of the Seine, a little south of the Pantheon. There are in this street four buildings that harbor scientific research establishments, three of these belonging to the Sorbonne (the ancient name of the University of Paris, dating back to the Middle Ages). Coming from the Pantheon one found on the left the *Institut du Radium*, on the right there was the Rothschild Institute of physico-chemical biology, containing the laboratory of Theo Kahn, then followed the *Institut Henri Poincaré* devoted to mathematics and theoretical physics, and then a relatively compact laboratory of physical chemistry, which represented the high status achieved by the great scientist Jean Perrin. The remainder of the street was taken up by a number of conventional apartment houses.

Joliot told me what I had expected: The efforts to find a position for me had encountered bureaucratic obstacles, but with a little patience matters would certainly be cleared up. After some further waiting I suddenly found myself the recipient of a one-year fellowship from an organization called "Alliance Israélite Universelle." I was somewhat annoyed to realize that I was now receiving charity; this was the more difficult because I had never before had any connections with Judaism or with its social organizations. But since I had not been consulted, I decided that discretion required silence. After a year I was transferred to the embryo, created by Jean Perrin, of the later C.N.R.S. (Centre National de la Recherche Scientifique) which eventually became a very large fund-disbursing agency of the French government for science, roughly corresponding to the American National Science Foundation but somewhat more comprehensive.

Fairly soon I found a place to work: I was assigned a small table in the library of the Institut Henri Poincaré, on the third floor of the building. I retained this for three years, until I left Paris for the United States. It was, I think, typical of how scientists were then treated in France (now their status is much improved). There were no facilities for leaving one's own books overnight; whatever I needed had to be carried in and out in a briefcase. The Institute was named after a great French mathematician; he was, by the way, the cousin of the politician, Raymond Poincaré, who played such a great role in history around the time of the First World War. Henri Poincaré had been a man of wide intellectual interests, which included a great deal of philosophy. His books on the latter subject, while somewhat formalistic, were widely read in my youth, and I knew them thoroughly. Poincaré, who died in 1912, had before his death become an ardent proponent of the theory of relativity.

There was in Paris at that time a group of remarkable men who directed physical science and its instruction; soon I came to know them. The most conspicuous among them was Jean Perrin. He had been, comparatively speaking, a self-made man. A provincial, the son of an army officer, he had graduated from the *Ecole Normale*, one of the two great schools (the other being the *Ecole Polytechnique*) which are at the pinnacle of the highly structured French educational system and whose entrance examinations are notoriously difficult. He had made a brilliant career in experimental physics that was ultimately crowned by the Nobel prize. His experiments to establish evidence for the kinetic theory of matter were as valuable as any done; he was the first man to obtain a precise value of Avogadro's constant, the number of hydrogen atoms in a gram of ponderable matter. Perrin with his carefully trimmed mustache and goatee, always well dressed, looked the embodiment of a man of distinction; he was also quite ambitious politically and at one time was made Under-Secretary of Education. I soon realized that he had a very strong personality and, in his younger years at least, must have been a man of penetrating intellect; I began to suspect that the spectacular vanity expressed in his external appearance and in his political activity was a shield that protected him in the vulgar tumble of political battles in a country where personal vanity is one of the most common vices. Perrin was an ubiquitous figure around the Rue Pierre Curie; he always had a friendly smile and a "Bonjour Monsieur" when he saw me. He made great efforts to remember my name, but, being in his sixties, his memory seemed to falter; he always called me by the name of someone else, also foreign-sounding to him. He ultimately succeeded in impressing upon the rather parsimonious French political establishment the need for ampler subsidies to scientific research. But it was only after the war that his efforts bore extensive fruit.

Jean Perrin had a son, Francis, who was also a physicist. He was a highly intelligent and knowledgeable man who had also gone through the Ecole Normale, but was quite different in temperament from his father. He was rather dry, impersonal in his relations to others, with modest imagination. When I came to Paris, he had just been made professor of theoretical physics at the Sorbonne, at the young age of thirty-two. I was told that I should cultivate him since he was the man to whom I was closest in interests and competence. I made it a point to see him at intervals and to ask him questions or engage him in discussion, but these visits never seemed to progress much beyond rather formal audiences. Francis Perrin was undoubtedly one of the men, of whom I have seen many in my life, whose early development is kept back by the overpowering personality of a distinguished father. He came into his own only in middle life after 1950, when he was made Joliot's successor as the head of the French Atomic Energy Commission. His personality and his capabilities eminently qualified him as a high-level government administrator, and he maintained this position for many years.

A physicist who had his laboratory in the building for physical chemistry, and who belonged to the same younger generation, was Pierre Auger. He is known to science through his discovery of the Auger effect: An atom may have an electron removed from a tightly bound level, and it ordinarily responds by the dropping of an electron from a more loosely bound level with the emission of an X-ray; but the atom is on occasion capable of converting the energy internally and to eject a second, loosely bound electron. The study of the Auger effect was valuable in these days because it showed the interactions between electrons in one and the same atom to be exactly the same as those between electrons of separate atoms. Auger's sister had married Francis Perrin; Pierre Auger himself ended up as an administrator of no mean proportions but on the international scene: He was director of science for UNESCO for twelve years; then he became director of the European Space Research Organization.

A leading French physicist of that day was Prince Louis de Broglie. I could not fail to be introduced to him soon after my arrival. As he was the scion of one of the most illustrious aristocratic families which for three centuries had given France an almost uninterrupted series of military and political leaders, one was not surprised to find him a man of superb manners. But these were not such as to encourage a closer approach. As I eventually learned from the two or three people who worked with him personally, he was a total hermit who lived attended only by a manservant. After de Broglie had received the Nobel prize in 1929, a chair of quantum mechanics had been created for him at the Sorbonne. In this capacity he had an office in the Institut Henri Poincaré, but he was almost never found there. He did regularly attend the weekly sessions of the Academy of Sciences, of which he was later secretary for many years. He transmitted numerous small papers of mine to the Academy for publication, of which I shall speak later. After the famous thesis, de Broglie's scientific output consisted almost entirely of an interminable series of books; but since none of these seemed to contain another stirring idea, they had little lasting effect.

Since it was clear enough that Joliot was the moving spirit, and to all appearances the only one who had brought me to Paris, I made it my business to specialize in the structure and dynamics of atomic nuclei. Not that I had a unique passion for this subject, but it seemed the proper thing to do, and, in fact, the transition from the kind of research I had done before, to the application of quantum mechanics in the nucleus, was achieved readily enough. When I came to Paris, Mme. Curie was still alive and could now and then be seen in the laboratory, but the leadership was then in the hands of Frederic Joliot and his wife, Irene, Marie Curie's daughter. The couple had assumed the double name Joliot-Curie. At that time the work they were doing on nuclear

Jean Perrin, drawing from life by Elisabeth Korn, 1930

physics was just coming into the foreground of interest for many physicists; I was aware that in moving into this field I might find myself in competition with such giants as Bethe and Fermi, but I felt that I was under a strong moral obligation to work on whatever was most useful to the Radium Institute.

Madame Curie was then sixty-six and a somewhat shadowy, frail figure. Given her almost mythical character, one left her as much alone as was feasible. Now and then she came to seminars where she sat in the front row, almost never speaking. She was always picking at the skin of her fingers which peeled incessantly from radiation damage sustained earlier. She did in the summer of 1934, but the news of her death and of the funeral was kept strictly private, so that those like myself, who were not intimate with the family, learned it only from the newspapers. The medical post-mortem showed complex causes of death, but it also showed that the end was greatly accelerated by the sudden onset of pernicious anemia, a radiation-related illness.

The romantic story of Marie Curie travelling from Poland to Paris at age twenty-four to study physics is too well known to repeat here. Two years later she passed as the first in her class the licentiate in physics (corresponding roughly to the baccalaureate in the U.S.) and a year thereafter the licentiate in mathematics, also at the top of the class. Two years later again, in 1895, she married Pierre Curie, eight years older than she. Curie would in any event be counted among the very great men of physics, although the second area of his scientific inquiries and productivity (the first had been magnetism) was entered and covered jointly with his wife Marie. They created the term radioactivity, which "stuck" with the public. It seems to me silly to inquire "who did what" in the scientific cooperation of a married couple; who can penetrate into such privacy?

In 1896 the French physicist H. Becquerel had discovered that the element uranium emitted a "radiation"; that is to say, any chemical compound containing uranium when put next to a photographic plate wrapped in dark paper, photographically blackened the plate; also, if an uranium compound was placed next to a charged electroscope, the latter was rapidly discharged. At that time physicists had learned that this effect indicates ionization of the air that can only be effected by certain radiations. The further elucidation of the phenomena of radioactivity was due to the combined efforts of the Curies in Paris and of Ernest Rutherford in England. Marie Curie's painstaking years-long work of chemical fractionation first established that she was faced with

a spontaneous transformation of elements into each other—the fulfillment of the alchemist's dream. She discovered several new elements:
polonium, actinium, and most significantly, radium. Rutherford, born
and raised in New Zealand, who was then professor at Manchester
(1898–1919) and later in Cambridge, investigated and clarified the
nature and measured in detail the properties of the radiations emitted
by these elements. Later, Rutherford's school produced Nobel laureates
with the ease with which a naturalist may find new species of beetles.
He had early predicted the existence of a particle, the neutron, with
about the same mass of the proton but without an electric charge, and,
in fact, he publicly insisted for years that this hypothetical particle
would be found some day.

    In January 1932, the Joliot-Curies made a highly significant experi-
ment in which they bombarded some light elements, beryllium, boron,
and a few others, with alpha-rays produced by a powerful source of
polonium. They found that this induced a secondary emission that was
very penetrating; they interpreted the radiation as energetic gamma-
rays. A particularly intriguing observation was that if their radiation
detector was covered with a layer of material containing hydrogen, a
material such as paraffin, there was an even more powerful secondary
radiation than usual. While the Joliots reported this as a remarkable
phenomenon worthy of further study, James Chadwick, working in
Rutherford's laboratory, recognized in it the tell-tale marks of the
neutron. Since this particle has the same mass as the proton, it can, on
a head-on collision, communicate all its speed to a proton, whereas in
collision with heavier nuclei only part of the speed can be transferred.
Chadwick also had better measuring equipment than the Joliots, a
proportional counter, at that time still rare in the nuclear laboratory.
Chadwick's announcement that he had discovered the neutron appeared in print just seven weeks after the original note of the Joliot-
Curies. There began then, in the Radium Institute, an intense study of
the secondary radiation induced in light elements by the proximity of a
radioactive source. This led, just two years after the near-discovery of
the neutron, to the basic discovery of artificial radioactivity: Instances
were found in which the counters continued to click even after the
primary radioactive source had been removed. The Joliot-Curies
published this result in January 1934, and thereafter the mechanism
became easy to understand: New, radioactive isotopes of known light
elements had been created. Since the chemistry of light elements is well
under control, research broadened rapidly. Joliot himself with his

lively imagination recognized at once the great importance this discovery would have for the study of chemical and, in particular, biological processes through the use of radioactive "tracers," a set of nuclei (isotopes) which are chemically indistinguishable from some given species of element but which make their presence known by the emission of radiation that can be readily detected. The preparation of such tracer elements is now a large industry except that the tracers are made by irradiation in nuclear accelerators, not by putting the material to be transformed next to a source of naturally radioactive material. In 1935 Chadwick received the Nobel prize for physics for his discovery of the neutron, and the Joliot-Curies obtained concurrently the one for chemistry for their discovery of artificial radioactivity.

Although the rapid rise of Frederic Joliot happened to coincide with my stay in Paris, I could never discover the slightest change in his perfectly free and natural relations with me or, for that matter, with others. I soon developed into a great admirer of Fred's, as he was called by everyone. He came to represent for me that mixture of simplicity, directness, personal engagement, and practicality that is the product of centuries of French life, so often transmogrified by the professorial term, "civilisation." Frederic Joliot[1] had been born and brought up in Paris in a family of the petty bourgeoisie. The father had worked his way to modest comfort from narrow circumstances, but there seemed to have been little that presaged greater things to come. The father as a young man was in sympathy with the Paris Commune of 1870, and when its adherents were severely suppressed, he had to lie low for a while to escape persecution. Fred's mother, a native of the Alsace, was a strong personality, very much opposed to any kind of parochial nationalism. So Frederic Joliot first came by his later left-wing and cosmopolitan views through family channels.

After completing high school, Joliot entered the School of Physics, as it was generally called, its official title being *Ecole Supérieure de Physique et de Chimie Industrielles* operated by the city of Paris. This school had been founded in the later decades of the nineteenth century when the rise of industry made the training of corresponding professional people important. But it was not what a school of that title would have been in most other countries. It was highly intellectual, and the teachers were superb. Foremost, among them was Paul Langevin, director of studies for physics, who can safely be described as one of the greatest French scientists. Joliot, who previously had an excellent but not superbly brilliant record, blossomed out; in particu-

lar, his ability as an experimentalist showed more and more clearly.
The school, of course, while it had great qualities was not on the same
social level as the "Grandes Ecoles," the Normale or the Polytechnique, where one was sure during one's student years to make the
acquaintance of the future leaders of the French establishment. After
Joliot had decided to concentrate on physics rather than chemistry, he
became a pupil of Langevin, who recognized his genius. After graduation from the School of Physics, Joliot did his year of military service.
Before the year was quite over, he came back for a visit with Langevin,
to discuss his future. Langevin said: "Would you like to work in the
Radium Institute; I know Mme. Curie, of course, and would be glad to
recommend you. Go there and introduce yourself in a few days." When
Joliot appeared before that world-famous woman, he was almost
trembling, but she quieted him, asked him a few questions, and then
said: "Could you start work tomorrow?" Joliot, who was in uniform,
said: "I have still three weeks of military service before me." "What is
the name of your colonel? Let me settle that with him," said Mme.
Curie, and Joliot started the next morning. He could not help becoming acquainted with Mme. Curie's daughter Irene, who also worked in
the laboratory in an official capacity. They fell in love and were married
within a year.

I got to know both of them rather well. Fred Joliot had a quite
uncanny ability for dealing with people, a gift not often associated
with the scientific temperament. From my first long conversation to the
last time I saw him three years later, I always had the feeling that I had
a staunch friend in Fred, and I never found it possible to doubt the
reality of that feeling. Joliot's biographer, Pierre Biquard, tells a story
which vividly illustrates this quality: A few years after the war, the
French Atomic Energy Commission, then headed by Joliot, had
decided to build their technical installations near the hamlet of Saclay,
some distance south of Paris. There had to be meetings with the local
populace who understand the value of that work for the country's
industrial and military future, but so shortly after Hiroshima and
Nagasaki could not help being very skeptical, if not hostile. It took two
appearances of Joliot before these assemblies, and then they said: We
have complete confidence in this man; we will accept him as our leader;
he will lead us in the right direction.

Joliot's relations with others, based on his remarkable openness,
were far from a one-way street. I remember one incident that impressed
me very much; it may have been a year after I had first met him. That

Frederic Joliot

morning I found him in a bad mood. "Why are people so nasty," he said. "Why do they claim that I don't love my wife, and that I have married her just for the sake of my career. But I do love my wife. I love her very much." Nobody who knew Irene could doubt that her scientist-husband's love for her was the most natural thing. While she was by no means pretty in a conventional sense, she had very regular features, and below the somewhat cool exterior one could sense a warm personality, probably capable of much passion. Irene was a fairly accomplished sportswoman and outdoor person, and in this respect she had a great deal in common with her husband. As distinct from so many women in the professions who seem to have a mannish streak, I always felt that Irene was an essentially feminine type. Then, however, Irene had had a most unusual experience early in life: When she was seventeen, the First World War broke out. Mme. Curie soon engaged in an extraordinary enterprise, entirely on her own initiative: She was determined to give the Allied troops the benefits of a "radiographic" (i.e., X-ray) service. At that time many surgeons had never even heard of X-rays. Marie Curie created a mobile X-ray unit, consisting of a large private automobile in which she installed an X-ray machine and an electrical generator with the car's motor being used to drive the latter. She saw to it that as many of these units as possible were improvised; she gave courses of instruction to prospective operators and tried to get the proper ministry to organize the whole enterprise; in the meantime she drove one such unit closely behind the front lines to stop wherever there was a field hospital and to help the surgeons there. Irene was forever at her right hand. Nobody but a woman of Madame Curie's celebrity could have operated in such an individualistic fashion in the middle of a war; she was then terribly famous as the only person, and a woman at that, who had received two Nobel prizes. The impression upon young Irene of all these events must have been indelible. When in 1956 Irene died of leukemia, few experts doubted that it was the delayed result of this early but protracted exposure to X-rays.

The later life of this couple, the Joliot-Curies, was devoted to technological, educational, and political activities. Politically, both were active members of the Socialist party. Joliot's technical interests had become captivated by the idea of a nuclear reactor whose principles seem to have been perfectly clear to him by about 1939. He bought all the "heavy" water he could get from the power station in Norway, the only place in the world where it was then produced; for a lengthy period he also collected all the purified uranium he could lay his hands on. The distinguished British physicist P. M. S. Blackett states in an official biographical sketch after Joliot's death that there can be no doubt that the first functioning nuclear reactor would have come into existence in France had it not been for the German invasion.

In 1939, when the Germans succeeded in encircling the Maginot Line and marching into France, everyone had left Paris since there was no point in being in the way of street fighting or a bombardment, neither of which, fortunately, took place. After things had become somewhat stabilized, there was a parting of the ways. Perrin, father and son, spent the remainder of the war in North America, as did many other Frenchmen. Joliot chose to return to occupied Paris and to work at the Collège de France where he was a professor. This is a venerable institution of advanced learning and teaching whose members are outside the rigid discipline of the French educational system. Joliot was interrogated by the Gestapo about his uranium and his heavy water; he told them the truth: He had given the uranium to the Ministry of Armaments and didn't know where they had hidden it. So far as the heavy water was concerned, two of his collaborators had taken it to England some time earlier. The Germans made Joliot promise that he would not do any war-connected research, and they forced him to accept several German research workers in his laboratory. He assigned working space to them and then left them alone. Irene had succeeded in escaping with the two children to Switzerland where she remained until the end of the war. The name Curie being so famous, the Hitlerites did not dare molest Joliot, as they did his teacher Langevin,[2] then considered the dean of French scientists. Langevin was put in prison for several weeks, where he was treated like a common criminal; then the French government was forced to retire him from his position, and he was obligated to live under police supervision in Troyes, a small town some distance from Paris. There ensued a constant pilgrimage of distinguished Frenchmen coming from Paris and knocking at his door. A few months before the end of the war Langevin escaped to Switzerland.

Joliot at once became active in the Resistance. This was particularly nerve-racking for a man so much in the public's eye. All the work had to be carried out in secret under the very eyes of the German police and their French collaborators. When the Germans converted a French factory to the production of war materiel that could be shipped to the German front, the factory was blown up at night a couple of weeks later. This is, I believe, a typical case of the things the Resistance did.

Marie and Irene Curie

In the spring of 1942 the physicist Jaques Solomon, who was the son-in-law of Paul Langevin and an ardent Communist, was arrested by the German police and executed before a firing squad. Since the Curie and the Langevin families had been on terms of intimate friendship for several decades, this was more than Joliot could bear: He applied to the then clandestine Communist party for membership and was immediately accepted. A little later Solomon's wife, the daughter of Langevin, was deported to Auschwitz. But since she was not of the Jewish "race" she was apparently not "exterminated." I have read some letters of hers written from Auschwitz, but do not know what happened to her. Pierre Biquard, Joliot's biographer, and a close personal friend, quotes him (p. 70 of the English translation) as having said frequently: "I became a Communist because I am a patriot." At the end of the war, an Atomic Energy Commission was set up after the American model. Joliot was made its director; he was, of course, the guiding spirit who managed to get things started. In 1949 he successfully started up the first French nuclear reactor. But he was not about to become a turncoat who would abandon the Communists. He remained an active Communist to the end of his life and made numerous trips to Russia in the 1950s. This was from the beginning a hopelessly difficult situation. France was an active member of NATO, the period being that of the Cold War when in the U.S. even a loose connection with Russia or anything Communistic was taken as a sign of high treason. The right-wing part of the French press staged a violent campaign of criticism against Joliot which even spilled over into the American press. The rationale was simple enough: An avowed Communist could not be tolerated as the head of Atomic Energy in a major NATO nation. Eventually, the French Government yielded: In 1950 Joliot was relieved of his position, and Francis Perrin groomed as his successor. The work of the Atomic Energy Commission was then already in full swing. Francis Perrin acquitted himself exceedingly well and was somewhat later confirmed as High Commissioner.

It is my impression that it was these events which broke Joliot's spirit. From his viewpoint all this was rank ingratitude from the country for which he had so valiantly and successfully labored for so many years. Frederic Joliot, whatever his great assets and his defects, was always a very ambitious man. In the 1950s he began to feel the exhaustion brought about by the tensions of the Resistance work and by the activity of building up the French Atomic Energy establishment; his health deteriorated. He suffered a severe case of viral hepatitis that left him in a weakened condition, and then Irene died, who had given him two fine children. Two years later, in 1958, he died of internal hemorrhages at age fifty-eight. There seems to be unanimity among the medical men that radiation effects played no major role in his death.

Joliot's biographer, Biquard, entitles one chapter: "Joliot, Rationalist and Communist." He could readily have added: "Pacifist." Joliot spoke a great deal about these last two issues, communism and pacifism, in the later years of his life. I have never been able to see how these several "isms" could be made compatible. But there was Joliot's practicality and simplicity. Many times he told me: I am a simple man, a man of the people; I do not really feel comfortable with the intellectuals with whom my lot has thrown me; I really relax only when of an evening I sit around the fire with a bunch of Breton fisherman. I never had the impression that there was even the slightest degree of affectation in him when he said that. And while he undoubtedly allowed his emotions to drive him in a direction that eventually clashed with the dominant policy of his country, that is not the way I see him. I remember him as Joliot, the practical man, who could design experiments of formidable simplicity and could deal with every man he encountered. Charles de Gaulle, who had appointed Joliot as High Commissioner of Atomic Energy in 1945, was in power once more in 1958; he ordered a State Funeral for Frederic Joliot, attended by masses of Frenchmen.

If today I meet an American who has just returned from Europe, he or she will almost invariably complain of how cold, if not hostile, the French are to tourists. This, I think, is a misjudgment. They are merely indifferent. Julius Caesar already commented on the curiosity of the inhabitants of France. But there is a counterweight to curiosity in the form of the highly vaunted French rationality, not as innate as curiosity but more of an acquired trait. If a Frenchman saunters along the Champs-Elyseés, he soon encounters every variety or representative of his three or four billion fellow humans. It is clearly not rational to get acquainted with all or even most of them. French family relations are notoriously warm but relations that go beyond the family or beyond one's own trade or profession are not usually cultivated. For a foreigner living among Frenchmen, this can sometimes be awkward. In my case it amounted to my developing few social relationships with Frenchmen in my three years in Paris—although there were a few French Academicians of Jewish background, some of them well known, who with their children made a determined effort to meet and help the refugees from Germany.

By the fall of 1933, I was, of course, not the only scientist who had found his way from Germany to Paris. But I was the oldest one, approaching thirty, and in a privileged position because I was on excellent terms with the Perrins and Joliots, the acknowledged leaders of French physics. Every couple of weeks another young man would arrive, and when they were physicists, they were usually sent to me. My god-given helper in the effort to help those people was Jean Langevin, the older son of the great physicist and a physicist himself. He had a position at the School of Physics, not too far from the Rue Pierre Curie, where he usually could be found in his office. He was a chip off the old block, with an excellent mind and a heart of gold. No effort was too big or too small for him to consider whether there was a niche in Greater Paris into which a man of given talents and a given experience would fit. I then took the man around to his destination, and if nothing was available for him, as was very often the case, I took him to the Alliance Israélite. They would at least keep him from starving, which was usually the most I could do. It was impressive to see this flow of talented people which only began to let up by early 1936. I could not forget what Francis Perrin had told me once, very early on: "I don't understand these Germans. Why do they want to kill off science, the cow that nourishes them?" Clearly, this was beyond the scope of his French rationality.

One of the rather annoying aspects of my life was the table in the Institut Henri Poincaré that served as my desk. The library where it was located was under the authority of a "concierge," a wizened, middle-aged veteran of the First World War who had been given this job since he was unable to do harder work. At precisely noon, no more than a minute earlier or later, the concierge would announce in a loud voice: "Closing time, Messieurs." He would wait impatiently for a minute or two until everyone had left, then lock the door, and open up again at two o'clock with the same infallible precision. I realized that I could do nothing about this until I was much better established in Paris, in another year or two, say. By then, however, I planned to emigrate to America, and I didn't think it fair to my French colleagues to indulge in the major bureaucratic operation of acquiring an office of my own, only to relinquish it a few months later.

I did not have a specific group with whom I shared my luncheon. But there are innumerable small restaurants in the Latin quarter that serve a tolerable meal at a modest price. In such a restaurant, the regular menu is invariably accompanied by a pint of the common French red wine, which can only be avoided by a formal refusal. (For myself, I found it a poor idea to consume alcohol in the middle of the day.) After such a repast it was not nearly two o'clock when my office would have reopened; so I adjourned to an outdoor table at one of the large cafés on the Boulevard Saint-Michel where a group of German refugees used to assemble. There were usually between half a dozen and a dozen of us, men and some women, mostly academics, with intellectual interests or at least pretensions. The group was not very stable, people came and went. Most of them had Jewish antecedents, but some were liberals or left-wingers for whom life in Germany had become all too unsafe. There were many rather interesting characters, and those meetings were never boring. Many of the people I met had parents that were either wealthy, or else distinguished in the German scheme of things. Still, it made me feel somewhat odd that I was the only one who could count on a steady monthly income practically forever, tiny as this income might be. All the others had to live on what they had been able to smuggle out, on investments outside of Germany by their parents, or on income from occasional jobs. Much of the conversation was about who would go where, and how; the luckiest tried the United States; others went to South America or to South Africa, and not a few to Israel. Once I met a man who had many social contacts. He told me about Polish Jews he had met who were literally starving to death in Paris. There were some large cafés where the counters were piled high with croissants from early morning till late in the afternoon. These poor wretches would go and filch a few croissants while the kind-hearted waiters would obligingly look the other way.

In the milieu of my coffee-house friends, sexual promiscuity was universal; it was the one thing that made life bearable. Since everybody lived in hotel rooms, there were no practical complications; one asked a girl whether one could accompany her to her hotel, or else the girl asked a man to escort her; the rest came by itself. I remember how I met during my years in Paris two very nice girls, each the daughter of a well-known French professor of Jewish background, but they seemed so extraordinarily staid compared to the uncertain and adventurous life my refugee friends were leading that the gulf between us appeared inconceivably large. In the spring of 1934 I met a girl in the café who had just come from Germany and who impressed me greatly. She was younger than I, pretty, and intelligent, with what I thought was a very pleasing personality. She had clearly been carefully raised in a good Jewish family of a small South-German town. She had come to Paris to visit a sister, but the girl had very little money of her own. We "fell" for each other promptly, and after a few days I asked her to come with me on a vacation at the French Riviera, a day's trip from Paris by rail. We rented a charming cottage overlooking the blue Mediterranean, with the lights of Monaco visible at night in the distance. We had a wonderful time, but at the end of a week my money ran out, and we were forced to return to Paris. I am sure the girl expected me to propose to her, but the eternal foe of true love, my rationality, prevented me from swearing any rash oaths. That in turn hurt the girl's feelings, and a few weeks later she went to Israel. I do not know what became of her thereafter.

True social contacts with Frenchmen were rare and hard to achieve. There are two that I clearly remember, and for all I know they were the only ones I ever had. The first occurred in about August, 1934, when Frederic Joliot asked me to visit him in his family's summer home in the Bretagne (Brittany). The place was a little fishing village called Arcouest (or L'arcouest) on the north coast of that peninsula. There I found a whole colony of houses inhabited in summer by Parisians at some distance from the fishing village proper. Mme. Curie had a home there; so did the Joliots and the Perrins. There were some accommodations for temporary guests, and I was quartered in one of these. Life was very informal, everyone was left to his own devices. One could fish, sail, swim, take sunbaths, read, or just loaf, as one wished. The only formal event was dinner in the later afternoon taken at a long table at whose head sat papa Perrin, carefully barbered as ever, clothed in studied negligence with loosely fitting summer garments. Apart from the Joliots, there were about half a dozen younger couples around and occasionally some of their more grown-up children. I knew none of these, but it turned out that they all were connected with the Sorbonne.

There was one personage, however, who made a deep impression on me, so much so that I remember him vividly to this day. His name was Charles Seignobos, professor of history at the Sorbonne, and the original discoverer, many years earlier, of that hideout, Arcouest. When I first saw him, I estimated him to be about sixty, but recently I looked up his name in a reference book and found him to have been eighty that year. He had an impressive line of historical writings to his credit. He appeared now and then at these dinners and promptly showed himself as one of those who must compulsively dominate any company in which they are. Even old Perrin, never a very vociferous person, was noticeably more quiet around Seignobos.

Seignobos was the representative of a vanishing species, the only one of the kind I ever met, of that ancient occupation, so typically Mediterranean, the rhetorician or orator. It is a very high art indeed, whose master must deal with the language as well as with the content of the language. A cultivated Frenchman can enunciate his speech, so that the words flow off his tongue like drops of honey in that caressing, almost sensuous manner to which the French language so readily lends itself. In addition, Seignobos was also a master of style, and French style is unique, quite different, for instance from that of the English language. French does not have such a rich vocabulary with many synonyms, as does English; instead, a French word takes its meaning, partly at least, from the tissue of the phrase in which it is used. Hence the French language is, in a manner of speaking, composed of phrases rather than of words; the proper use of phrases requires erudition, a knowledge of the context, literary or historical, in which a phrase assumes a particular meaning. Needless to say, M. Seignobos was a master at this (although I am hardly qualified to judge him). His colleagues have criticized him, as I read later, for not being modern and critical enough in his historiography; but for me it represented the revival of a Mediterranean past, of classical antiquity, that my teachers in high school had certainly not presented to me in a similarly engaging form.

The second social event took place in the winter of 1934–1935 when, quite unexpectedly, I received a formal invitation to a Sunday afternoon reception at the house of Duke Maurice de Broglie, older brother by seventeen years of Prince Louis de Broglie. Maurice had done systematic research in the science of physics many years before his younger brother; he had a laboratory devoted to the study of X-rays that had established a very solid position in the French scientific world. There was only a small crowd at this affair; I recognized two people of my own generation whom I knew personally, one of them was L. Leprince-Ringuet, who was then beginning to develop a substantial reputation as an experimentalist specializing in the physics of cosmic rays. The people I saw were not the same crowd that I encountered daily in the Rue Pierre Curie although some degree of overlap might have escaped me in the commotion of a social gathering. This experience brought home to me the frightening depth of the split of French society into two camps, the Right and the Left. Joliot and all his friends were clearly men of the Left. The Perrins were by long tradition members of the Radical-Socialist party which, in spite of its flamboyant name, had become a very moderate party of petty bourgeois, although it still considered itself as mainly a party of the Left. Here now was the Right, the nationalists and the traditionalists. It seemed clear to me that a rumor had gone around that M. Elsasser was a friend of Joliot's and quite possibly a rising star. Still, there seemed a remarkable spirit of *noblesse oblige* in socially welcoming a person who had but fairly recently arrived from abroad, and was closely associated with a prominent figure of the Left.

This cleft between the Left and the Right had been building up very gradually in France. The history books agree that it first came to the surface at the outbreak of the "Affaire Dreyfus" that shook the French world as nothing had done for decades. Alfred Dreyfus came from a Jewish family of the Alsace; he had embraced an army career and in 1894 was a captain assigned to duty with the General Staff. He was suddenly arrested and accused of having sold military secrets to a "foreign power." This scandal lasted for several years and was fully laid to rest only after a high Court of Law had declared Dreyfus innocent in 1906. In honor of the French nation I should add that the Dreyfus affair has been the only outburst of political anti-Semitism in modern French history.

Prince Louis de Broglie was not at his brother's party. He almost never went into society. He was, in fact, one of the most restrained, nearly asocial, and withdrawn persons I have met. But when Louis de Broglie did get involved, his ancient breeding showed clearly enough: One could no more conceive that he would be vulgar than that he would be condescending. De Broglie had passed the war in the French Army as a lowly wireless operator. When the war had ended and de Broglie was ready to follow his brother in the study of physics, he was already past twenty six, and he was in his early thirties when he was far enough advanced to think of a thesis. A French Ph.D. thesis is much bigger than the corresponding American species; whereas the American thesis is taken as evidence that a person can do research work under suitable broad supervision, a French thesis is meant as a piece of original research done by the author with some breadth and depth. The chairman of Louis de Broglie's Ph.D. committee was Paul Langevin. At that time Langevin was professor at the Collège de France, and as such had the greatest freedom in choosing both his collaborators and the subjects of his research work. Still, at that time, around 1924, before Schrödinger had made it into a respectable branch of mathematical physics, the set of de Broglie's ideas, extraordinary and challenging as they were, were also highly speculative and "far out." Since I knew de Broglie's thesis myself at this early stage (before Schrödinger, that is) I venture to say that only a minute percentage of physicists would have had both the vision and the courage to accept such a set of ideas as the subject of a thesis. I have often asked myself what I would have done had I been in Langevin's situation. I believe I would have followed the vast majority who would have said that while such a discovery ought to be elaborated, a thesis should be centered on a more conventional problem. And where except in France could one have seen an aristocrat with a pedigree a mile long supported by a genius who was a son of the people and a communist in all but formal party membership (which latter he acquired after the war, shortly before his death)? Here, one saw advanced a proposition that steered science into a direction different from the one it had held for 250 years, since the days of Newton. Langevin was a friend of Einstein's and of many other leading physicists; there is no question that Langevin's moral support was largely responsible for de Broglie's work joining the scientific mainstream almost at once, instead of first being forgotten and then rediscovered years later, as has happened so often in history.

There were two ways for a physicist working in Paris such as myself to make one's results known: One was through the French Academy of Sciences which published a weekly report known throughout the scientific world as *Comptes Rendus*, the initial words of a lengthy title (meaning simply *Reports* in English). Then there was the *Journal de physique*, a regular periodical published by the French Physical Society edited at the address of the School of Physics. Since there was no formal scheme for the review of papers submitted, they were simply printed as they came in from, or through the hands of, a person well known—the vast amount of technical work needed to issue a scientific periodical was done by Jean Langevin, if my recollection serves me right.

When I had arrived in Paris I was intensely aware that my own publication record was quite poor for one aiming to be a professional research scientist. I had often been hesitant and inattentive, if not downright negative toward seeing my work in print. As psychologists would undoubtedly say, I had had "inhibitions." Now in Paris, I realized I had another last chance—undeservedly, but there it was. The rules of the *Comptes Rendues* said that the length of a note could not exceed 2-½ printed pages, and this was rigorously enforced. Since the pages were large and had two columns, that space was really enough to formulate clearly any ordinary communication. Another rule forbade more than five notes per year for any one individual author. After I had written my first note, I went to Louis de Broglie, who was closest to my own interests and who, as a member of the Academy, could submit it in my behalf. He told me that he had not the slightest wish to read my manuscript; if he ever had any desire to read what I had written, he could always do this later at his leisure in print. I should hand my manuscript to him before the start of the Academy's session, which took place at the same hour of the afternoon at the same day of each week. Then, a week later I went to the official printer of the Academy where an envelope with the proofs of my article was waiting for me. Having corrected these, I had only to await the next issue of the *Comptes Rendus* a week later. By that time I had learned my lesson about the need for publication for a future research scientist: In my three years in Paris, I tried to publish my five notes in the *Comptes Rendus* every year. Looking back at them now, they do not seem as bad as this somewhat cynical story of their origin might make me believe; doubtless they benefited greatly from the rapid progress of nuclear physics in these years. In addition, I wrote in that period seven somewhat larger articles for the *Journal de physique*, and never thereafter did I feel any undue bashfulness about publishing ideas or results that I considered worthwhile. In accordance with the decision I had made when I came to Paris, I concentrated fully on the structure and dynamics of the atomic nucleus.

An atomic nucleus consists of a certain number of "nucleons" (a collective term embracing both protons and neutrons, particles of comparable mass). The number of nucleons can vary from one, the proton itself that can be the nucleus of a hydrogen atom, to well over two hundred for the heaviest elements known. At that time Niels Bohr's school in Copenhagen had decided that the nucleus was a homogeneous agglomeration of nucleons without further internal structure; this was known as the "liquid drop" model of the nucleus. There was considerably empirical evidence that some truth inhered in this model; but I had developed certain doubts (on evidence that would be too long to quote), and I thought that eventually the nucleus would be found to have a degree of internal structure. I decided to follow up this idea, and a large part of my efforts in France was spent on it. In the fall of 1933, K. Guggenheimer, a physical chemist, came to Paris from Berlin. He found a temporary position in a laboratory of the Collège de France. Since everyone in physics at that time was beginning to question how the nucleus was held together, he and I couldn't help meeting on this topic. He had a great deal of knowledge of how molecules are held together starting from atoms. There are many analogies with nuclei but no identity, since the energies involved in the nuclear case are a hundred thousand times larger than in the molecular case. Still, from ordinary chemical reaction kinetics, one thing was clear. Variations of binding energies of the nucleons would in many cases be reflected in nuclear "abundances." Abundance is a technical term for the relative proportions of different kinds of nuclei. This was significant information because the abundances of many sorts of nuclei had been measured. I proposed a joint piece of research, but we were unable to agree, and in the summer of 1935 Guggenheimer by himself published two articles on the binding energies of nucleons in the *Journal de physique*. Some months later he told me that he had found a place in England. He disappeared, and since neither of us was much of a correspondent, I soon lost track of him. I had, in 1935, found a trick to obtain, at least approximately, the binding energies of individual protons or neutrons from the directly measured disintegration energies of the very heavy, naturally radioactive nuclei. This enabled me to show in detail how beyond the end of a nuclear shell the binding energy of a nucleon suddenly decreases to as little as a third or quarter of the preceding value. I was satisfied that I had established the existence of shells, although it soon became clear that they were not simply analogous to the shell of atoms. Later, the numbers of nucleons at which shells were closed, 2, 8, 20, 28, 50, 82, 126, became known as "magic numbers," but since I was not a party to the jargon of Los Alamos, I know not much about the origin of this term. I did some other theoretical work on nuclei in that period; one piece, jointly with Francis Perrin, was a theoretical explanation of the exceptionally large capture cross sections for slow neutrons which certain nuclei had shown. Here, we had no head-start over several others whose results came out in print about the same time as ours; as one could have expected, Hans Bethe was among them, his treatment being not only more extensive and general but also a couple of months ahead of everybody else.

The deeper physical understanding of the forces between nucleons that brought about the nuclear shell structures became possible only two decades later when as a result of the Manhattan Project and the tremendous growth of nuclear research in universities all over the world that followed it, the forces between nucleons began to be understood in quantitative detail. In 1963 the Nobel prize for physics was divided between Eugene Wigner, who obtained one-half which he had deserved long before, and two people who had between them worked out the theory of nuclear shell structure. They were a German theoretical physicist, Hans Jensen, and an American, Maria G. Mayer. This was the same lady who had been a Ph.D. candidate of Max Born's in Göttingen just after me; but we had not seen each other in the intervening years. In an article that Maria Mayer wrote in the journal *Science* (vol. 165) in 1964, she duly quotes my earlier contributions to this problem but also points out, perfectly correctly, that the underlying mathematical theory could not possibly have been understood before the knowledge of nuclear interactions had sufficiently advanced. which occurred only in the 1950s.

I have been asked often in my life whether I did not regret having "come so close" to the Nobel prize. My answer has always been that there would have been too high a price to pay for a purely external decoration. After all, this would have implied that I would have had to remain a full-time nuclear specialist and would have been involved in all the activities that led to Hiroshima, Nagasaki, and to all other untold disasters that still hang over the heads of mankind. I could have no idea of this, of course, at that earlier time, since nuclear fission was not discovered until 1938, when I had already taken leave from research activities in nuclear physics.

The deaths, in part sacrificial, of the various members of the Curie and Joliot families were not entirely in vain in one special respect. Today, the French have their flourishing, rather well-endowed, and, what is most important, relatively autonomous C.N.R.S., their Center for National Scientific Research, that is contributing greatly to science.

8

Passage to the New World

By the fall of 1934, my situation in Paris had been stabilized. I had been appointed to a small position as "investigator" on the budget of the budding French Science Center and, given the circumstances, this was likely to last almost indefinitely. This, in turn, brought home to me the need for making a personal decision about the future: If I settled in France and started on a career as a French public servant, I would certainly want to become a French citizen, sooner rather than later. But I quickly learned that this was only possible if I did two years of French military service, after which time I would instantly be made a citizen; under any other circumstances, I would have to fight almost forever with a bureaucracy determined to keep me out. There were good historical reasons for this: France, a country of about forty million people at the outbreak of World War I, had long ago so reduced its birth rate that the population was stationary. But the war had been terrible; there were about four and a half million casualties, of whom nearly two million were dead or missing; it was by far the most cruel bloodletting the country had undergone since it had been conquered by Julius Caesar, or since the black death in the Middle Ages had decimated it. This had left a social vacuum, an absence of the competitive pressure that prevails in healthy societies. Here was the cause, as far as I could see, of the extraordinary ingrown character so evident among the academic people of my acquaintance. It would clearly be a few more years before I could learn the language thoroughly enough to acquire a social ambiance beyond the circle of the German refugees and an occasional French Jewish family.

One thing I very much appreciated in the meantime, even as a relative outsider, was the remarkable historical continuity in French life. I began to understand that a "classical" education was far more meaningful in this environment than it had been where I grew up. History, beginning with the ancient Gauls and Romans, was in the air here; one was inescapably surrounded by it on all sides. There was far more historical continuity in France than I had ever observed or was ever to see elsewhere (never having lived in England).

Then there was my alternative: to go to the United States. This possibility became more difficult once I found myself in a research position paid by the French government. In that period, all over the world, employment, even in scientific research, had become extremely hard to get. Having acquired a stable position in France, however small, I could no longer ask any one of my American acquaintances to assist me to go to the United States; this would have been interpreted as a reprehensible show of egoism.

Between 1933–1935 I thought a lot about these alternatives, but it was my parents' situation that made me decide to try my luck in America. By 1934 my father, then in his early sixties and ill, had retired, and my parents had moved to a small house they had built in the Black Forest. But by that time the direction of the Nazi policies had become clear: In the midst of a worldwide depression, a country that fifteen years before had been defeated in a major war, was furiously rearming—and, in part at least, the property of the non-Aryans was paying for it. The non-Aryans were a larger group than those classified by religious denomination as Jewish, since in the preceding century of vast economic expansion many Jews had moved and married into the middle and upper classes, often with a change of faith. The growing war machine had to be fed by the property of these people. I foresaw that before long my parents would lose their house and soon thereafter all other property, and finally their retirement income. I did not know anything about extermination camps for Jews; in fact, it was not until the end of the war that I read of these in the newspapers. But I felt almost certain that in a very few years my parents would be reduced to indigents, deprived of home, income, and normal medical care. There was also my sister, but I did not have any serious worry about her. She was a type quite different from me: easygoing, sociable, and with many friends. I thought she would manage to leave when the time came, and she did.

But it was absolutely impossible even to mention my parents' predicament to any Frenchman: I tried it only once and was greeted with uncomprehending laughter; this was a problem clearly much too far from their circle of interests. Once I had come to the United States, American law entitled me to bring my parents into the country. This made me decide to make every effort to go to the United States, even if I could not get any assistance from my scientific colleagues. A few years later, I found that my foresight had been fully justified. Early in 1939 my parents were enabled to go to England for temporary residence, pending their passage to the United States, helped by the unselfish efforts of a Protestant clergyman of their acquaintance in Germany, and by British Quakers. About a year later, they came to America and later lived in Chicago with my sister.

Eventually, with the help of the aforementioned friend of our family, the wealthy Swiss banker Mr. Kaufmann, who had excellent connections in the United States, my affidavit was settled to the satisfaction of the U.S. consul in Paris; after the usual bureaucratic delays I received an immigration visa in the spring of 1935. At that time large German steamers still went to New York regularly, and my parents bought me a ticket on one of these. I took the boat from Le Havre to New York early in the summer of 1935. The ambiance on the boat itself was one of subdued nazification; it was the last closeup view of this phenomenon I ever had. On the boat I became acquainted with a girl from Chicago named Margaret Trahey who was returning from a vacation visit to some old friends of her family in Austria. We seemed to understand each other well from the beginning. She was reading *The Search* by the British novelist C. P. Snow. It contained the story of a talented young man who, rising from small circumstances, becomes a physicist in academic research. It had appeared just recently and was the beginning of Snow's literary career after he had himself started adult life as a research physicist. I was the first representative of that species Margaret had met; that, of course, helped greatly in our getting acquainted. She invited me to visit her and her family who lived in Chicago; I did this a few weeks later. Margaret had become the private secretary to an exceedingly wealthy man, a Mr. Pullman, heir to the sleeping-car fortune. Her father was Irish, her mother was Scotch, and both had been born in Europe. Margaret, who was the eldest of four, helped to maintain her mother's household.

I still remember vividly, as if it were yesterday, my first look upon the Statue of Liberty when the steamer entered New York harbor. I think that only those who have undergone years of oppression and persecution can fully appreciate what this means to an immigrant: the chance to begin life over again without the impediments that Europe throws in the way of everyone who is not born into a privileged social class— and how many are? I had myself grown up under favorable economic circumstances, but certainly not under similarly favorable social ones.

When I arrived in the United States free immigration had been stopped, but the country still accommodated itself to the reception of persecuted minorities, and still occasionally does today. But in such political matters it is the spirit that counts, not just economic considerations. Comparable conditions, after all, prevailed in South America, but there seems to be little there that corresponds to the reception of the downtrodden masses at the feet of the Statue of Liberty.

Disembarkation at New York was uneventful. Two days later I visited an old acquaintance from Europe, I. I. Rabi, at Columbia University. He arranged to have me stay in a dormitory room on the Columbia campus; he also introduced me to Harold Urey, then also at Columbia, whom I saw often many years later in La Jolla. Urey was, I think, one of the great men of that period; his book *The Planets* was the first work to put the study of the solar system on a solid scientific foundation, by combining classical methods of astronomy with modern chemistry and physics. Without Urey's work the later exploration of the moon and solar system by rockets would have been more a showpiece of technology than a true scientific undertaking. I also met Dean Pegram, an older and most impressive man, very tall, with a stern but fatherly air. He was the moving spirit behind the scientific development of Columbia University in these days; he, together with Vannevar Bush, was at the helm of much of the American scientific establishment during World War II. Although Pegram remained in New York during the war, his later participation in the Manhattan Project was important. A little later I went to the Bell Telephone Laboratories to visit Davisson with whose work I had had some connection ten years earlier (see Chapter 3). That laboratory had been set up in some commercial lofts at the south end of Manhattan; it was puny compared to the sprawling present-day Bell Telephone Laboratories in New Jersey that teem with tousands of scientists.

While I met these men and a number of others, I was, of course, alert for possible employment, but it was clear enough that there was none. In fact, it soon became obvious that most Americans had not succeeded in developing a sufficiently hard shell against such vicissitudes of life as seeing one's fellow men out of employment. The reaction to being told this was in most cases somewhat cringing, like that of a man who, faced with a begging leper with open sores, tries to escape without appearing too callous. Clearly, life in America was altogether different from life in France, where centuries of tradition had led to a psychological attitude that made it much easier to deal with almost any contingency, including one's neighbor's troubles. Here, lack of employment touched a raw spot that many otherwise decent people just could not handle, even with all the goodwill in the world.

From New York I travelled to the University of Michigan at Ann Arbor, where I planned to attend a summer course given by Enrico Fermi. This trip was my first experience of America outside of New York; and that town, clearly, was not typical. In Ann Arbor I was lucky to meet a colleague of mine, David Inglis, a theoretical physicist whom I had known two years earlier in Pauli's Institute in Zürich. He and his wife Betty were the first young American intellectuals that I met on their homeground. They lived on a modest income but had a car, of course. David had been born and raised in Ann Arbor. In the month that I spent there, I often saw this couple; they succeeded in introducing me to many of the minor aspects of American living, the nuances that are not explained in the guide books and which make one feel more at home than any number of printed pages. The one literary exception is de Tocqueville's famous *Democracy in America*, that I read early in my stay. The first volume, at least, is full of penetrating observations about Americans and their way of life and thinking that is not matched in any other work.

In high school and during my early college years, I had read many generalities about the United States. These writers invariably thought of the United States as a large-scale replica of the modern European national state. This gives a completely false image of American reality, economic, political, and psychological (de Tocqueville, by the way, does not fall into this trap). The European national states, even those which were formed only fairly recently, such as Italy and Germany, are the present outward form of a millenial reality, whereas in the United States almost nothing and almost no one's American ancestry dates back for more than 200 years. All citizens of the United States are fully aware that almost everyone's ancestors left home to escape intolerable or at least highly unsatisfactory economic or social conditions. The "melting pot" is very much a reality: At the foundation of the Republic in 1776, the population was about two and a half million, a little over one percent of that of the bicentennial in 1976. The immigrants came from two dozen European nationalities, plus the Africans whose forebears arrived as slaves. The psychology of the American people that resulted from this rapid development has been described to perfection by de Tocqueville who wrote in 1830; it does not seem to have changed at all since then. The one aspect of the American mind that impressed

me most, very early on, was its cosmopolitanism. Europeans also are
now beginning to acquire this point of view, but very slowly. There is a
background of breadth here that, I believe, represents the best in
America. Nobody can be sure of the economic future; however, I feel
confident that its spiritual future as the leader in the struggle for
human brotherhood is still largely to come. For a time this was
obscured by a tendency toward brute politico-military domination of
most of the world by the United States; but this phase, fortunately, has
not lasted too long. If during my stay in France I was most impressed
by their sensitivity (*la delicatesse du coeur* is a term frequently used by
French writers) I was now, among Americans, deeply impressed by
their generosity. This character trait can be made more intelligible,
although not, of course, "explained," by American history. The
frontiersman was accustomed to meeting every kind of foreigner who
might have barely mastered the English language but who shared the
same dangers with him: the wilderness, the elements, and the Indians,
except for the few instances when the latter were peaceful. The most
violent economic ups and downs have been incessant in American life;
hence, no one counts on the future. The prospect of an uncertain
economic future does not breed despair or cynicism as it does so often
in Europe. The well-known proverb, "three generations from overalls
to overalls," often expresses the attitude of the average American
toward wealth. There is thus another side to the American psychology
apart from the preoccupation with getting rich, but it is "other" not
"otherwordly," as it was through so much of European history. But
this aspect of the American character is still largely unrealized; I have
little doubt that it will someday be transformed into major achievements in history.

But to return to Ann Arbor: I was attending Fermi's lectures and
came to know him personally to some degree. He was speaking about
the theory of electrons in metallic conductors. His lectures were
extraordinarily elegant and full of admirable mathematical tricks; but
at that time I felt that he had not found it possible to prepare himself
fully. Since Fermi had just emigrated from Italy, this seemed not too
surprising, especially since his genius could not be hidden by any
presentation. Fermi was perhaps the most scientifically gifted of all the
physicists I have encountered. In the few personal contacts we had, he
was invariably simple and modest, a posture that is, of course, easier to
assume for a man who is fully conscious of his superior abilities than
for lesser men.

After the summer session in Ann Arbor, I went to Chicago where I visited extensively with Margaret and her family. We became sufficiently well acquainted to correspond frequently after my return to Paris. While in Chicago I introduced myself to the famous physicist, Arthur Compton, who was the leading experimental man in physics in Chicago at that time. He had discovered what became known as the Compton effect for which he had received the Nobel prize in 1927. The Compton effect is probably the most spectacular phenomenon to show that light is not simply a wave motion but exhibits corpuscular properties. The Compton effect is a scattering of X-rays that can be interpreted only in terms of a collision between an electron and light, which latter must be considered as a quantum with a given amount of momentum; if, on the other hand, one treats the X-ray as if it were a light-wave, no understanding of the Compton effect results. That day in 1935 I had a fairly lengthy and pleasant scientific conversation with Arthur Compton, but when I mentioned incidentally that I was looking for a position in the United States, he became highly emotional. He told me that he considered it unethical to give positions in the United States to Europeans while many American scientists were still unemployed. He had just sent back home again a young German physicist named Wilhelmy who had been visiting on a fellowship, although this young man had a few months ago met and married an American girl. It so happened that I knew Wilhelmy; he was the nephew and assistant of Dessauer, the man who ran an institute in Frankfurt that studied the biological applications of radiation (see end of Chapter 4). A couple of years later I heard the sad ending of this story from Mrs. Wilhelmy whom I had befriended by then: Her husband, she told me, returned to Germany where he was soon drafted into the army. But this didn't last long: Being of rather delicate constitution, he died of the exertions of a forced march a short while thereafter. This event must have struck Arthur Compton rather severely, for from that moment he was always the first and the most vociferous among those who helped displaced scholars from Europe. At the end of my stay in Chicago, I returned to New York to take the boat back to Europe for another year in Paris.

During this period, some months after my return, I once had a conversation with Frederic Joliot which I remember vividly. At first, we were just chatting, having nothing too serious in our minds. "You know," said Fred suddenly, "nuclear physics is just the kind of activity that could be organized like an industrial enterprise. There should be one man for each type of machine, one man to run a particle accelerator, one who runs a Wilson cloud chamber, one who runs photographic counters, and so on . . . , and one man in the middle who thinks and then tells the others to perform various experiments. This would speed things up tremendously." I realized quite well, of course, that he was just fantasizing. And, of course, as in many dreams, the dreamer was placing himself in a central, controlling position. But, nevertheless, I felt that there was also much truth in Fred's fantasy, and if it was possible to imagine nuclear physics in this manner, reality, too, would very likely move in that direction—as it has done in the past forty years. Nuclear physics has increasingly become a mixture of large-scale technology and high-powered mathematical analysis with little relation to things that can be visualized simply and handled by individuals. With my apparently inborn tendency toward individualism, I found this prospect slightly frightening, and I thought about it often in the months that followed. Fred himself never slowed down enough in his own life to realize this idyllic picture of the man in the middle.

Since my prospects of being accepted in nuclear research in the United States were evidently slim, as my first trip had shown, I began to think seriously about another specialty. By that time I had already developed in embryonic form many of the philosophical ideas that are discussed in Chapter 6. I began to think that much of the science of the future would be concerned with the study of complex systems. The ideal place for studying complexity would, of course, be in biology. But for me biology, which requires much chemistry, seemed too remote. I later approached biological subjects by way of certain semiphilosophical ideas that I have outlined in Chapter 6. Beyond atomic and nuclear physics, I had learned astronomy and mathematics as minor subjects in my Ph.D. examination, and had also done some independent reading in astronomy. It occurred to me that in geophysics I could indulge the study of complex systems, and largely, moreover, with the tools of the theoretical physicist and some knowledge of astronomy. It was also clear, with the rapid development of aviation and the rise of worldwide shipping and communication, that governments would invest in geophysical research. These speculations were, in fact, vindicated in the years that followed. I did not consider that military operations would also become worldwide and would totally and qualitatively alter the nature of warfare and international relations.

As I formulated plans for my next trip to the United States, I decided to visit California, specifically Pasadena, where the California Institute of Technology, which had been founded around 1920, was an already famous and still rapidly growing institution. Furthermore, California was not then as crowded as it is now. I decided to cut loose from my moorings in Paris, go to California, and try to "sink or swim" there. (In the event, matters at Caltech were more straightforward than I had expected.) Next I wrote to Robert Oppenheimer about my circumstances, about my first trip to the U.S. in 1935, and about my intention to go this time to Pasadena. I knew that he had been a professor in Berkeley since leaving Göttingen nine years earlier and that he also spent two or three months in the spring of every year at Caltech. He answered promptly—it was our first exchange of letters—and tendered me a double invitation: First, I should go to visit his father, who would be advised of my coming, when I came through New York. (His mother had died a short time before this.) Then I should spend a few days at his ranch in New Mexico on my way to Pasadena. I accepted both.

There was no technical difficulty to my returning to the United States after I had once formally entered as an immigrant. Correspondingly, I felt none of the emotional stirrings of my first setting foot in the Western hemisphere. Shortly after my arrival I called Robert Oppenheimer's father, and we agreed on a time for a visit. He had a large apartment in a rather elegant residential district of Manhattan. The father, Julius Oppenheimer received me in a very large room that contained his desk, among other things. I had to exercise all my self-control to look at him and not at the magnificent paintings on the walls. But gradually I managed to count three van Goghs and three Gauguins, which in these opulent surroundings could only be certified originals. Clearly, Robert Oppenheimer had not grown up in an average middle-class household. The father, a businessman, was very much a man of the world in his meeting with me, at ease himself and able to set his guest's mind at rest. He very soon directed the conversation away from generalities and to my own person. It seemed to me that he was not just animated by courtesy but was really interested in finding out what "made me tick." Presumably, he did not see many young Europeans. After about half an hour he took me to another room where tea and refreshments were served, and I then took my leave. My friend Charlotte later told me that during her first visit to the United States she had experienced on a number of occasions the hospitality of this warm-hearted and generous household.

I had stayed in New York for a few days without contacting any colleagues and had used this time to get better acquainted with that marvelous and complex city. But I was more anxious to go on to Chicago, where to none of the family's surprise Margaret and I announced our engagement. A year later she left her position in Chicago, came to California and we were married. By that time Margaret's family no longer needed her assistance and later on, between our two small incomes, we could manage in a very modest style. Considerably later we had two children, a girl and five years later a boy. After seventeen years of marriage which gave me the deepest happiness I have experienced in my life, I lost Margaret under extremely tragic circumstances; I did not remarry for ten years.

In 1936, after some weeks in Chicago, I took the westward train that goes to Albuquerque and Los Angeles. This railroad line passes at some distance from the city of Santa Fe; I had been told to get off the train at a smaller station in that neighborhood. Robert Oppenheimer was waiting there and took me in his elegant sports car to his ranch in the Sangre de Cristo mountains, on the east side of the Rio Grande valley. Through some clearings in the pines, one could occasionally see the mountain range on the valley's western side, the region where the Los Alamos Laboratory was later to rise. Oppenheimer had bought his ranch very soon after returning from Göttingen and later had spent most or all of his summers there. He had assumed a regal bearing, that showed clearly when he was surrounded by the three or four students whom he had invited to the ranch. The one that seemed closest to him was Robert Serber, who eventually became a theoretical physicist of stature and taught for many years at Columbia University. Robert Oppenheimer was outwardly unchanged but seemed in much better health than I remembered. He was very self-assured and natural and moved at ease among the small group which surrounded him, and which he dominated effortlessly. I had never before realized how much of an extravert Robert was. (The terms introversion and extraversion had been coined by Jung around 1910; he had emphasized that they are genetic traits that have little to do with intellectual capability. In fact, Jung uses scientists corresponding to those two types as examples: The extravert has mastered masses of data and then succeeds in putting some empirical order into them; the intravert creates in his own mind a picture of reality and then projects it upon the external world, modifying it in the process until it fits the facts.) As I learned later in Pasadena, Robert Oppenheimer knew by heart every one of the many hundreds of nuclear reactions that had been discovered by then; he not only remembered them almost instantly; he also remembered the quantitative details and the place where they had been published. With these skills and his fabulous ability for dealing with people, he was ideally suited to preside over one of the most phenomenal engineering developments of recorded history, the invention of the atomic bomb.

For the day after my arrival, Robert had arranged a trip on horseback through the surrounding mountains. We left after breakfast, and I was told to climb in the saddle of a somewhat elderly, extremely gentle horse on which I merely had to relax. After about half an hour, I learned that it was unprofitable to try to direct the beast which, clearly, was an expert in climbing about the extremely rocky countryside. We returned in the midafternoon. I was exhilarated by the magnificence of the country but quite tired from the altitude, the open air, and the unaccustomed exercise of riding. Robert was as fresh as if it were early morning and said that now I must try a chili drink that he prepared himself according to an old recipe. Chili is, of course, Mexican red pepper commonly used as a condiment; I tried in vain to refuse. A mouthful of the vermilion fluid tasted like I thought sulfuric acid would taste, and I spat it out by a mere reflex action. Oppenheimer informed me that I had passed the first, but failed the second part of the initiation ceremony at the ranch.

I am not quite sure whether it was at this occasion or somewhat later in Pasadena that I first encountered Robert's younger brother, Frank. He and his wife, Jackie, are among the most charming people I have met. Frank had made the mistake of following his brother in becoming a physicist. He had also adopted Robert's leftist political leanings. But whereas the latter was extremely discreet about these interests, Frank was not. He frequently boasted about his "proletarian" sympathies. He did not seem to be aware of how unrealistic this was, but there was no question about his simple sincerity. In place of an automobile, he drove a small truck. The truck was not just meant to indicate the proletarian leanings of its owner, but was also very useful for what was then one of the most fashionable sports in the area: excursions into Baja, California, a desert-type country with some very beautiful scenery. Baja had then only dirt roads and no settlements with telephones, or even without them, so that a person could easily get lost and never be heard of again, in this peninsula that is nearly 1000 kilometers long. Frank Oppenheimer's troubles started during the McCarthy era when his brother's name began to appear frequently in the headlines. He was eventually ousted from a professorship of physics at a state university. Thereafter, for many years he operated a ranch in New Mexico where his children grew up, but years later he returned to a university.

After I had relaxed for a few days at Oppenheimer's ranch, I took the train to Los Angeles. After arriving in Pasadena I introduced myself to a physicist there, Jesse DuMond, to whom a common friend in New York had given me an introduction. Jesse was kind enough to show me around the campus and introduce me to various people, among them Linus Pauling, the famous chemist, then still young but already the head of the chemistry department. Pauling almost at once offered me a place in his laboratory. I thought about this proposal for a couple of days but feeling that I had no background whatsoever in chemistry, I decided to refuse. This, I think, was one of the wiser decisions I made in my life.

In time Jesse and I became good friends. I remember many occasions when Margaret and I spent an evening or a holiday with him and his family. Jesse, who was a physicist, was independently wealthy and had come to Pasadena on his own to try to work in the laboratories of Caltech. He had been given space, but Robert Millikan, the head of Caltech, flatly refused to give him a salary under these circumstances. This was altogether in style for there were many stories about Millikan's parsimoniousness, usually connected to his Scotch descent. Only after many years did Jesse acquire a professor's title, and eventually even enough space in his laboratory to have some assistants working with him.

But this was much later. In 1936, Jesse made an appointment for me to see Millikan, my first introduction to this remarkable man whom I was to see a good many times thereafter.[1] At that first occasion I did not think it made sense to waste the time of so high an administrator; I very briefly told him that I had been forced to leave Europe by the political events and that I was looking for a position in the United States. I explained that I was a theoretician who had worked in atomic and nuclear physics, but that I was quite willing to consider alternate forms of research; for instance I was somewhat interested in geophysics. "If you want to do geophysics we can use you," said Millikan. "If you want a place in nuclear physics or in astrophysics, I can do absolutely nothing for you." (Note: Ever since the foundation of the nearby Mount Wilson Observatory, whose offices were in Pasadena, this region had become the mecca of astrophysicists.) I was prepared for this and

had therefore suggested geophysics as the alternative. Millikan continued: "If you are serious about geophysics, I can promise you that I will
find some salary for you." Although it eventually took him the better
part of a year, Millikan kept his word. The salary was infinitesimal, but
it kept me from starving. When I started to work, the rather general
term "geophysics" was specialized in my case to "meteorology." Of
this I will speak in the next chapter.

It was sometime later that Millikan told me the history of his
involvement with geophysics: During the First World War he had been
director of the Signal Corps laboratories. The Signal Corps is the
branch of the Army in charge of all communications, and at that time
radio, or "wireless" as it was then called, was just beginning to acquire
the central role for military communications in action which it has
increasingly had ever since. But radio communication is affected by the
atmosphere and by other conditions of the earth, the solid earth as well.
At that time there were no specialists in geophysics in America who
could deal with these problems. This sparked Millikan's interest in all
of geophysics; thereafter, he conceived it as one of his missions to
provide the United States with research men and research facilities in
geophysics. The high point of this endeavor was his success in
bringing the distinguished seismologist, Beno Gutenberg, from Germany to Caltech in 1930. The institution has been a leading center of
seismology ever since. When I went there, Millikan was actively
engaged in developing meteorology, and since he took great personal
interest in it, I had occasion to talk to him now and then during my five
years' stay in Pasadena.

Millikan was one of the most extraordinary men I ever encountered.
His forte was not original thought but subtle and controlled strength
in everything he did, and he did many things—Millikan was a human
powerhouse. I have never seen anyone who could work the way he did.
When younger he had done the oil-drop experiment on which his
scientific fame rests. The oil drop, minute in size, is kept from slowly
falling through the air by means of a suitably adjusted electric field; for
such drops usually carry an electric charge acquired when they are
produced by spraying the fluid. This method had been known and used
for a few years when Millikan improved all its technical aspects to such
a degree that no doubt was left of the charge's occurring in multiples of
a small unit, that of the electron. The inventor of the method, named
Ehrenhaft, professor in Vienna, fought for many years with Millikan
because the method which he had invented did not give such clearcut

Walter Heitler, Robert Millikan, R.H. Fowler, Marie Curie, Werner Heisenberg, and Léon Brillouin at the Rome Conference on nuclear physics, October 1931.

results in his hands as in those of Millikan; Ehrenhaft claimed that it was impossible to prove the existence of electrons in this way.

But by the time I met him, Millikan had abandoned this work to study cosmic rays. This was no accident; it was, I think, in part the attraction of the term "cosmic" that appealed to him in later life. It was a trait rooted in Millikan's personality: When one came to know him better, one could recognize two contradictory trends in his make-up. On the one hand, he tended to be genuinely modest, no doubt due to his being the son of a clergyman with strict views. For instance, when in 1921 he was offered the presidency of the then novel Caltech, he insisted that his title be changed to Chairman of the Executive Council. But then, once he was at the head of a privately financed institution, he realized the necessity of successful propaganda to keep money flowing in. This corresponded to another side of his personality. He was forever giving speeches about science and the exploration of Nature, sonorous and somewhat lyrical. Science and Religion was one of his preferred subjects, presented before wealthy audiences, and I came to admire the way specific technical details of science were embedded into a beautiful fog of oratory. He had become quite famous for this trait. Once, when a new building was being erected on the campus, someone had painted on the wooden fence surrounding the site: Jesus saves. Two days later the students had elaborated on this; it said underneath: But Millikan gets the credit.

I came to be somewhat acquainted with Millikan's secretary, who occasionally showed me his appointment calendar. Every half-hour was blocked out, and frequently filled, from ten in the morning until the middle of the afternoon. When I called up this secretary to ask for an appointment, I almost never had to wait more than twenty-four hours before seeing him. The technique of these appointments was remarkable: Millikan opened the door of his office almost precisely at the set time. He remained standing while I stated my business. During this he gently guided me toward his big window where we could stand and lean against the sill; when Millikan did not look at me he looked pensively out of the window. I found this a much better arrangement than sitting on a chair and looking at the big man across a desk. Slowly then, Millikan began to move around the room inducing me to follow him, and suddenly I realized that I was facing his office door and that this was the sign my interview was over. After leaving, I was astonished to realize that all but three minutes of the appointed half hour had passed.

As I remarked, Millikan's working power was almost beyond belief.
When I came to Pasadena, he was in his late sixties and had slowed
down a little, but only a little. There were many stories about Millikan
when he was somewhat younger: The graduate students that worked in
his laboratory could expect him to drop in not infrequently around
midnight, clad in his tuxedo, coming from a party which his position
had required. But he was almost as lively as if it was still morning, and
the students had learned to be prepared for such visits. One peculiar
aspect of the man was his seeming inability to understand that other
men did not possess his superhuman stamina. When he first came to
Pasadena, he had planned to make Caltech entirely a graduate school
in pure and applied science, but this was too one-sided and soon an
undergraduate college was added, also concentrating on science. This
remained small, however, with an enrollment of not more than a few
hundred. There was one severe problem plaguing this establishment:
The suicide rate among undergraduate students amounted to an
average of about one a year, sometimes two. This was often discussed,
of course, by the faculty, but little could be done about it without
"lowering the standards" as the academic phrase goes. Millikan and
his collaborators were far from ready to do this.

During the worst years of the economic depression, around 1930,
Caltech, which had rapidly expanded, suffered a severe financial crisis.
For a time it seemed that bankruptcy was unavoidable. But Millikan
was equal to the crisis. He arranged a large banquet to which he invited
several hundred of the wealthiest people in the Los Angeles area. The
purpose was to present the future plans of the Institute. Millikan spoke
at the end, unveiling scientific as well as architectural plans. Then he
expressed his regrets about the one aspect of Caltech that he felt was
inadequate, its community relations. In order to improve these, he had
decided to create a new position, that of Associate of the California
Institute of Technology. Associates would be kept abreast of the
Institute's doings and would yearly be treated to a banquet similar to
the present one. Associates, in order to obtain that title, would have to
obligate themselves to pay $1000 a year for twenty years. Many people
joined up and the Institute was saved. This story was told to me with
glee one day in Pasadena, and I cannot vouch for its details. But the
Associates certainly existed in my time.

A man such as Millikan did, of course, dominate the spirit of the
institution even without wanting to. With his terrific strength he
sometimes reminded me of a bear who wants to embrace a human

friend and crushes him instead. But Millikan was no dictator. In his later years, shortly before I came, he had mistakenly over-expanded the physics department. He had brought from Europe two men who were good, productive scientists, but certainly not first-rate; furthermore, they showed little capacity for adapting to the traditional Anglo-American style of living and thinking to which most of the faculty adhered. They had, therefore, developed few personal or social contacts among the faculty, and as a result the physics department revolted. They passed a resolution that in the physics department, already too large in proportion to other departments, no further appointments of younger people should occur. I feel confident (although I was never told this) that Millikan brought my case officially or unofficially before the department and was turned down with respect to any future faculty appointment. But somewhat later I was given a place in the physics building, first to do my research, which at that time comprised a lot of drafting, and a couple of years later even to do some experimentation. I retained such a room until I left Caltech in 1941.

Millikan's high intellectual standards must be judged in the light of that period. They were, of course, a striving for excellence, but they were also something else: a striving for outstanding performance in a purely mechanical, or else quite mechanically intellectual, sense. This was the era when Henry Ford succeeded in offering a personal automobile to the majority of citizens who then spent their spare time repairing and beautifying that automobile. Some miles away, in Hollywood, Charlie Chaplin had become a unique celebrity by playing the role of the little man baffled by too much machinery. There was something immensely refreshing in all that simplicity. I enjoyed very much the positive aspects of that period, coming as I did from an old and over-sophisticated continent.

It was against this background that Millikan's effort to create a new type of intellectual leadership ought to be considered. Caltech had from the beginning been a school of quantitative science, specifically of physics, chemistry, and some quantitative biology such as genetics. This undoubtedly corresponded to Millikan's idea that intellectuals of this stripe after being educated in first-rate schools would go out and spread the spirit of quantitative science and the objectivity that goes with it throughout industry and eventually throughout all of American society. Millikan was eminently successful in his enterprise. During the 1930s his students began to populate American universities, and his high standard of technical competence and devotion to science were imitated throughout the American educational system, especially in its top strata. The great flowering of American science that has occurred in the past half-century was in no small measure brought about by Millikan's inexhaustible strength.

He was equally extreme in selecting his faculty. Competence was the exclusive criterion, primarily judged by the amount of scientific production turned out by the individual. That such scientific minds are often not too well adjusted did not bother Millikan in the least, so long as their oddities did not interfere with the running of the organization. He told me once: "You are a producer; if you were put on the top of a mountain you would still produce." I think of this as the highest compliment that I ever received about my qualifications as a scientist. By the time I arrived in Pasadena, Millikan had deputized the administration of chemistry and biology to Linus Pauling; but Pauling was too young to threaten Millikan's paternalistic rule of the whole institution. He wanted his people isolated from more mundane preoccupations and involvements, and this aim was pursued successfully until the end of the Second World War when science had risen to the top of the social order, and Millikan had retired. He had always "played by the rules," which included bowing out without protest when his time had come.

It goes without saying that during my years at Caltech I became acquainted with the faculty in physics and mathematics; among theoretical physicists there were then Richard Tolman, the cosmologist, and Paul Epstein, who, although born in Russia, felt quite at home in Pasadena. But these men did not play any significant role in my life, either personally or scientifically.

When I had settled the outlines of my future activity with Millikan, I decided that it would be wise not to leave nuclear physics too abruptly. I made the acquaintance of Charles Lauritsen and his capable group of research students who represented nuclear physics at Caltech. Among these was William Fowler, an experimentalist who later became well known for his studies of nuclear transformations in the stars. Lauritsen himself was a remarkable person: He was a Dane, had grown up in a provincial environment, and attended a local technical school. He came to the United States when he was twenty-four; he then made a living from commercial activities as an electrical engineer. But his passion for science was too strong. In his middle thirties he came back to Caltech as a Ph.D. candidate, was retained there, and rose rapidly through the ranks of the faculty. When I met him, he had a modest nuclear accelerator running, and his crew of students were at the forefront of the study of structure and dynamics of nuclei then going on in the world. Lauritsen was a very reticent and outwardly difficult man, more than a bit shy and hard to be casual with, but underneath this he had a strong and very sound personality. This appeared clearly later during the Manhattan Project and its aftermath, when he sided with James Franck in condemning the United States government's warlike posture in the use of the atomic bomb.

Lauritsen's laboratory ran smoothly, and the students were inspired by him to a deep dedication to their task. Since I knew quite a bit about nuclei myself, it was easy for me to converse with them about that science. I came to be well acquainted with them; they were pleasant company, and I owe them one skill that is indispensable in the United States: They alternated, with a little bit of prodding on my part, in teaching me how to drive an automobile. (It was a little later, early in 1938, that Margaret and I bought our first automobile, a somewhat aged Model-A Ford.)

As I became acquainted with these students I found out that their official theoretician was Robert Oppenheimer who spent two or three months in Pasadena every spring. But in the summer of 1936 his annual spring sojourn was quite a few months away, and when he did arrive in the spring of 1937, I had already become deeply engrossed in the physics of the atmosphere, which seemed rather a "weird" subject to nuclear physicists, including Oppenheimer. Since by then I had ceased to read the rapidly progressing literature in nuclear physics, this gradually estranged me from the otherwise congenial crowd of Lauritsen's laboratory. Eventually, I lost touch with them.

In the spring of 1937, Margaret gave up her position in Chicago and came West to look for employment. After a number of weeks she did succeed in finding something that was tolerable although not too well paid, and we got married. Shortly after Margaret had arrived in the spring of 1937, I invited Robert Oppenheimer to have lunch with us in a restaurant, so that the two could get acquainted. On that occasion he gave what I can only call a flawless performance of a perfect gentleman and an accomplished cavalier. Margaret was floored; in the middle-class environment of Chicago, whose manners were shared even by the very rich at that time, she had never seen anything comparable, and it took her months to get over it. I myself, while deeply impressed by the extraordinary mastery of his performance, realized also how far we had grown apart: Oppenheimer, by dint of having instructed a talented section of the American population for ten years, had had the pragmatic aspects of his mind very much reinforced. He practiced his pragmatism by his social and intellectual adaptations. It was his tragic fate—as it was that of the American people, a circumstance all too often ignored—that his main achievement, the most spectacular feat in science and engineering in America, was building a weapon. That there is some relationship between this destructive outcome and the extreme preponderance of pragmatism we see all around us does not yet seem to have occurred to American thinkers.

But I should, perhaps, conclude this part of my story on a lighter note: Some time after we had been married, Robert Millikan got wind of this fact. He complained rather pointedly to my friend, Jesse DuMond, about it, saying that a young man had no business getting married before he even had a steady job. Jesse rebutted rather acidly: It was unfair to ask a man at age thirty-three to postpone marriage just because he had not yet achieved academic tenure, a condition equally suffered by the majority of his fellow creatures.

9

Earth Science

It appeared from my conversations with Millikan that he wanted me to join the fairly new Meteorology Department. He later managed to achieve a contract with the U.S. Department of Agriculture, based on the outline of future research that he had from me. The Weather Bureau, then a part of the Department of Agriculture, came to administer this contract. My own knowledge of meteorology at that time was nil, but I did not find it difficult to read a couple of textbooks superficially and find unsolved problems in which I could put some of my accumulated knowledge of atomic physics to good use. I soon settled on an investigation of the effects of far infrared radiation upon the atmosphere. Millikan arranged that, by the summer of 1937, my salary began to flow at a small but steady rate. Up to that point, I had been living in Pasadena on loans.

Next, I should explain far infrared radiation and its effects upon the atmosphere. The facts were at that time well enough known to physicists but had so far almost entirely escaped the attention of students of the atmosphere, the meteorologists. A solid body emits, just by virtue of its temperature, a certain radiation, the so-called black-body radiation, spread over an interval of wavelengths and with a pronounced maximum at a certain wavelength. For the sun (temperature of 5500°C), this peak wavelength lies in the middle of the visible part of the spectrum, whose wavelength extends from about 0.4 microns (violet light) to 0.7 microns (red light). (One micron is one thousandth of a millimeter.) When the temperature goes below that of the sun, the peak of the black-body radiation is displaced in a regular fashion to longer waves. For a moderately hog piece of iron say 1000°C, the peak lies at a wavelength of the infrared that is well beyond the visible range, but we can see the end of the spectrum which makes hot iron appear in a reddish glow. The same type of radiation also exists for a solid at ordinary temperatures but the peak radiation is still farther out in the far infrared, at a wavelength of about 10 microns.

The earth as a whole must be in "radiative equilibrium," that is, it must on the average absorb as much of the sun's radiation as it sends out to space by its own far infrared radiation. The main constituents of the atmosphere, nitrogen and oxygen, are transparent in their infrared spectrum, but the chief minor constituents, water vapor, carbon dioxide, and ozone are not. If the atmosphere is sufficiently moist, it can absorb and then re-radiate an appreciable fraction of the earth's far infrared radiation, say one third of it or more, much more for a sufficiently moist atmosphere. Furthermore, a cloud acts as if it were a solid-body radiator (which in fact it is, since the cloud consists of water droplets). Some related phenomena are well known to everyone: Below a clear sky with a very dry atmosphere, as in the desert at night, the ground gets very cold overnight, whereas in a moist climate, especially with a cloud deck overhead, there is little cooling. Also, the atmosphere if it absorbs radiation from the ground will be warmed up. The power of this infrared radiation comes largely from the fact that this "radiative heat transfer" goes on continuously all the time, twenty-four hours a day one might say, and toward all directions. And so, while the radiative effects are small over a short period of, say, an hour, they become appreciable when they extend over many days or weeks.

These were the known qualitative facts, but almost nothing was known of a quantitative nature. For some years preceding, the American Meteorological Society had passed resolutions that were addressed to the American Physical Society, to the effect that research should be done on far infrared radiation in view of its importance for the atmosphere—but nothing at all was done. The far infrared spectra of the gases involved, especially that of water vapor, have an extraordinarily complicated structure which was then known to a small number of specialists; but this knowledge involved among other things quantum mechanics, which was clearly not familiar to meteorologists. The basic material pertaining to infrared spectroscopy had been gathered and presented in a remarkable reference work by the physicist Gerhard Herzberg, with whom I had become acquainted in Germany. On Hitler's advent he was forced to leave Germany since his wife was Jewish; he went to Canada where he had a brilliant career. Starting from Herzberg's book, I made it my business to analyze the properties of far infrared atmospheric radiation from first principles, as it were. After fairly lengthy calculations I would end up with tables and graphs which a practitioner could use to find the heating or cooling of the atmosphere when he knew the distribution of temperature and moisture. This work with all its ramification occupied much of my time for about four and a half years in Pasadena, from 1937 until I left in the fall of 1941.

This time was, in a way, a unique period in my life: After having had for nearly twenty years the hot breath of Hitler at my neck, I had succeeded in escaping to a climate where such extreme brutalities did not exist; moreover, I had found a congenial wife. With all this the pinched material situation did not matter too much. I needed a time of rest and recovery to catch my breath for future activities. In spite of its subdued external tenor, this period was also, in fact, extremely fruitful. I had plenty of time to think, and it was during this time that I developed the two basic ideas that have dominated the scientific activity of my later years: the ideas that led to the theory of the earth's magnetic field, about which I will speak a little later, and those about the relationship of organic life to physics, especially quantum mechanics, whose background, so far as it lies in my own experience, I have previously expounded in Chapter 6.

After I had done this work for a few years, involving mostly calculations and drafting, the frustrations that had formed around my previous inability to do experimental work began to resurface. But this time I was in a quite different position. I had by then befriended a man who was a most successful experimentalist: John Strong. At a young age he had made a reputation for himself with a book, *Methods of Experimental Physics*, that was illustrated by an artist and showed a vast array of tricks invaluable to the experimentalist. I was always surprised at how well John and I understood each other despite our radically different backgrounds. We were about the same age, but John had been born and raised on a wheat farm in Kansas, which fact he mentioned now and then with considerable pride. He was a specialist in optics, especially infrared optics, and in this capacity he was associated for many years after the war with what was then a great center of optical research, the physics department of Johns Hopkins University.

John Strong had an important assignment at Caltech: At that time the large five-meter (200-inch) reflecting telescope to be installed on Mount Palomar was being constructed. Strong's task was to fashion a reflecting surface for the front side of the disk. The time-honored method of doing this had been to precipitate metallic silver from a solution of silver salts by a chemical process. But by then, another method proved advantageous: "sputtering" metallic aluminum upon the surface in a very high vacuum from aluminum wires that are heated by an electric current. Strong succeeded after some trials in achieving this for the big disk. Once the mirror is aluminized, the process does not need to be repeated for several years.

In my conversations with John I learned a great deal about the requisites for successful experimentation. Not that we discussed specific techniques or specific details; but I began to understand how one goes about performing a successful experiment. John taught me that much of the critical work is in the planning; one must break down the whole procedure into a number of little steps and then learn to master each step completely before proceeding to the next one. If one ever decides that a particular step is easy enough to skip, it is almost certainly there that the procedure will break down. Only years later did I learn that this had long been known to philosophers as the Cartesian Method. But then, John was no philosopher who reasoned deductively from general principles; he was a pragmatist with an inductive bent, and, of course, he had a natural passion for gadgetry, like so many Americans of his generation.

After I had become well acquainted with John, I decided to overcome my own lingering sense of frustration by carrying out an experiment myself. In 1940 I measured the far infrared transmission of the atmosphere along a set of paths up to 300 meters in length. I built all the equipment except for the mirrors with my own hands. The measurements were done on a stretch of flat earth next to the campus, usually reserved for athletic pursuits; the temperature and moisture along the path were continuously monitored. I wrote up the results and had them published in a meteorological journal. I was proud of this achievement although I realized that as a contribution to experimental science it was miniscule; but it restored my self-confidence and also made me realize that the American ambiance had a relaxing and stabilizing influence on me. I also understood that I would never be more than a third-rate experimentalist—so I stopped then and did not perform experiments later.

When I first came to Pasadena the Meteorology Department at Caltech was only about two years old. It consisted essentially of one young man, an assistant professor, roughly my own age, named Irving Krick. This gentleman was highly intelligent but not primarily a research man. His interests were essentially practical and commercial and since he was thoroughly aware of this, we got along very well; we both realized that our spheres of interest did not overlap and proceeded with corresponding courtesy. Krick had gone into meteorology on the advice of a relative with more academic leanings. While still very young, Krick had the ingenuity to devise a scheme for forecasting the weather in the Los Angeles area for the benefit of the movie industry: In that region a very low and thin cloud deck usually forms overnight and then dissipates during the morning (this was, of course, before the days of smog). The disappearance of these clouds is produced by the heat that the sun supplies as it rises. Krick was able to show that one could compute the time when the cloud dispersed if one knew the temperature and moisture of the air, the height of the cloud deck, and the wind. This required only the most elementary principles of physics (little more than the gas laws and energy conservation). Krick installed a weather forecasting service for the movie companies which was very popular since it saved them a lot of money. Usually a major film requires dozens and sometimes hundreds of "extras" who are paid by the hour. Krick's service enabled the companies to have the extras assemble just before they expected the clouds to break instead of a fixed hour of the morning. This activity netted Krick a lot of money and it was simple work that could mostly be delegated to clerks; so Krick turned to developing the instruction in meteorology shortly before I arrived. During the war he was part of the team that forecast the weather for the Normandy invasion; after the war he left Caltech and set up a private forecasting service in the Middle West.

My time was my own in 1936, and I decided to take the regular course in meteorology. It consisted of two parts, a class in "synoptic" meteorology and one in "dynamic" meteorology. I soon recognized that the latter was just a branch of theoretical physics which I could learn by myself in less time than it took to sit through the course; so I limited myself to synoptic meteorology. There were then about twenty students in this course, virtually all of them career officers of the armed services who had been sent to Pasadena for training as weather officers. They appeared in civilian clothing throughout; I never saw them in uniform. The students of this class were a new type to me. As military men, they were, of course, well aware that in a few years they might have to fight against Hitler. They were very well behaved young men in their twenties but not precisely talkative, even among each other. I certainly did not have much success in starting a conversation with my neighbors.

Every day each student sat at a drafting table on which a rather large map was placed. This map showed the outline of the United States and some surrounding territory in feeble print; on it the weather data (temperature, pressure, etc.) had been entered for stations all over the country, as they were transmitted daily over the weather teletype service. They were entered daily on a master map and then transferred to the individual maps by a duplicating process. The task of each student was to draw by pencil the isobars, curves of constant pressure, the isotherms, curves of constant temperature, to mark regions of precipitation, recognize fronts, and do whatever analysis could be done for the purpose of a short-term forecast, usually for a day or less ahead. Later we proceeded to plot and evaluate such upper-air data as were available. I did learn much about the peculiarities and the vagaries of the earth's atmosphere, and there was a great deal to be learned. The mechanics of flow in the atmosphere is utterly dominated by the effects of the earth's rotation. (To appreciate this, one has only to remember that the speed of a point at the earth's equator owing to the earth's rotation is about 470 meters per second, vastly superior to the speed of any wind.) As a result of this, the laws of motion on the earth (in the atmosphere as well as in the ocean) are radically different from what they would be if the earth did not rotate. I found that past experience in mechanics was of little avail when one studied the weather; one had to follow the motions as inferred from the weather maps and retrain one's mechanical intuition almost from the start.

On every weather map there appear regions of low pressure and regions of high pressure. The low pressure, for instance, indicates that in such a region the column of air that produces this pressure is less dense; hence it must be warmer than its surroundings. For high pressure it is the reverse. (There are no "bulges" on top of the atmosphere, as one might naively think.) Thus, the air in a low-pressure region tends to rise as an effect of what is called buoyancy; conversely, the air of a high-pressure region tends to sink. In the absence of the earth's rotation this would simply lead to a rather slow inflow into low-pressure regions and outflow from high-pressure regions. But the effect of the earth's rotation is very powerful; it bends the motions into a near-circular pattern as shown in Figure 2a. The circulation is in opposite directions for the two regions. The diagram of Figure 2 shows in a schematic manner the way any ordinary weather map looks. One further phenomenon is extremely common: the appearance of so-called fronts. During the atmosphere's streaming, masses of air are often carried north from warmer regions; nearby, another mass of air may be carried south from colder regions. This is

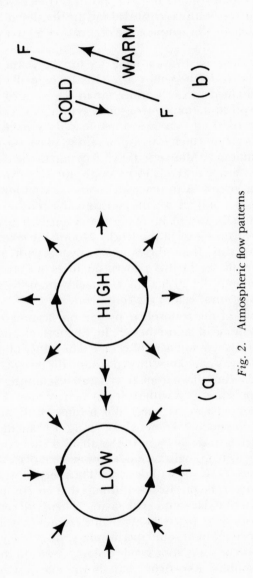

Fig. 2. Atmospheric flow patterns

shown schematically in Figure 2b. Now the air coming from the south is warmer and that coming from the north is colder. When the winds continue, a discontinuity is created along the line designated by FF. (In practice, the change in temperature occurs over a layer of air about 1 kilometer thick.

At a front there is always a tendency for the warm air to rise by buoyancy relative to the colder air. This leads to the falling-out of moisture contained in the warmer air in the form of droplets, and eventually to precipitation, rain or snow, as the case may be. Hence, the identification of fronts on a weather map is a major part of the weatherman's art in which forecasting rain is, of course, of the highest practical significance. Moreover, the eastern part of the United States in particular has a hot reservoir to its south, the very extensive Gulf of Mexico; if air circulates in that neighborhood even for a few days, it becomes very hot and filled with moisture. There is a corresponding cold reservoir in the vast plains of northern Canada. The weather of the United States to the east of the Rocky Mountains takes on a certain "dramatic" quality from these facts. Anyone with a little poetic imagination will see in this pattern an incessant struggle between masses of hot and cold air flowing alternately from the south and the north into the central belt of the continent.

The motions of the atmosphere present one feature common to all large-scale motions of fluids; they are highly unstable, usually leading to a spontaneous development of eddies. The father of modern scientific meteorology, V. Bjerknes, proved around the turn of the century by mathematical means that a front gives rise to instabilities in the form of nascent low-pressure areas with the proper circulation (Fig. 2a, known to the meteorologist as cyclones). But because of the nature of such instabilities, one doesn't know where along a front they develop. A front may stretch from Texas in the south all the way to Maine in the north, but the meteorologist cannot know at what place along a line of 2000 kilometers a cyclone will develop. Thus there arises the inability of the forecaster to be precise about things that are conspicuous to the public, such as rain. He cannot risk saying: There will certainly be rain at several unspecified places along a line from Texas to Maine. But should he predict rain at some specific place, he is likely to be wrong; the rain may occur some appreciable distance away, to the disappointment of the public. Experience has shown that just increasing the density of weather stations and the number of observations helps little since the difficulty lies in the instability of the atmosphere which cannot be remedied. But forecasting the weather over longer periods, months or years, is a different matter altogether. There are many variables that influence the behavior of the atmosphere; one group of these comes from the coupling of the atmosphere with the ocean, which has so large a mass that it acts like a heavy flywheel, a huge reservoir of energy connected to the atmosphere and stabilizing it.

Modern meteorological analysis of the short-term variety, such as I learned in Krick's class, had been developed by the Norwegian Vilhelm Bjerknes and by some of his students, roughly 1890–1910. The central idea was that the weather in middle geographical latitudes is determined by the interaction of masses of warm air moving north from subtropical regions and of masses of cold air moving south from near-polar regions. Very conspicuous phenomena are the fronts along which the warm air rises, resulting in rainfall. These ideas were introduced to the United States by a remarkable personality, Francis Reichelderfer. He had joined the U.S. Navy as a young man and had remained in it for twenty years, rising to commander. Reichelderfer recognized the need in the age of aviation for a competent meteorological service, and succeeded in inducing the Navy to send him to Norway to study Bjerknes' methods. He subsequently spread this knowledge among the armed services and among the civilian agencies of the government concerned with the weather. In 1938 he left the Navy to become director of the Weather Bureau where he served with distinction until his retirement in advanced age. I have pleasant recollections of several meetings with Reichelderfer over the years.

I was led to nurse many thoughts about the atmosphere as I drew my weather maps in Krick's laboratory. I continued to draw such maps for a year and a half each day that Krick's staff provided copies with the raw weather data entered on them. From this exercise I gained a very thorough understanding of the idiosyncrasies of the earth's atmosphere (which proved eminently useful in my later work on the earth's magnetism). I also began to think about these matters along philosophical lines, but this bore little fruit. I did learn from experience that the earth's atmosphere is full of unpredictable contingencies at every level of its scale, and this fact, encountered daily, gives the meteorologist a feeling for the nature of reality radically different from that of the laboratory scientist who with some diligence can hope to ban contingencies almost entirely from his work bench.

The divergence in points of view between a man aware of the roles of contingencies in the world and one who is not is well exemplified by the story of the encounter between Napoleon and Laplace, the famous theoretical physicist. When Laplace had finished his great tome on celestial mechanics he wrote to Napoleon asking permission to dedicate the work to him. The result was an audience, and on that occasion Napoleon asked: "And where is God in your celestial system?" Whereupon Laplace: "Your Majesty, I do not require this hypothesis." This anecdote has always seemed to me to illustrate brilliantly the difference between the man of action whose survival, and even the survival of his ideology, depends on the mysterious contingencies of battle, and the sort of physical scientist who has succeeded in a realm in which contingencies are irrelevant.

These years of studying meteorology brought home to me for the first time the importance of contingencies in many human activities. Everyone knows that contingencies occur in daily life. But the appearance of major contingencies in most fields of science is not taken for granted; in pure physics one makes successful efforts to minimize their incidence. Many bad misunderstandings, even ideological differences, arise because two parties may have acquired an habitually different attitude toward contingencies. Ever since Descartes ushered in the age of enlightened rationalism over 300 years ago, such conflicts have been common, and little has been done to overcome them.

In the spring of 1938 I received an invitation to lecture at the Meteorology Department of the Massachusetts Institute of Technology. This department was then headed by Carl Gustaf Rossby, born in Sweden, educated there and in Norway, who had come to the United States in 1926 and had risen rapidly. Rossby was a firebrand in whom an exceptional ability for generating and spreading enthusiasm was combined with a very high skill for mathematical and physical analysis. He was surrounded by a bevy of students who worshipped him; many of these eventually achieved high positions in the American meteorological community which was to become so important in an era when first military and later civilian aviation was to be one of the country's major assets. I came to know Rossby and some of his pupils well during this summer, and we had many fruitful discussions about the dynamics of the atmosphere.

Earlier that year, when I first received Rossby's invitation, my wife and I decided to make the trip to Boston and back in our automobile. When I recall this trip today, it seems to me that it was a particularly favorable period for such an adventure. A few years earlier, both the cars and the roads were so imperfect that one had to expect major technical breakdowns and delays for unforeseen and lengthy periods. Today superhighways are everywhere, and crossing the continent by car is hardly more of a human experience than it was earlier to cross it by railroad. To see the vast variety of American scenery in a short compass of time without having to rush can be the unique experience of a lifetime, as it was for us. On the return trip we took the southern route, through St. Louis and Albuquerque. The last part of this trip has remained vividly in my memory. We wanted, of course, to see the Grand Canyon that lies somewhat north of the road. We left the main highway by a side road that leads to a small settlement called Cameron. At that time it was a trading post operated by the federal government for traffic with the Navajo Indians. On our arrival we found that a tribal election was in progress. The Indians had come from far and wide to elect a new chieftain under the government's supervision. Since the Navajos were totally illiterate at that time, the government agent had assigned a color to each candidate. Each member of the tribe was given paper strips of different colors and voted by depositing a strip of the appropriate color in the ballot box. We saw many of the Indians that had come in for this event; they seemed to be in a state of absolute wildness. They would look at us from a distance with the furtive glances of a deer surprised in the open. They seemed to be natural creatures more than fellow human beings, somewhere in the transition between a state of wildness and that system of organized customs that we call civilization. When I was last at the Grand Canyon a few years ago there were many tiny houses in the neighborhood of Cameron with equally tiny irrigated gardens. The Navajos, clearly recognizable by their facial features, were garbed in the white man's overalls and each drove a tiny Ford truck. However, I cannot visualize the psychic effect of this acculturation process.

We drove along the southern rim of the canyon to the place called Grand Canyon proper, with the world-famous panoramic view. We then travelled due west for about a day passing through one of the most desolate sceneries on earth, nothing but extreme desert with barely a dried-out sagebrush or two in sight—until eventually one arrives at the top of Cajon Pass where the road begins to descend to the California plains. The view of this panorama with its wide sweep, with all its greenery, with the signs of peace and prosperity appearing suddenly all along the horizon, after we had travelled endlessly through a moon-like landscape, is one of the archetypical American experiences, not to be forgotten.

Some months after my return to Pasadena, a new face appeared among those involved in meteorology. It was a Captain Maier sent by the Army to supervise a government contract to build radio-meteorographs, arranged by Millikan. This apparatus consists of small meteorological measuring devices, for pressure, temperature, and moisture, whose readings are fed into a very small short-wave radio transmitter. The latter had a miniature electronic tube and was energized by a minuscule storage battery. The whole assembly weighed only a fraction of a pound and could be sent aloft by a balloon.

Maier at once proceeded to set up a regular assembly line for the series-production of these small devices, not yet then a routine tool. He engaged a crew of three or four young people for this primitive industry, a graduate student or two and some outsiders with an interest in tinkering. Maier was the successful product of military leadership training: bluff, aggressive, and always present when technical difficulties arose. He was totally prepared to meet any difficulty by direct action. I came to know him well and we liked each other, although Maier never abandoned that shield of personal reserve which a military career man has learned to use outside—and perhaps even inside—an officer's club.

Since Maier had the enthusiastic backing of Millikan and apparently had easy access to him, it could not fail that he tried to add me to his working crew even without having to compensate me properly. Before long I spent half my time with Maier and his crew building meteorographs in large numbers. The vicissitudes of this project first afforded me an insight into some of the administrative problems that beset Caltech as they do every young institution. The Meteorology Department was part of Aeronautical Engineering and was housed in the corresponding building. I had gone there daily to draw my weather map, but my own desk and later laboratory space were in the physics building some distance away. The Guggenheim Aeronautics Laboratory, as it was called, was then headed by a very outstanding man, Theodore von Karman, who had come to Pasadena from Europe in 1930 after an already brilliant academic career. He had been born and raised in Hungary, had come as a young man to Göttingen, where he had obtained a Ph.D. in mathematics, and had gone on to teach and do research in applied mathematics and mechanics at a German engineering university. In addition to being a superb scholar by the most rigorous criteria, von Karman was also an excellent administrator and a man of the world who could deal with all sorts of people as the need arose. He once told me how difficult it was for him to keep his laboratory going on the very slender basis of its fixed income; he had to do frequent testing work for aircraft companies, which interfered with the more fundamental research work he himself liked to see advanced.

Not long after I met von Karman, he remarked to me that there were more interesting studies than what he called in a slightly contemptuous tone "the thermodynamics of the atmosphere." He explained that there were many problems in hydrodynamics, especially in turbulence, that could be greatly advanced by the skill of a competent theoretical physicist. I turned a deaf ear to these entreaties and to a series of similar ones later. I felt no desire to give up everything I knew by then about modern physics to become an aeronautical theorist, either in industry or in a university. As a result I never became closer to von Karman; he never, for instance, invited me to one of his famous social parties. Gradually, then, I began to see that von Karman had accepted meteorology into his laboratory as an accommodation to Millikan who in turn believed that he was doing a patriotic duty by fostering its development. I also began to see that my small position and my failure to be promoted were not based on any weakness in Millikan's character (or mine for that matter) but were simply the by-product of a protracted political accommodation between two very outstanding scientists who were also most skillful administrators—I was the link of least resistance.

As I gradually recognized the realities of this situation, I began to look for other employment but with little success. Positions were then still rare in the wake of the Great Depression, and, furthermore, I had no money to travel to look around for opportunities. Once during those years, it might have been in 1938, I asked Robert Oppenheimer whether he could help me obtain a teaching job at one of the other campuses of the University of California, particularly the Los Angeles campus. His answer was precise and to the point: "We do not wish to encourage graduate teaching outside of Berkeley." This was almost the last time I saw Oppenheimer until shortly before his death (as told in Chapter 3).

My position in Pasadena came to a rather ludicrous end in 1941. Early that year I was travelling to Washington on some business connected with my research. There I found Rossby again, who had been made assistant chief for research of the U.S. Weather Bureau. He took me to dinner at the Cosmos Club and brought me up to date about his current situation: As head of the Weather Bureau's research activity he, Rossby, had obtained control of scientific meteorology in the United States. But he found the task almost overwhelming and had decided to delegate the control of the western part of the country to a deputy: He had picked me as his deputy. I didn't know what to say and remained silent. I thought these ideas to be sufficiently phantastic that they would take care of themselves when confronted with reality. But I was not quite right.

Some two or three months later I went to see Millikan's secretary to make sure that my contract had been extended for another year. "You better see Dr. Millikan," she said. But Millikan told me to see von Karman. This was ominous because von Karman had never before taken any part at all in the administrative affairs of Meteorology. When I came face to face with von Karman, he told me that he had been in Washington some weeks earlier and had spoken to Rossby. Rossby had told him that the Meteorology Department at Caltech was just inadequate, being headed by Krick, who was a commercial entrepreneur and would never be a scientist; but they had an excellent man right on the spot, namely Elsasser. He, Rossby, had already discussed with Elsasser his future functions. Von Karman promptly reported to Millikan that Elsasser had tried to mobilize the federal government to obtain for himself a position at Caltech. Rossby had given emphasis to his ideas by declaring that the contract from which my salary was paid would not be renewed.

The game was clearly up. I recognized that I had been a pawn in a struggle between two giants, and I understood why Millikan had seemed so embarrassed when he sent me to see von Karman. There was no sense in asserting my innocence; I walked out of von Karman's office and considered myself "fired." The main thing, I felt, was to move east, where, with the war coming on, the greater opportunities were. I wrote to Charles Brooks, the professor of meteorology at Harvard University. He was in charge of the Blue Hill Observatory, a small building in the south of Boston that had been given to Harvard in the nineteenth century, when an observatory on top of a hill was considered a great advantage for studying the weather. Brooks, a climatologist, always had a few young people compiling tables of various data; I had counted on some of these small funds being given to me. Brooks almost at once agreed, and very soon Margaret and I packed our few belongings into the back of our car and drove off to Boston. I stayed there until early in 1942, writing a small book, a monograph on atmospheric radiation which Brooks published in a series he edited.

Rossby, who had a bad conscience, had most of the edition bought up and distributed free to meteorology students. But I did not see Rossby again.

In Pasadena I had been able to think at length about some of the major unsolved problems of the earth as a whole as they appeared to a physicist. The exploration of the earth's body had come into its own when seismological stations were first established in the 1890s. During the succeeding decades, the main features of the earth's interior became visible. The most important of these is a sharp boundary located about midway between the surface and the center of the earth. The region inside this boundary is called the earth's core. All information obtained over the years without exception confirms that this core is liquid. The part lying outside the core's boundary is called the earth's mantle; we have no reason to doubt that the mantle consists of rocks similar to those seen at the earth's surface. The core cannot consist of molten rock since its density is too high. Hence geophysicists early suspected that it was made of molten metallic iron, since pieces of metallic iron are often found in meteorites that have fallen from space. These conclusions (mantle being some sort of conventional rock; core consisting of molten iron; the two separated by a sharp boundary) were increasingly confirmed over the years as the pieces of this puzzle fell into place. By now, almost a century after the first seismographic stations were set up, we have a very thorough and quantitative knowledge of all the mechanical properties of the earth's interior, which means also of the variation of these properties with depth.

There is one characteristic of the earth as a whole that is not yet included in this scheme—magnetism, a property studied scientifically since 1600 when the Englishman Gilbert published a book, *On the Magnet*. Gilbert said that the earth behaves as if it were a bar magnet, magnetized along the earth's axis. But mysterious deviations from the regularity of the earth's magnetic field were later discovered; for instance, mariners found to their dismay that the magnetic needle often does not point exactly to the north but a few degrees away from it. To confound things, these irregularities not only differed from place to place, but in time also if one waited for some decades. Therefore physicists began to speak of the "secular variation" of the earth's magnetic field ("secular" meaning here long-term). In the first half of the nineteenth century, the famous mathematician Gauss, in Göttingen, analyzed the earth's magnetism still further: He showed that if one knows the magnetic field all over the earth's surface, one can mathematically divide this field into two parts, one part whose sources are inside the earth's surface and a second part whose sources are outside it. Gauss had already concluded that the overwhelming part of the field originates from sources inside the earth. But throughout the nineteenth century there was no clarity about the nature of these sources. Toward the end of the century, knowledge of the properties of matter had advanced sufficiently to eliminate "molecular" magnetization of the type observed in ordinary bar magnets. The evidence is perfectly clear that this form of magnetism occurs only at low temperatures and not at the higher temperatures that one has every right to expect inside the earth.

Two kinds of speculation were then taking the place of knowledge: First, many theoreticians believed that this inability to explain the earth's magnetism was a reflection of our inability to systematize the traditional classical field theories. In such theories two kinds of fields existed, gravity fields and electromagnetic fields; while both are clearly produced by ordinary matter, no connection between them is known. A significant group of physicists, with Albert Einstein at their head, believed that a theory must eventually be created in which large bodies such as the earth are magnetic by the very fact of their rotation. When I last had some contact with Einstein, in Princeton after the war (he was then in his late sixties), he still showed a strong emotional attachment to such ideas, though he was no longer prepared to fight for them.

The only alternate idea was that there must be electric currents flowing in the earth's core, which was then generally admitted to consist of molten iron. In the end, this idea turned out to be right, but the nature and origin of these currents had still to be understood. Some years before this, the true nature of the earth's magnetism had been illuminated by a highly significant discovery: The discoverer was George Hale, the founder of the Mount Wilson observatory, near Pasadena, where he had erected two "heliostats," telescopes specially adapted to observe the sun. These instruments allow the observer to select small regions of the sun's disk and study them in detail. In 1908 Hale discovered that all sunspots have large magnetic fields. This was first inferred from a splitting of spectral lines that arises in a magnetic field and that is utterly characteristic of magnetism; later, other confirmations of the magnetic nature of sunspots were found. The magnetic fields of sunspots are very strong, such as are produced on earth only by very powerful electromagnets. But while in such magnets the field is strong only in a small region, a few centimeters across, the magnetic field of a sunspot extends over its whole area, which is often many hundreds of times greater than the entire area of the earth's surface. One thus deals with truly gigantic amounts of magnetic energy. Beginning about 1950, the astronomer H. Babcock made a systematic search for other magnetic stars and over a number of years found almost a hundred of them. But a fixed star can be identified às magnetic only if a large magnetic field prevails over an appreciable fraction of the star's surface; the sun for instance does not have strong enough fields to be recognized as magnetic if it were some light-years away, as all ordinary stars are.

In the discussion that followed Hale's discovery, the distinguished British physicist J. J. Larmor said that there could be no doubt now that the sun's magnetism was due to a "dynamo" effect. The term dynamo is used by engineers to describe those machines, found in every power station, that convert mechanical motion into electrical current, that is to say, the conventional rotating generators. Although Larmor vaguely suggested that the earth's magnetism might well be explained along similar lines, there is not a single article about any of this in the scientific literature from that time (1909) until my own series of papers appeared in 1946–1947. This has always struck me as strange. Not that there was no research on the earth's magnetism, but all such activity centered exclusively on the minute and rapid variations of the field that are caused by electric currents flowing in the upper atmosphere (the ionosphere). There seems to be only one explanation for this absence of discussion: The limited number of those who are qualified to handle the solution of problems of theoretical physics was absorbed by the two main streams of inquiry then existing, relativity and quantum theory. But this again seems to imply a warning, namely, that no simplistic ideas will ever "explain" the history of science.

When I became deeply involved in the problem of the earth's magnetism, around 1940, I felt strongly that I was pioneering, since there existed no theoretical literature in this field. Early on, I spent a lengthy period going through very numerous models that might conceivably be invoked for the explanation of the earth's magnetic field. The result was unambiguous: There was no model that even remotely gave an adequate numerical magnitude (within factors of a hundred or a thousand, say) except a dynamo model, and that one came out just right. I then developed a strategy, which was to tackle the problem in two steps. The first step would be to assume as given a constant main magnetic field and calculate how motions, especially

eddy-type motions, of the conducting fluid of the core would modify
this field. This approach was also taken independently, a little later, by
the British geophysicist E. Bullard. Could this produce the slowly
variable fields observed in the secular variation of the magnetic field?
Indeed, such eddies could. Then I constructed mathematical machinery that could describe the field as it was generated by currents inside
the core. From this I could derive rules about the character of the fluid
motions needed to produce the observed field. At this point my
knowledge of meteorology turned out to be invaluable. Without my
knowledge of the dynamics of the atmosphere I would assuredly have
been unable to develop a theory of the earth's magnetism, a view
confirmed later by a very knowledgeable meteorologist friend.

When the time is ripe, however, such successes rarely come to one
man alone. I had a competitor whom I did not know at the time except
for reading his articles. This was the Swedish physicist, Hannes Alfvén.
He had some years earlier written a book entitled *Cosmic Electrody-
namics* in which he systematically treated the phenomena that arise
from electromagnetic fields in the vast expanses of the universe. Alfvén
later received the Nobel prize for this work. His strength was in an
extraordinarily rich and also extraordinarily disciplined imagination
that he applied to problems similar to those which arose in my own
work. For one thing, he succeeded in formulating in mathematical
terms the principle of amplification of a magnetic field by a fluid, the
details of which, while implicit in my calculations, had escaped me.
Alfvén's theory says that if the electrical conductivity of a fluid is very
high, then a magnetic field is carried along as if it were "frozen" into
the fluid, that is to say, it is deformed as if it were attached to the fluid
particles. The result of this mathematical analysis is that the best way
of amplifying a magnetic field is by a fluid motion that contains a
"velocity shear," a concept illustrated in Fig. 3. On the left of that
figure there appears a "velocity profile" which indicates that as one
goes down on the page the velocity increases. The particles farther
down travel faster and hence farther to the right than the particles
higher up. The effect of this upon a magnetic field of suitable direction
is shown on the right of the figure. Assuming that to begin with the
magnetic field is as described by the dashed vertical arrows, it will then
be stretched by the fluid motion as shown by the solid lines. One can
readily see that the vertical field assumed to exist at the start has been
augmented by the horizontal field that increases proportionally to the
time.

The equations governing the motion of an electrically conducting fluid had been well known for many years. They had simply not been studied because they are so complicated that it is very difficult if not impossible to obtain simple and precise mathematical solutions. Even at this writing, thirty years later, the efforts of a number of brilliant mathematicians have not led to anything remotely simple. At that time, I could only follow the problem into some of its ramifications and show that the numerous and detailed observations of the field with its secular variation on the one hand, and the numerous results from the mathematical theory on the other, matched each other perfectly.

In this endeavor I found support from unexpected quarters. There was a physicist, E. H. Vestine, who for several years had been studying the earth's magnetism at the Carnegie Institution of Washington. During the war he did computing work for the military. In that period, before electronic machines had been invented, he had assembled a group of young women who did the computing routines. Toward the end of the war, he had a brilliant idea. Before dissolving his group he directed them toward an exhaustive evaluation of all the geomagnetic data to which he had access, and whose number was already large. On the basis of these data, he and his assistants constructed worldwide

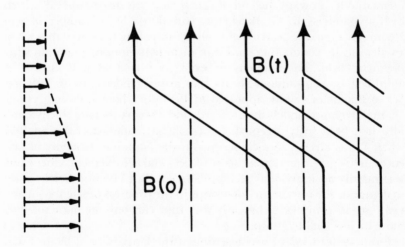

Fig. 3. Stretching of magnetic lines by shear flow

magnetic maps, consisting of lines of constant rates of secular variation. The resemblance of Vestine's maps with ordinary weather maps is
uncanny; this removed much of whatever uncertainty I still had.
Furthermore, by using these maps I could determine a value for the
average speed of fluid iron in the core; it turned out to be 0.03 cm/sec. A
fluid particle endowed with this speed can move through most of the
core in a thousand years.

The chief part of my theoretical work on the earth's magnetism was
done during the war. I had plenty of time on the weekends; especially
toward the end of the war. I used many weekends to work on this
problem, to do calculations and write articles which appeared in print
just following the war. After the war I had occasion to meet John von
Neumann again, who was then at the Institute for Advanced Study in
Princeton. Since hydrodynamics had long been one of his major
concerns, I decided to interest him in the problems of the earth's
dynamo. I then lived close enough to von Neumann to manage to visit
him regularly, for about an hour once every two or three weeks. In the
beginning he listened to me with great interest but refused to believe
me; like everyone else at that time he said that to create a magnetic field
by fluid motions alone was a way of "pulling oneself up by one's
bootstraps." But I persisted and in the course of perhaps a year I
succeeded in convincing him that my arguments were mathematically
unassailable. Toward the end of this period, the distinguished British
hydrodynamicist K. G. Batchelor, stimulated by a number of von
Neumann's remarks, carried out calculations which showed that when
an electrically conducting fluid is in turbulent motion, a random stray
magnetic field that happens to exist in this fluid will always be
amplified by the random shears that are engendered by turbulence.
When Batchelor's work appeared in 1950, the "bootstrap" objections
against dynamo models disappeared, and a few years later the dynamo
idea had been fully accepted. I was officially notified of this in 1957
when I was elected to membership in the National Academy of Sciences. This gave me a strong sense of personal achievement, since mine
was mainly an individual accomplishment. But I do not thereby want
to denigrate the importance of groups in the progress of science—many
tasks are so complex technically that they can only be mastered by a
more or less sizable group.

From 1950 to 1956 I was teaching at the University of Utah. I will
come to this period of my life in more detail in the next chapter. Then,
early in 1956 I moved to the Scripps Institution of Oceanography in La

Jolla, a suburb of San Diego. This institution is one of the two places where oceanography in the United States originated, the other being the Woods Hole Oceanographic Institution on Cape Cod. There I came to know oceanography and its social background. This might seem a strange mode of expression; certainly no one would speak of the social background of, say, either seismology or meteorology, which had been created as branches of science by some hardy physicists who sought to apply their knowledge and skill to the earth. But much of oceanography had been born as a plaything of the wealthy. One of the earliest promoters of that science was the first Prince of Monaco who, after having grown very rich from his casino, had purchased a large yacht and had used it to explore the Mediterranean. From this grew one of the first oceanographic research stations, at Monaco; later, La Jolla underwent a quite parallel development. It had been selected as a center of oceanographic activity because of geographical advantages by men who were on the faculty of the University of California in the early years of the century; in the same period the town had developed into a highly exclusive retreat of the very wealthy, under the leadership of the Scripps family, heirs to the Scripps-Howard newspaper fortune. When I arrived in La Jolla, the severe social exclusiveness had somewhat eased, but its remnants were still visible everywhere. It disappeared later, in favor of a more egalitarian style of life, as the result of an extensive building activity and of the growth of the new campus, then called University of California San Diego. But in the early days some of the scientists at the Scripps Institution were very wealthy people indeed.

Oceanography, as I soon learned, is a conglomeration of three different sciences held together by the need for a common technique. These three are known as physical, geological, and biological oceanography. Physical oceanography is the study of the ocean's currents and waves and greatly resembles meteorology. The effects of the earth's rotation on ocean currents are just as overwhelming as those in the atmosphere. Geological oceanography is the exploration of the ocean bottom, a study that is complicated by the overlying water. This requires, especially at some distance from land, the use of high-pressure technology which was then growing by leaps and bounds, and by now has led to the exploitation of submarine petroleum and other mineral deposits. These disparate branches are held together by a specialized technology. I remember vividly how this was brought home to me on my first day in La Jolla, when I was shown to my office. The room was rather small, but this defect was compensated by an infinite prospect over the blue expanse of the Pacific. On my way to the office, I had seen a peculiar column-like contraption of metal two meters high, looking almost like a torpedo that someone had set on its rear end as a museum piece. I asked what this was. Oh, I was told, it was an ocean thermometer, designed to measure water temperatures as function of depth. Inside, it contained a chamber communicating with the outside water. A plate of glass covered with soot is mounted in the chamber. An aneroid barometer and a bimetal thermometer end in a point that moves over the soot scraping a line into it. After use, the glass plate is removed, corresponding temperatures and pressures are measured, and a fresh plate is installed. I was told that anything more delicate, if thrown routinely on a rope over the side of a rolling and pitching ship would be shattered. Here was a clear indication that one had to become a seaman first to be an oceanographer. Later, I spent a day now and then as a guest on board a smaller oceanographic research vessel, but I remember more seasickness than science.

In 1959, three years after I had arrived in La Jolla, I had an unexpected encounter. Fritz Houtermans, whom I had not seen for over thirty years, suddenly appeared, invited by one of the local scientists. Houtermans was at that time actively engaged in applying the newly developed experimental methods of atomic and nuclear physics to the knowledge of the earth. He stayed for several weeks, and, as we became reacquainted, he told me about his intervening life which seems extraordinary enough to be recounted. He had been a senior assistant at the Polytechnic School in Berlin when Hitler came to power and, with his numerous left-wing connections, he could only save himself by leaving at once. He found a place in an industrial research laboratory near London, but was rather unhappy there. Two years later he took a position at the Physico-Technical Institute in Charkov, in the Ukraine, where I had been earlier (Chapter 4). But in 1937 there occurred the famous mass arrests throughout Russia by Stalin's police and Houtermans was among the victims. His wife, Charlotte, discovering that her husband had been taken to Moscow, and realizing that in Russia families of prisoners are cut off from all support, took her two small children and, on the strength of her German passport, escaped by train to Riga, then still outside Russia. From there she sent letters and telegrams to friends, and later managed to reach Copenhagen and eventually the United States. Here she taught physics for a great many years at a well-known women's college on the Eastern seaboard.

Houtermans was kept a prisoner in Moscow for two and a half years without being brought to trial. But he was intensively interrogated. In this procedure, which he vividly described to me, he was kept standing for many hours under the intense glare of klieg lights. There were three interrogators at a time, replaced by another team every two hours; whereas he remained standing. The longest such ordeal lasted uninterruptedly for eleven hours; when he fainted and collapsed, he was revived by a bucket of cold water thrown over him. It was clear that the interrogators themselves were under heavy pressure to produce results, that is to say "confessions." The pressure became so brutal that he finally succumbed and "confessed" to being a German spy. Immediately, of course, he was urged to divulge the names of his contacts. This was a little delicate because one did not wish to drag in the name of an innocent person, even inadvertently. Fritz indicated that he had contact with two officers of the German general staff and named two men who had once led the Prussian insurrection against Napoleon, names every German schoolboy knows by heart. They were duly noted. But the most cruel punishment, Fritz told me, was solitary confinement, to which he was subjected for a great many weeks. He reckoned that he could survive this with his spirit intact only if he kept his mind determinedly busy. But he had neither books, nor paper, nor pencil, nor any other implement, only his mind; so he conceived the idea of developing mathematical number theory in his head. He succeeded in acquiring a rather considerable mental facility in this and found many intriguing results. Later, when he was freed, he visited a distinguished mathematician and told him about these results. He found that many of them appeared in the textbooks of number theory as theorems found by famous men; unfortunately, he had not arrived at unknown results.

In the summer of 1940, while the Russians and Germans still respected their nonaggression treaty, Houtermans was extradited to Germany. There he had to lie low but remained unmolested; he managed to survive the war with the help of minor activities which were arranged for him by some of his colleagues who had not succumbed to the Nazis. Finally, in 1951 he obtained a position again. It was the professorship of physics at the cantonal university of Bern, Switzerland. The Swiss cantons, corresponding in size to our counties, have a high degree of sovereignty. They govern their own financial affairs and the richest of them have their own universities. When Houtermans arrived, physics consisted of a professor's salary and a lecture room in an ancient building. But science was then riding high in public esteem, a few years after the explosion of the first atomic bomb. By the sheer force of his personality and by clever use of his innumerable connections in the scientific world, Houtermans succeeded in coaxing the burghers of Bern into financing a splendid new physics building and letting him populate it with faculty members and assistants. Most of the work of this laboratory concentrated on geophysics. This was the situation when he visited La Jolla. But it was evident that he was in decline. He had taken to drinking, and he died some years later.

Let me now go back to geophysics. It is quite fair to say that everything about the earth's body, with the exception of its geometry, became accessible to thorough scientific analysis only in the twentieth century. The turning point was the discovery of radioactivity around the turn of the century, which made radioactive "dating" possible. Its basis is that certain radioactive nuclei disintegrate with extreme slowness, at a rate requiring many millions of years. If one can measure the concentration of the original nuclei and that of the final ones in a rock, one has a quantitative indication of the length of time the rock has been solid and undisturbed. The time span of ordinary geology, in which rocks can be identified by the presence of numerous fossils, came out to be 600 million years, although fossilized primitive algae have by now been found to be as old as three to three and a half billion years. By similar methods the age of the present solar system is now rather well determined to be four and a half billion years.

Earlier, there had been a strange prelude in the nineteenth century. It was almost entirely the work of one man: William Thomson, better known as Lord Kelvin, one of the greatest of physicists. He contributed as much as any other man to the establishment of the Second Law of Thermodynamics and to the kinetic theory of matter, that is to the idea that heat is a motion of molecules. Kelvin was also very active in electricity; he designed the best measuring instruments then known and he did much work on improving submarine cables, the chief means of international communications at the time. Since Kelvin also had a very gentle disposition and was a spirited teacher, it is not surprising that even during his life he had a formidable reputation. It was said that there had been no one quite like him in England since Newton.

Kelvin had argued that since the earth, being hot on the inside, loses heat to the surface at a known rate, it must formerly have been hotter and at some earlier time too hot for ordinary geological processes. He calculated the maximum time available for geology as certainly no more than 100 million years. He then did similar calculations for the sun and found that the energy store allowing the sun to radiate at its present rate would be exhausted in twenty million years. But he thought the former estimate for the earth was more reliable. He then stated rather clearly that geologists with their less rigorous methods must conform to the clear and precise deductions from the unalterable laws of nature as known to physicists. He was supported in this endeavor by his friend and colleague Tait, who was less famous but more strident in such assertions.

This was most uncomfortable for geologists, who were well aware that hundreds of millions of years were needed for geological history. By the middle of the nineteenth century the doctrine of uniformitarianism had been generally accepted: This is the idea that geological processes have been occurring throughout the past at the same slow and steady rate that can be observed today. Uniformitarianism was also important for Darwin and his followers. Darwin's notion of evolution required hundreds of millions of years. To make these long periods palatable, in *The Origin of Species* Darwin gave an example of a remote geological date, when the erosion of a certain landscape in England had begun; this led him to a time 300 million years in the past. But under the influence of Kelvin's writings, he omitted this figure from the last few editions to appear in his lifetime.

Its English setting made this battle even more significant. In the nineteenth century geology was one of the major sports of English gentlemen, who wanted to explore the countryside. Hence, the controversy between Kelvin with his anti-uniformitarian views and the geologists, too awed to reply properly, could not be confined to groups of specialists but reached the general public; lengthy articles about the age of the earth appeared in British general magazines and were widely read. The geologists waxed hypocritical and tried to "doctor" their data to conform with Kelvin's prescriptions. Kelvin continued his fight against uniformitarianism for over thirty years. But Kelvin's arguments collapsed with the discovery of radioactivity around 1900. We now know that the earth's internal heat comes to some extent from radioactivity and that the sun's radiation is sustained by nuclear processes deep in its interior.

It was only many years later, on reading a book by the American historian of science, J. Burchfield, entitled *Lord Kelvin and the Age of the Earth*[1] that I began to understand how the blithe use of quantitative but ill-founded conclusions from physical principles by Lord Kelvin had left long-lasting psychic scars on earth scientists.

Geologists had long since realized that they had no very satisfactory idea of the process of mountain building. But it was clear that most mountains had been raised in rather well-defined periods of geological history and that the older mountains had been much flattened by erosion in later ages. A physical basis of what geologists call tectonics, that is the dynamics of large rock masses, began to emerge in the 1950s and 1960s.

The beginning of a novel approach to the physical problems of geology was made in 1915 when the German geophysicist Alfred Wegener published a book in which he introduced the hypothesis of "continental drift" that, in one form or another, has been with us ever since. Wegener's ideas were not flights of fancy but were based on solid geological findings, mostly in the southern hemisphere. These findings showed quite clearly that South America, Africa, Australia, and the Indian peninsula had once formed one coherent continental block which had then separated and moved slowly apart; this is the chief example of continental drift. Similarly, Wegener indicated that North America and Europe had once hung together; the Appalachian chain that crosses the North-American continent then extended directly into the so-called Caledonian chain of Great Britain and Norway.

All of this is rather confidently accepted by the majority of geologists today, some sixty years after Wegener. But in view of the confusion created by the collision with Kelvin, the evidence had to be very clear to be accepted, and gradually it has been made so. One key to understanding these processes is their slow speed, which is much too small to be measured directly. It has now been determined by indirect methods in great detail, and it turns out to be rather uniformly of the magnitude of several centimeters per year. No wonder, then, that the motion cannot be directly observed. But over tens of millions of years, the displacements become large indeed.

When Wegener appeared on the scene, practically nothing had been known about the deformation of solids. The property of crystalline solids to deform permanently under sufficient forces is known as their "plasticity." The forging of iron is a familiar example. But forging was not of much interest to nineteenth-century physicists. The very first quantitative experiment on plasticity was made in 1911. But progress was slow until the connection between plastic deformation and the behavior of atoms in crystals was established through the discovery of atomic dislocations in 1933. In the decades that followed, many physicists in industrial laboratories and in engineering schools began to study plasticity systematically. Some of this work could not fail to leave its impress upon geology, and in due course geology was thoroughly modified. There arose a new model of the mechanics of mountain building and of other geological processes which combined Wegener's semi-empirical ideas with the results of modern solid-state mechanics. This model is now widely known as "plate tectonics" and is universally accepted among students of the earth.

When from 1962 I taught the fundamentals of the mechanics of solids to graduate students of geology (see next chapter) who on the whole did not have a strong background in mathematics or physics, I felt that closer contact with an expert would be very helpful to me, and I remembered that my old friend, Egon Orowan (of whom I have spoken in Chapter 5) who was then professor of mechanical engineering at MIT, was indeed an expert in this field. I got in touch with him, and we began a scientific correspondence which lasted for a number of years thereafter. I benefited very greatly from this since Egon not only thought like a physicist but also had a long-standing, active interest in geology. Whenever, in preparing for my class I encountered a question where the interpretation of the geologist and that of the physicist were at variance, I called upon him and invariably received a satisfactory reply. This interchange also kept my mind alert for the physicist's problems in this field, and during these years I made several minor contributions to this area of research and was able to stimulate some of the younger people with whom I happened to be in touch.

Alfred Wegener's drift model had at first been very unfavorably received by the majority of geologists who considered it extravagantly speculative—except for the geologists of the southern hemisphere where the evidence is very powerful indeed. At about that time H. Hess, of Princeton, had begun to investigate the physical and chemical conditions of the ocean bottom where the study of mantle motion seemed simpler than on the continents. It increasingly appeared in the 1940s and 1950s that the effects of overturn of the earth's mantle are more clearly visible under the oceans than they are on land. But nothing was known about details of the ocean bottom until that time; this is one main reason why the older geologists found it so difficult to arrive at even a qualitative model of mountain building. Another reason is that nothing was known about the mechanics of solid-state deformation, that is about plasticity.

Geologists had early recognized a comparatively thin layer at the surface which they called the "crust." Before anything was known about the geology of the ocean bottoms, crust designated mainly the continents. The material of the continents was found to be less dense than the material in the mantle, by about one sixth. As a consequence of this, the continents "swim" in the mantle the way a log of wood or an iceberg swims in water. As the ocean floors became open to exploration in more recent times it turned out that there was only a thin layer on the ocean bottom, some 3–4 kilometers deep, that can be thought of as the "oceanic crust." Near the continents, however, there is often a much thicker layer of crustal material that forms what is known as the "continental shelf." The depth of the deep ocean basis is about 5 kilometers; the mantle begins at a depth of about 8–9 kilometers. Since the continents protrude from the mantle by $\frac{1}{6}$ of their total height, they go down to a depth of about 50 kilometers where the density rather suddenly increases. This gives rise to the Mohorovičic discontinuity (abbreviated Moho) named for the seismologist who discovered it.

With these facts in mind, it is not too surprising that the main convective activity (bringing heat up by motion) is under the sea floor. There are two kinds of conspicuous features: One consists of submarine mountains, called ridges, which are bigger and higher than any mountains on the continents. Using the technique of submarine echo soundings, these have been thoroughly explored in recent decades. The ridges form an elaborate worldwide system; we know that they are the locus of "upwellings" where material rises from the deeper mantle and then, near the surface, begins to spread sideways. The second feature are deep valleys, called submarine trenches, where the mantle material goes down. For reasons that we do not yet understand, almost all of these trenches are along the circumference of the Pacific Ocean.

Even these few glimpses will show how the encounter of geology with physics, started early by Kelvin's false criticism, had now led to a fertile marriage. Add to this the tremendous exploration of the geology of other planets that arose through modern rocketry, and one sees that the prospects for unravelling the history of the earth as well as of the solar system are bright indeed. This kind of inquiry gives us a chance to investigate the apparently quite involved history of our physical surroundings which ends by unveiling complexities that hardly anyone could have conceived a century ago.

10

The War and Thereafter

During the period I was working at the Blue Hill Observatory, the United States entered World War II following the Japanese air attack on Pearl Harbor. Three months later, early in 1942, I received a telegram from the U.S. Signal Corps Laboratories at Fort Monmouth, New Jersey, saying that I should promptly report there for duty. The telegram was signed by the personnel officer, but I remembered a half-forgotten conversation with Captain Maier a year or so earlier when he had told me that I would hear from him in case of war. Later, I found that Captain Maier had become Colonel Maier and was now the director of the laboratories, with thousands of soldiers and civilians under him. Naturally, I saw nothing of him, except for two occasions to be mentioned later.

Some weeks before this telegram arrived, I had completed my monograph on infrared atmospheric radiation and was awaiting the proofs. Charles Brooks, the director of the Blue Hill Observatory, generously proposed to read the proofs for me, so that this need not detain me. I took my leave from Brooks, then my wife and I bundled up our little daughter, six months old, packed our meager belongings into our automobile, and drove off to Fort Monmouth. This is a string of military compounds distributed over several small towns along the coast of central New Jersey. On arrival, I presented myself as a meteorologist; I was given a classification in the civil service, and a salary corresponding to my age, education, and experience, which at once lifted me to a comfortable level well above the very narrow one I had lived on before.

I soon found, however, that the Signal Corps no longer had much interest in meteorology, a subject that had been taken over by the Air Force, which was at that time still a struggling branch of the Army; it reached its independent status, parallel with the Army, only a few years later. One day I was summoned to the office of Colonel Maier, who at once began to tell me that the Signal Corps had a desperate need of electronics engineers and that he was planning to make me into an electronics specialist. I protested, not so much against the fact, but because I disliked the military way of doing such things; but Maier simply told me that this was war and that I had to obey orders. He added that he knew me to be a physicist and dismissed me; my career as a meteorologist was over.

The next day I found myself in the quartz crystal division, one of the largest and most active branches of the laboratory. Quartz crystals play an important role in modern warfare; they serve to stabilize the frequencies of radio transmitters, of which thousands are used simultaneously on a modern battle field. Only this stabilization prevents the many channels from interfering with each other. The pieces of crystal needed as raw material came from Brazil. It was a lucrative trade: I was once told that during that war over a billion dollars' worth of quartz crystals were imported; with the value of the dollar at that time this represented an industry of formidable proportions. The supply of raw quartz in Brazil is by now nearly exhausted, but in the meantime industrial methods for synthesizing quartz crystals have been developed.

I also found myself at the head of a small group of younger people. Individualist that I am, I did not relish the functions of a bureaucrat which this entailed. I had been living in an ivory tower most of my life and did not realize that the value system of most people is centered on ideas different from my own. Thus, one day I was surprised holding a soldering iron in my hand by an inspector from the Civil Service Commission. He rebuked me quite severely for stooping to such inappropriate manual efforts; for such work, he said, the government could hire people for half of what it paid me. While I rapidly learned electronics in this work, I was clearly in a semi-industrial activity: For the duration of the war, the Signal Corps had taken over the technical supervision and inspection of the industries that built quartz crystals into radio circuits.

About a year later, an emergency arose that required the help of men versed in meteorology, of whom the Signal Corps had by then rather few. There had been serious trouble with an initially baffling phenomenon called "anomalous propagation." This turned out to be based on the fact that radio waves, especially short waves, are affected by the moisture in the air which bends (refracts) the trajectories of the signals. Under certain conditions they are bent downward and eventually hit the ground, whereupon they are reflected and rise into the atmosphere again. This would be innocent enough except that it seriously interferes with the ability of radar to measure distances of targets. Radar is used to guide artillery fire which becomes quite ineffective when directed to a wrong distance. This had caused great difficulties in the early part of the war when radar was first extensively used. Research showed that anomalous propagation occurred only under very special meteorological conditions; there was no way of avoiding the diagnostic tools that allow the specialist to recognize these conditions.

After I had been detailed to study this problem, I wrestled with it for some time in vain. Eventually, I was called into the office of Colonel Maier. He told me that higher levels had decided to turn the problem of anomalous propagation over to the National Defense Research Council which had set up a "Radio Wave Propagation Committee." The Signal Corps was willing to release me for service in the technical office of that organization. I breathed a sigh of relief that I am sure was mutual; Colonel Maier must by then have realized that Elsasser was not the best raw material for the military life. The new office was set up in one of the upper floors of the Empire State Building in New York, and it was there that I spent the remainder of the war, together with half a dozen other technical people. During this time I wrote, in the simplest and clearest words I could muster, a pamphlet for the use of technical personnel explaining the meteorological origins of anomalous propagation, how to recognize it, and how to make such use of radar sets as one still could under those conditions. Illustrated by a very capable artist, it was printed in tens of thousands of copies and widely distributed to the technical branches of the Allied armed services. This was my one individual contribution to the war effort.

With the Allied victory in Europe and the surrender of Japan after atomic bombs had been dropped on two of its cities, the war came to an end. I learned about the existence of Los Alamos and Robert Oppenheimer's role from the newspapers; hitherto, I had had only a vague inkling of this whole development.

After the end of the war, the office where I worked was to be disbanded within a few months. This put me in a difficult situation since I had lost my connections with atomic physicists a good many years ago, and felt no great desire to return to meteorology. In desperation I scoured the job advertisements of the newspapers for engineers' and physicists' openings, but soon realized the inefficiency of such behavior. I finally remembered that I had become acquainted with a member of the Radio Wave Propagation Committee who was a vice-president of the Radio Corporation of America (RCA). I also happened to know that not long before a highly placed physicist, who was acquainted with my research work, had spoken favorably about me to the Committee. On the strength of this information, I called the man from RCA on the telephone and asked him outright whether he would be interested in placing me in the RCA laboratories at Princeton. He was very friendly, and after about a week I was working there as an assistant to a man who was a specialist in antenna design. It soon became clear, however, that testing antennas was not my favored line of work. I had lost no time in making the acquaintance of a few of the many physicists who worked in the laboratories, and after some weeks I managed to be transferred to a section supervised by Dwight O. North, a theoretical physicist, who was called Don by everyone, even his wife, from the initials of his name. Before long, the Norths and the Elsassers became friends and remained so; I am still in touch with them. Don told me how he had graduated from Caltech in the midst of the Depression; it was, of course, unquestioned that a theoretical physicist coming from that school would enter college teaching, but there were simply no teaching jobs available. So Don finally took an industrial position with RCA, and when some years thereafter that company concentrated its research facilities in the Princeton laboratories, he went there. He established a reputation by becoming a specialist in what is called electromagnetic "noise," but when I joined his group, he had switched to studying the properties of solids used in electronic solid-state devices. He had succeeded in effecting this change but slowly, against the intense resistance that any large organization opposes to a man who tries to be more than a one-track specialist.

I found a very congenial group among Don's collaborators and friends in which I felt at home. While I did have to forget more than ever the European residues in my manner of thought and speech, by then I was sufficiently Americanized to do this. After some months I also felt I had adapted sufficiently in my work to be considered a useful member of the group, and I began to feel secure. Nevertheless, it was a little late in my life to make a permanent switch to industry: I had always lacked that particular skill with gadgetry and that eye for the practical which, being partly inborn and partly strengthened by one's early environment, makes the applied scientist successful. I began to look about for an occasion to return to the teaching profession.

After staying about two years at the RCA Laboratories, I succeeded in obtaining an appointment as associate professor of physics at the University of Pennsylvania in Philadelphia, rather close to Princeton. There I developed a graduate course in mechanics which later became my mainstay in teaching; I also wrote a review article, for physicists, "The Interior of the Earth and Geomagnetism," that appeared in 1950 and made me known to my American colleagues. I had been told by friends when I took the position in Philadelphia that I would find an ingrained political constellation which would make a protracted career there unattractive. I found this to be true, so I kept my eyes and ears open. In the spring of 1950, I received a letter from the chairman of the physics department of the University of Utah: Would I be willing to join their faculty in order to develop a graduate program in physics? The University of Utah is in Salt Lake City; it is a state university and should not be confused with Brigham Young University in nearby Provo, a denominational college run by the Mormon Church. I had been in Salt Lake City during the war, sent by the Signal Corps on a mission to a nearby military installation, and had been impressed by the singular beauty of that part of the world, and by the cleanliness and orderliness of this city in the middle of the desert. I tried to find someone among my acquaintances on the East Coast of the U.S. who would have knowledge about the University of Utah, but I failed for a long time. Finally, an answer came from an unexpected source: Robert Oppenheimer. Since the end of the war, he had been director of the Institute for Advanced Study in Princeton, and while we ordinarily had no contact, he was extremely friendly on this occasion. He said: "I know that school very well, even though only indirectly. In my days at Berkeley, I had several Ph.D. candidates who had received their undergraduate training there. It is an educational institution with a very high scholastic level. You will not regret it when you go there." Coming from this source and said with that air of self-confidence which he had by then acquired, this seemed a very high and considered recommendation, and I soon sat down to write a letter of acceptance. Later that fall we settled in Salt Lake City. We had two children by then. We became acquainted with the local people, most of whom were members of the Church of Jesus Christ of Latter-Day Saints, as it is officially called, more commonly known as the Mormon Church. Mormons have been much maligned for their early adherence to polygamy, which came about because Joseph Smith, the founder of the sect, had a number of visions commanding him and his followers to take several wives. None of his followers liked the idea, but his authority was high, and they complied. Polygamy is very expensive, and only the richest and most successful men could ever afford it. Even so, it was not a social success. Once, some years later, I became acquainted with a middle-aged man of distinguished position who had, in his youth, known many people who had grown up under the system of polygamy; they had known the "houses with many gables" as the habitations of polygamists were called. He said the atmosphere in such a house was vicious and disgusting—it was a harem after all—and the Mormons were privately very happy when the United States Congress refused to admit Utah as a state of the Union until polygamy was officially abolished. This allowed the Mormons to claim that they had abandoned their tradition only under duress. But their many years of persecution at the frontier for their beliefs had given them a certain coherence as a group and a certain integrity as individuals that may account for the remarkable success of so many members of this numerically small group. They are in this respect somewhat like the Jews whom they in fact respect highly. I soon found that the secret of being accepted by Mormons on their home ground was simply to show genuine respect for their religious beliefs. I interpreted these in the sense of C. G. Jung as valid symbolisms and did not fail to express my respect and interest on suitable occasions. I was old enough to understand this; but I have seen several young men come to the University of Utah full of hope, only to lose their social foothold through little more than a few inadvertent sarcastic remarks about the "superstitions" of the local creed. The men in question usually left within a couple of years.

I found a number of young people in the physics department capable of becoming graduate students; several of them later obtained Ph.D.s under my supervision. Over these years I gradually taught a comprehensive set of courses in theoretical physics comprising all the classes then customary except one: quantum mechanics which was taught at that time by the most distinguished member of the faculty, the theoretical chemist Henry Eyring. He had been eminently successful in his research work on reaction kinetics. This together with his teaching abilities had earned him a prestigious professorial position at Princeton University. Henry came from an old Mormon family and was himself a devout Mormon. In 1946 he had been persuaded to leave Princeton to become dean of the then new graduate school. Eyring had

Robert Oppenheimer and John von Neumann, in front of the Princeton computer, ca. 1952

sufficient status in the community to engage in recurrent public debates, defending evolution against a local publicist who took the fundamentalist view that the scriptures had been explicit about the world having been created in 4000 B.C. He did so with considerable zest and gusto and with a pronounced sense of humor which endeared him to everyone in the university.

Let me, however, go back in time for a moment. Shortly after I had joined the RCA Laboratories in Princeton, I had contacted John von Neumann, who worked at the Institute for Advanced Study. As mentioned previously I had many discussions with him about the magnetism of cosmic fluids, including the earth's core. In the spring of 1950, when I had decided to move to the University of Utah, I asked von Neumann, who was then busy with the construction of the first large-scale electronic computer, largely of his own design, whether the art of computing was far enough advanced, so that an electronic computer would soon come onto the market which was small and inexpensive enough for me to have in Salt Lake City. He replied: "You are extremely lucky, the first such machine has just come out." I learned, then, from his story and the reports of others that von Neumann had such a formidable reputation that the commercial company, located in the Los Angeles area, which produced the machine had chartered a special airplane to fly a prototype to Princeton, set it up there to demonstrate it to von Neumann, and fly it back again. I inquired about the price and found that it was $25,000—which, I decided, was not too much, in these days of science's affluence, for a government agency to invest in my research. I constructed a somewhat contrived scheme which required extensive calculations on atmospheric radiation, too intricate to be done by hand; but after I had identified the appropriate government agency (a technical branch of the Air Force) I found that, as the saying goes, "the shoe was on the other foot": They were only too anxious to have the machines, about whose potential they were more than half convinced, tested by competent academic people; they would purchase the machine and loan it to me for some time, but they did not care in the least about which scientific problem I proposed to solve.

Early in 1951, a huge wooden crate labelled "computing machine" arrived in Salt Lake City. This was duly set up in a room next to my office. For the benefit of those of my readers who know someting about such devices, I should say that the machine contained relatively few electron tubes (transistors were not yet in general use) but contained somewhat over a thousand diodes which were plugged individually into clamps and could be changed as needed. It was frequently necessary to replace them, since, although the general ("logical") design of the machine was brilliantly conceived, its actual execution in terms of hardware had been hasty. As a result, diodes often burned out and had to be replaced, to the point where we never succeeded in carrying out any lengthy calculation. But this was also an advantage because it forced us to learn more about the design of such machines. It had a good-sized magnetic drum "memory"; it operated, of course, in binary arithmetic (with a pulse rate of 100,000/sec.). I also learned Boolean algebra, the formal logic of computing machines.

The most fortunate thing about this whole adventure was that I found a graduate student perfectly fitted to work on the machine: David Evans, the son of a well-established family with local traditions going back to the famous trek west from Illinois in 1847. He was far more mature than the average student, since he had spent part of the war and some of the post-war period, as a soldier abroad in the Army. Gifted in technical matters, he wanted first to become an atomic scientist, but after some effort I persuaded him to use this opportunity to specialize in electronic computers. After having fully explored the logical design and all the engineering details of the machine, and after having himself designed and built several elaborate extensions, he obtained his Ph.D. He then worked in the electronic computing industry, and later as technical director of the large computer on the Berkeley campus. When I saw him last a few years ago, he had returned to Salt Lake City where he was heading a growing manufacturing plant for computer accessories and was also teaching at the university's engineering college.

These early years in Salt Lake City were a turning point in my life. I had risen as high as I could in an academic career, although at a smaller university. I could, if I continued to be successful, move to an older, more prestigious university. This would necessarily be more competitive, and I doubted whether it would turn out to be a worthwhile aim. Moreover, I had achieved a considerable status in the local community. Professionally, the vicissitudes of my life, together with some personal choices, had given me a competence in several scientific fields. Now, having "arrived" in my late forties, I recognized the need to jettison most of these specialities in order to remain "on top" in one of them; this seemed to be the inexorable requirement of society. Instead, during these years in Salt Lake City, I decided not to become more of a specialist but to remain a generalist, a "natural philosopher," as I still like to express it. I have never been able to analyze the feelings that gradually led to this decision. Undoubtedly, I had been conditioned to a similar posture early in life, when the Teutonic environment to which I was expected to adjust had rejected me; thus, the idea that one can disregard the environment, which strikes horror in most people's heart, aroused no horror in me. Intellectually, I believe that much can be said for the posture of a philosopher. We tend to look with condescension and pity on that period of history, called the Middle Ages, when men were so concerned with their souls that they often ignored the external world. It seems today that most men are so embroiled in the external world that they have lost sight of the vast dimensions of the world of the psyche. The latter is usually referred to as speculative and hence "unscientific." The consequences of this one-sided attitude are seen in all of modern society: They appear in the prevalence of the technical specialist who lacks the redeeming virtues of a broader philosophy.

During these years in Utah, I became a natural philosopher, something of a maverick among scientists. Perhaps the tragic loss of my much beloved wife, Margaret, in 1954, strengthened this turn of my mind. Beginning in this period I began to write articles on natural philosophy, especially on the application of the ideas of theoretical physics to biology, several of which appeared over the years in the *Journal of Theoretical Biology.* I also wrote three books which I will discuss a little later. Since I did not, however, want to become a speculative philosopher pure and simple, I had to invent an appropriate technique of working: I divided my time into intervals from several weeks to several months in length during which I concentrated on only one of these subjects, and alternated. I found that periods of that size were long enough to permit strong concentration, and I continued this scheme throughout my later life.

Now let me return to the computing machine. Close involvement with it for two years had widened my horizon. I gained, by direct contact, some first-hand knowledge of what was called "cybernetics," more recently called "systems theory." I also kept my mental eye fixed on the potential for using the computer as a model of the brain. I was not, of course, a brain physiologist, but since few men know the thinking of both modern physics and brain physiology, I imagined that such a look might be of interest. Eventually, I decided to write a book informed by the philosophical ideas upon which I touched in

Chapter 6. The two first chapters of the book became a survey of the basic ideas and techniques of cybernetics, after which I went on to more philosophical notions. In 1955, after I had written the draft of an introduction for this book, I felt the desire to show it to a member of the biomedical community. I had by that time met some members of the university's Medical School, which was rather new and had been created by inviting a few prominent members of the Eastern and Midwestern medical establishment to Salt Lake City, and they, in turn, had recruited others. These men, therefore, represented a country-wide cross section of the biomedical community. I asked some of them whether they could recommend one of their number who would be willing to read my manuscript. It seemed that all the recommendations centered on one man, a relatively young professor of biophysics. He was described as the one person who, among practically oriented medical men, had some interest in theory. On speaking with him, I was favorably impressed and asked him to read my draft. He took it home with him and brought it back a few days later. His answer was brief and to the point—he had evidently thought the matter over. "I have read this," he said. "It is thought-provoking, in fact, extremely thought-provoking—but so far as I am concerned, I do not think, I observe."

In this man, then, I met for the first time the representative of a kind of mentality, extremely widespread among biologists as I discovered later, who, living amidst the most gigantic accumulation of data which the world had ever seen, proclaimed that salvation lay in more data. For a moment I thought that I had been mistaken about the qualities and competence of this person, but everything that I learned later confirmed that he was a capable and qualified representative of his profession. For me, this was, after a fashion, a rather shattering incident. It was the denial of science as a creative activity. I had for most of my life, ever since I could form opinions about such things, considered scientific research as a process in which observation was related by a reciprocal interaction with thought; observational result tended to modify thought, which in turn engendered suggestions for new observations, and so on, if not ad infinitum, then at least until significant knowledge had come close to its boundaries. This dynamic process embodied the advance of understanding in physical science—but now it seemed that in the life sciences the prevailing approach, the philosophy as it were, had assumed a quite different form. This discrepancy became increasingly clear to me in my later years; it sharpened my desire to remain in the fray about the philosophical interpretation of matters biological.

After the family had been in Salt Lake City for a couple of years, we bought a house not too far from the university. It was located on a quiet street with almost no traffic, so that the children could play safely. We soon learned that many of the older local families were concentrated in this neighborhood; they were rather wealthy and civilized people who preferred to live unostentatiously. Before long, my children had accustomed themselves to going in and out of the neighbors' houses and felt quite at home. The very day we moved in, a neighbor had appeared at the door to welcome us. I knew him vaguely since he was a professor at the university. He introduced himself as the "bishop" of that "ward" as it is called. Mormons do not have a professional clergy but divide their flocks into wards of several hundred souls, ideally no more than 800, presided over by a bishop, who is a layman and receives no pay for his activities. These are rather strenuous because the Mormon Church is no once-a-week affair, but a very elaborate machinery for social integration. Each ward has a large building that is both a place of worship and a social hall around which almost the entire social life of the group centers. There are frequent dances, dinners, movies, theatricals, and so on that sustain this collective life, and this seemed to me the most characteristic and unique aspect of the sect's existence.

The bishop had invited us to participate in this life as much or as little as we saw fit, and, of course, we tried to maintain cordial relations thereafter. But this led to difficulties some years later when I had lost my wife and was left alone with my children. They were by then very much at home in the neighborhood, so that their supervision was no problem for me. It was clear, however, that this would end before too long in our joining the Mormon Church. I felt no strong objection to this since I had become very fond of these people with their devotion to the simple life. But they did not confound this simplicity with a peasant's existence, as in so many sects who regard higher education as detrimental to the soul.

At the same time I felt a strong desire not to see my own individuality and the identity of my family dissolved in the Mormon collec'ivity. In this conflict the latter trend won, mainly owing to external circumstances: Earlier in my stay in Utah, I had received a letter from Roger Revelle, then director of the Scripps Institution of Oceanography in La Jolla, a suburb of San Diego. He had offered me a one-year appointment to get acquainted with his institution. I had not accepted, but it now occurred to me to ask Revelle whether a similar position, but one less limited in time, was still available. To my surprise he was most encouraging, and I soon learned why: Not many weeks before, the University of California had decided to open a new campus in La Jolla and had published this decision. A big industrial corporation, which owned the General Atomic Research Laboratory in La Jolla had then donated a large sum of money to the university to speed up this development through the rapid hiring of new faculty. I was, quite unwittingly, the first person who had availed himself of this bonanza, and I became the first professor to be appointed to the new campus. As I was told later, my case was a favorable one because if the plan to establish the new campus ran into difficulties (as indeed it did in the beginning, being delayed for three to four years) I could simply work in the Scripps Institution as a geophysicist.

The chief theoretician of the Scripps Institution was Carl Eckart. He had started by working in quantum mechanics and had been a professor at the University of Chicago; at the outbreak of the war, he moved to San Diego to take charge of research on submarine acoustics, in more practical terms, the technique of discovering hostile submarine boats. In this way, by developing a love for oceanography, he became an expert on hydrodynamics. He remained active in this work and lived in La Jolla for the rest of his life. He had been director of the Scripps Institution, but was not temperamentally inclined toward administration and had returned to his theoretical research. I did not know Eckart personally at that time, but it was clear that his views on my appointment might well be decisive. In the spring of 1956, Eckart visited me in Salt Lake City for a few days. Thereafter, the appointment formalities took their course, and in the fall of that year I moved with my children to La Jolla. For the first few years I became a member of the faculty of the Scripps Institution, since there was as yet no new campus.

I became acquainted with Roger Revelle, the director, who was a remarkable personality. Besides unusually versatile intellectual interests, he had more vitality than any other man I had ever met except for Robert Millikan. In a few years he had developed the Scripps Institution from a small research group with perhaps thirty men, to a very large organization with many hundreds of employees—but so successfully that he compromised neither the quality of the crew nor that of the research performed. This sudden growth made it possible for the institution to accommodate and employ the very large research vessels with their complicated gear that had begun to be used. There existed then in La Jolla a remarkable group of interesting personalities who had been attracted by the opening field of large-scale ocean exploration. I must restrain myself not to speak of them here, lest this account become too prolix.

In 1956, before I moved, I had finished most of the writing of my first book and completed it shortly after my arrival in La Jolla. It was entitled *The Physical Foundation of Biology*.[1] On the advice of a prominent theoretical physicist of my acquaintance I sent it to a well-known scientific publisher, who after many months turned it down without explanations. Meanwhile, an unexpected opportunity for publication had arisen. At that time Carl Eckart had married the widow of John von Neumann, who had died of cancer in his fifties. One day there appeared the head of Pergamon Press, a large London publisher, to negotiate about the publication of von Neumann's collected works. The man, Maxwell by name, had some spare time in La Jolla, and I managed to place a copy of my manuscript into his hands. Mr. Maxwell seemed a rather rugged autocrat: After having read my book he simply declared that he liked it and would publish it. It appeared in the spring of 1958. But a few months afterward, it became clear that the reviewers were not at all favorably inclined. A couple of them called me a "vitalist," not a negligible criticism among biologists. As a very famous biochemist (A. Szent-Györgyi) once wrote: "When a molecular biologist calls you a vitalist it is worse than when an FBI man calls you a Communist." This set the tone for all my later relations with biologists, who never seemed to regain a reasonable equanimity with regard to my ideas.

By then the La Jolla scene had begun to change, not to say to deteriorate. Not very long after I arrived, the University of California committed itself to an organizational program that foresaw three major centers with fully developed graduate schools: Berkeley, Los Angeles, and San Diego, together with a number of lesser, but still rather large, campuses mainly for undergraduates. With the population boom of the postwar generation ready to arrive at the university system, an entirely novel experiment was undertaken: the rapid development, over only a very few years, of a large university center which would be comparable in quality to the older campuses. La Jolla increasingly began to resemble a construction site superimposed on the beauty of a South seas island, which latter had always been a characteristic of the town. Then, a new building that could accommodate the nascent physics department was completed, and the prospective members of the department appeared one by one. They had been carefully selected and were undoubtedly men of a very high caliber, as befits a school that wanted to rank immediately among the leading universities of the country. They were on the average some twenty years younger than I. As I became acquainted with them, I was made intensely aware of the gigantic revolution that had occurred in the science of physics in less than a quarter-century, say between 1930 and 1955. The modern physics that had emerged, and of which these men were representatives, was worlds apart from the old physics that had for so long been called "natural philosophy" in the English-speaking world. It had little similarity to the style of an older world in which Ampere had, less than a century and a half before, conducted in his own garret his celebrated experiments that led soon enough to the invention of the electric motor. This new physics and its representatives were completely steeped in technology—no longer the heavy and clumsy technology of the steam engine it is true, but technology just the same.

It became clear to me that these men had gone through a quite different process of adapting to society from anything that had been required of me. I had begun with a vague and undifferentiated philosophical curiosity that had then been channelled into attention to specific scientific problems. These men were confronted with a vast and interlocking scheme of science-technology in which they had to find their niche, and they had done so. It was easy to see that the effects of this scientific revolution could not be reversed, anymore than Western Europe could have returned to feudalism after the French revolution.

During these years at La Jolla, I had gone to considerable lengths not to become involved in the political maneuvering, committee work, etc. that necessarily accompany the creation of a large new organization. Revelle, sensing this, had early created a niche for me within the Scripps Institution. Now, I was among physicists again, but the younger generation had taken over, and I neither spoke their language nor shared their interests. I decided that I no longer fitted into such a modern physics department. During the administrative rearrangements then occurring, I was offered a position of almost pure research in geophysics, outside of the physics department, which I was ready to accept, had not other events intervened.

Professor Harry Hess, the chairman of the Department of Geology at Princeton University, was anxious to see his department more deeply involved in geophysics and offered me a position as professor of geophysics. Under the circumstances, it seemed only sensible to inspect this possibility, so I made a trip to Princeton. I was struck by a peculiar

architectural arrangement: The geology department was in one wing
of a building erected early in this century, at a time when evolution had
agitated the academic world. Much of the research then had centered on
paleontology. Thus, the geology department was put in one wing of
this building and the biology department in the other. Since then the
biology department had proliferated as the geology department had
not, but the basic structure still remained: The entrance was in the
middle of the building, as was the library, one floor above. The latter
combined two separate libraries in the same large room, the geology
and the biology library. I decided that these were ideal conditions for
continuing my double life, part time geophysics and part time philosophy of biology, and I accepted the offer.

Moving offered no great technical difficulties since my children were
sufficiently grown, and the eldest, my daughter, was attending the
University of California. After two years in Princeton I married for the
second time; my new wife Susanne, a widow, was a cousin whom I
had known since boyhood.

During my five years in Princeton, I came to know several distinguished biologists, but my relations with many of them were often not
very smooth, even though there were no open arguments. The habit I
had by then assumed, of philosophical probings into the foundations
of biology made them uncomfortable—and no doubt it is to one who
aims to resolve a specific scientific question and does not want to be
distracted from it.

I began to appreciate the fact that life science had always had a
complexion very much like what I had seen physical science assume
only late in its existence, in my own lifetime: There was a bewildering
variety of specialties, many of them tied to specific practical questions.
It was sheer romanticism to think that this variety could be made to
yield to any kind of simplistic philosophical scheme. I could visualize a
practical man, a doctor, for example, with a waiting room full of
suffering humanity, who would have little patience for the contortions
of a philosopher's mind. But I also realized that the situation had
undoubtedly been the same in physics all along: Physical science has,
of course, always had its complexities and its practical implications,
and it was only by stripping off the accessories that physical scientists
acting as natural philosophers could develop the methods that led to
the major experimental discoveries and the great unifying mathematical schemes which constitute the grand edifice of modern physical
science. The situation in the life sciences was similar but far more

difficult: There was no evidence of a grand edifice, but there was clear evidence of a general unity of pattern in organic nature. But scientific insight into the structure of living things was quite new, and it had not yet congealed into a system. How could a man, even one living as late as the middle of the nineteenth century, who knew nothing about the chemistry of proteins, let alone DNA, develop adequate ideas on the nature of organic life?

I believe, nonetheless, that the situation in our own age is uniquely propitious because, for the first time in history, there is an altogether coherent abstract scheme—quantum mechanics—for representing the physical basis on which organic life rests. This needs only the working hypothesis that quantum mechanics is valid in the living organism, an idea to which no contrary observational result has ever become known. But there are armies of competent technicians with neither the broad experience nor the imagination to tackle fundamental problems who, in their frustration, become sceptics: "How do you know that the laws of quantum mechanics are universally valid? Something to the contrary may some day be discovered. Prove it, prove it." Having been raised primarily in the mode of thinking of physical science, these men do not realize that if biology is indeed the realm of the utterly and perhaps insolubly complex, then such notions as that of proof, pertaining to the simpler black-and-white world of mathematics, might no longer apply and the whole conceptual system of scientific analysis might have to be reconstructed.

I understood then more and more how much the present juncture in history calls for an overall reconstruction of science, one that leads from the old world of simplicity and universality centered on physical science, to a world of complexity and individualities centered on biology (using here the terms introduced previously, in Chapter 6). I also realized, of course, how difficult it was to effect such a reconstruction. I looked in vain to history for guidance. History does not repeat itself, only those who teach it may. I felt I needed a great deal of raw material even to begin such a reconstruction. But beyond this, it is obvious that an individual can do no more than present his results; it is up to the inscrutable processes of history to do the rest.

When I now and then looked back on the development of my own ideas, the road seemed clear enough: I had been exposed extensively to depth psychology, and this had convinced me of the irrational nature of the unconscious. I had generalized from this to the broader idea that all life had irrational aspects. This began to make sense only after I had

The author, ca. 1974

accepted the notion that any living thing was the locus of utter complexity. Such complexity was first of all structural, but one could readily conceive of its becoming logical, that is, of its preventing the success of such basic logical operations as for instance, the manipulation of classes, on which all scientific procedure must be based.

I had written my first book at the end of my stay in Salt Lake City. In Princeton I wrote a second book; a rather short one published by Princeton University Press under the title *Atom and Organism*.[2] But after it had appeared, I began to see how much I had fallen under the sway of what I shall simply call without excuse, "the establishment." I had not been explicitly hypocritical, but I found that I was flying with clipped wings, as it were. I had by then become something of a frontiersman of scientific endeavors in a more specific manner than I had been before, and the settled society in the rear no longer held the same attraction for me. I did not want to become a biologist, as those around me always seemed to assume, but wanted to maintain myself as a philosophical critic of the modes of thought of biologists, and for this I needed a suitable existence.

In 1967, five years after having arrived, I left Princeton for a research professorship in the Institute for Fluid Dynamics and Applied Mathematics at the University of Maryland, which is located in College Park, on the outskirts of Washington. I abandoned of course all the prestige attached to Princeton, but I was, for once, free to do whatever research I chose. I had no teaching obligations, but I repeatedly taught an intermediate-level course in the physics department. I also managed to keep my research interests in geophysics alive with an occasional publication on the deformation of the solid earth.

The main product of this period was my third book on the philosophy of biology. While writing it, I was rather worried about having a lengthy and tiresome struggle to find an adequate publisher. But it turned out to be simpler than I had expected: One day a gentleman entered my office and introduced himself as the representative of the Elsevier Publishing Company, a well known Dutch house. He had been told by a friend of mine of my interests and wanted samples of my writing to take home with him. I gave him copies of a large part of the final manuscript. I soon learned that there was a combine of three Dutch scientific publishing houses: Elsevier, North Holland, and Excerpta Medica. I received some letters from executives of this group which showed that they had read my manuscript and liked it. They finally decided that it should be published by North Holland, an old publishing company that had long since concentrated on specialties within or near theoretical physics. A contract was signed and the book appeared in 1975.[3]

In the summer of 1974, after having reached my seventieth birthday, I was duly retired from the University of Maryland. A few months thereafter, Professor Owen M. Phillips, chairman of the Department of Earth and Planetary Sciences at Johns Hopkins University, offered me a suitable post-retirement affiliation, called an "adjunct professorship," that entailed no formal obligations. I moved to Baltimore, only some fifty kilometers away, where I found the leisure to write these memoirs.

Notes

PREFACE

1. *World Who's Who in Science*, Marquis Who's Who, Inc., Chicago, 1968.

CHAPTER 3

1. "Adiabatic" is a technical term of the physicist designating impermeable to heat.

2. There is a difference between my recollection of these events and that of Max Born, both of them put to paper some decades after the facts. I might make my own situation clearer by saying that these events loomed large in my then very young life since they were my first contact with a major research problem.

3. The ideas about Einstein and his role in the history of physics are subjective; they are views formed over many years but without my studying historical criticism concerning Einstein's role.

4. Constance Reid, *David Hilbert*, Springer, Berlin-New York, 1970 (in English).

CHAPTER 4

1. Klein, Martin J., *Paul Ehrenfest*, North Holland Publ. Co., Amsterdam, 1970.

2. This monumental multi-volume work in the German language, begun in 1898 and continued for about a quarter-century, owed a

very great deal to the organizational genius of Felix Klein. He succeeded in persuading the leading men in Germany and adjacent countries to write the chief articles. Klein himself edited the volumes on Mechanics, Sommerfeld those on Physics; its fructifying influence on theoretical physics in the early decades of the century was tremendous.

3. I have obtained information from an autobiographical sketch contained in vol. 3 of: Laue, Max von, *Gesammelte Schriften und Vorträge*, F. Vieweg & Sohn, Braunschweig, 1961, 3 vols.

CHAPTER 5

1. Fig. 1 has been reproduced from p. 41 of: W. T. Read, Jr., *Dislocations in Crystals*, McGraw-Hill, New York, 1953, by permission.

2. Scott, William T., *Erwin Schrödinger, An Introduction to his Writings*, Univ. of Massachusetts Press, 1967.

3. Eddington, Arthur, *The Philosophy of Physical Science*, 1939, reprinted by Ann Arbor Paperbacks, Univ. of Michigan Press. This little book stands in my opinion well above anything ever written on that particular topic.

CHAPTER 6

1. Whitmore, Frank C., *Organic Chemistry*, van Nostrand, New York, 2nd ed., 1951, pp. 2–3.

CHAPTER 7

1. Biquard, Pierre, *Frédéric Joliot-Curie*, Engl. Transl. Souvenir Press, London, 1965.

2. Langevin, André, *Paul Langevin, mon père*, Les Editeurs Français Réunis, Paris, 1971.

3. Quoted from the article "Panama Canal," *Encyclopedia Britannica*, 11th ed., 1910.

CHAPTER 8

1. I have tried to reproduce the stories circulating about Millikan as I heard them; I have not read his autobiography nor consulted other printed sources.

CHAPTER 9

1. Burchfield, Joe D., *Lord Kelvin and the Age of the Earth*, Science History Publications, New York, 1975.

CHAPTER 10

1. Elsasser, Walter M., *The Physical Foundation of Biology*, Pergamon Press, London and New York, 1958.

2. Elsasser, Walter M., *Atom and Organism*, Princeton University Press, 1966.

3. Elsasser, Walter M., *The Chief Abstractions of Biology*, North-Holland Publishing Co., Amsterdam and London; and American Elsevier Publishing Co., New York, 1975.

Index